East Turkistan's Right to Sovereignty

East Turkistan's Right to Sovereignty

Decolonization and Beyond

Rukiye Turdush

LEXINGTON BOOKS

Lanham • Boulder • New York • London

Published by Lexington Books
An imprint of The Rowman & Littlefield Publishing Group, Inc.
4501 Forbes Boulevard, Suite 200, Lanham, Maryland 20706
www.rowman.com

86-90 Paul Street, London EC2A 4NE

British Library Cataloguing in Publication Information Available

Library of Congress Cataloging-in-Publication Data Available

ISBN 978-1-66692-726-9 (cloth)
ISBN 978-1-66692-728-3 (paperback)
ISBN 978-1-66692-727-6 (electronic)

Contents

Acknowledgments

Judging the legitimacy of the East Turkistani people's right to choose sovereignty requires first determining whether they qualify to advance their claims. The Chinese government has used every possible tactic and the most heinous of human rights crimes—genocide—as a final solution to disqualify East Turkistan's legitimate right to choose sovereignty. As an ethnic Uyghur myself and an observer of the political history and current situation of East Turkistan, I feel compelled to write this book about East Turkistan's right to choose sovereignty. This is not only a refutation of China's false claims that Xinjiang (aka East Turkistan) is an integral part of China but also to educate readers who care about concrete evidence, as well as international security and justice regarding the cause of East Turkistan. Furthermore, the objective is to advocate the legitimate rights of Uyghurs and their entitlement to nationhood and to establish the East Turkistan state along with other Turkic people in the region, rather than tolerating extermination or assimilation by China. This book develops the idea of my 2020 self-published draft article "Right to Self Determination of East Turkistan" with Grin publishing. Thank you to Dr. Erkin Ekrem, professor at Hacettepe University in Turkey, and Dilyar Musabay, the president of East Turkistan Youth Congress, who expect me to turn my draft article into a book.

Even though I am confident with my knowledge on East Turkistan issues, proficient with qualitative research methods, and have a long-held desire to write a book for the people who never gave up hope for East Turkistan's independence, I acknowledge that I am not a disciplined scholar, that English is my fourth language, and that I have previously never written a book in English. I was very hesitant to write this book in English. When I started writing my first chapter, I could not imagine that I would complete this book. I must thank God for giving me the knowledge, analytical skills, and courage to continue writing and for blessing me with numerous helpful people that allowed me to publish this book.

Most importantly I want to express my heartfelt gratitude to the Uyghurs who have been martyred and who sacrificed themselves for the sovereignty of East Turkistan. It was their unwavering commitment and lengthy battle for this cause that inspired me day and night to study and research for this book. I also want to thank my brother, who was murdered by Chinese settlers twenty years ago. I saw him constantly in my dreams, looking at me with pride from heaven. It made me determined to finish this project and believe in the powerful contribution it could make to the literature on East Turkistan issues.

Words cannot begin to describe my appreciation for my beloved mother, Ayshe Qadir, who was unable to return to her home country and passed away. She would have unconditionally supported me more than anyone for this book if she was still alive. I am also grateful to the spirit of millions of Uyghur women who are currently imprisoned in Chinese detention camps. I repeatedly had strange nightmares of being trapped in Chinese concentration camps with other Uyghur women, while people in the free world did nothing and merely watched China's propaganda of me alive in the camp. These dreams felt like messages from those trapped in the concentration camps, and I felt guilty for not doing enough for them. This compelled me to continue writing for the liberation of these women, men, and children imprisoned there.

I would like to deeply thank the many brave Uyghurs in East Turkistan who found ways to contact me, trusted me, and provided invaluable information about the current situation in East Turkistan. I cannot thank these people by name; in all but a few rare instances, I use pseudonyms in the following pages to maintain participants' confidentiality—as many of these individuals are still in East Turkistan or are immigrants in countries where they are not fully protected yet. I also extend my appreciation to the camp survivors and many Uyghur refugees in the diaspora who allowed me to interview them and share their personal stories.

I also need to deeply thank the hundreds of Uyghur parents in the Uyghur diaspora who provided their children's photos as well as detailed information about their children in East Turkistan who have been forcibly separated by the Chinese government and locked away in concentration camps. I am grateful for these parents' consent to use their precious children's images. However, I did not use these pictures due to publication expenses.

My work draws on the groundwork laid by previous legal scholars and historians of related subjects on East Turkistan issues. Of course, I bear all responsibility for any deficiencies. The ability to read the works of these historians and legal scholars in multiple languages has been beneficial to my intellectual growth in this field. Respectfully, I want to express my gratitude to those scholars. I would also like to salute the Uyghur and other Turkic populations in exile for their intense desire for the independence of East Turkistan.

I owe a significant intellectual debt to Eric Schuessel, the distinguished young scholar who deeply understands Uyghur and Chinese history. He did not refuse my requests for help and enthusiastically read the whole manuscript despite his extremely busy schedule. He saw the value of this work's underlying project and encouraged me to publish it. His empirical critiques fortified my arguments. He even polished up my wording and sentence structure without changing their meanings. The manuscript that I gave him very much improved through his patient editing. During the intricate publishing process, he always guided me, and I will never forget it. Without his assistance and encouragement, I never would have been able to write an excellent book proposal and catch the attention of the publishers at Lexington. I cannot thank Eric enough for his amazing editing of this book.

I owe appreciation to Dr. Christian Gudehus, professor at Ruhr-University Bochum, who invited me to give a speech in his class and provided me a chance to connect with his lovely student Joy Dinkelman, an advocate for humanitarian causes. I am indebted to Joy Dinkelman for correcting my grammatical errors in several of my early drafts. Her patience and kindness are invaluable.

The manuscript's anonymous reviewer, Dr. Charles Burton, praised the book in his extensive appraisal and highly recognized my work. After learning his name, I feel privileged to be able to express my gratitude in this manner.

Furthermore, I owe so much debt to my acquisitions editor, Eric Kuntzman, and his wonderful editorial team who accepted my book proposal and patiently answered my every question about the publishing process. Without Eric Kuntzman's sincere, enthusiastic help and professionalism as well as his availability 24/7 during the publishing process, this book would never have been published. His guidance and mentoring provided me invaluable knowledge of the publishing world that I knew nothing about. I deeply thank my assigned editor Arun Rajakumar, the project manager of Deanta. His patience and thoughtful copy editing for every page amazed me. I appreciate Lexington Books editorial's punctuality in getting this book into print.

A special thanks to Nijat Turghun, a grad student of East Asian Studies at Stockholm University, my Uyghur brother who works with me to advocate the Uyghur genocide on many occasions. He urged me to never give up on the seemingly impossible task of improving my writing.

Finally, I extend a huge thanks to my youngest son Berkalp Birlik who passionately asked me to write a book about the political history of the Uyghurs' homeland in English so he could read it and more thoroughly understand his mother's home country. Despite his busy high school graduation years, he did all the chores at home, making it possible for me to write this book. I feel proud and appreciate his artistic skills for designing cover art of this book. I also thank my lovely husband for always believing in me, my eldest son for when I needed someone to talk to, and all the many friends who pushed me to be a better writer and researcher. Thank you for having great patience with me and my hectic schedule and for being on this journey with me.

Introduction

After World War II, self-determination entered international law as an essential principle. This principle guaranteed independence for many states subsequent to the dismantling of European empires. Ironically, it also aided the emergence of a new Chinese empire through Communist China's colonial domination of East Turkistan. *East Turkistan's Right to Choose Sovereignty* picks on this failed decolonization by investigating the national aspirations of East Turkistan's people across their long historical relationship with China. It is specifically concerned with the legitimacy of those national aspirations in the context of colonized states' right to self-determination and the potential for oppressed people in colonized territories to achieve "remedial secession."

East Turkistan's Right to Choose Sovereignty addresses the status of East Turkistan's self-determination in the context of global decolonization and beyond by providing an analysis of the colonial history of East Turkistan as the root cause of China's genocide. Through contextual, historical, and legal perspectives, it presents arguments concerning the region's illegal occupation, its long history of resistance movements, China's failure to provide constitutionally guaranteed internal self-determination and autonomy, and the discursive and practical dimensions of the ongoing genocide. It argues for East Turkistan's right to choose sovereignty on the basis of international self-determination law.

EAST TURKISTAN

East Turkistan is located in Central Asia. It borders China to the east along the narrow Gansu Corridor. The rail distance between East Turkistan's capital city of Urumchi and the Chinese capital of Beijing is 3,800 kilometers. It takes five to six hours to travel that distance by airplane, making Urumchi closer to Budapest than to Beijing. East Turkistan is a vast territory of 1.6 million square kilometers. The region has rich petroleum, natural gas, iron, coal, cotton, and other significant metallic and nonmetallic resources. Not long ago the region's main population consisted of the Uyghur ethnic group, as well as Kazakhs, Kirgiz, Uzbeks, Tatars, Hui Muslims, and Mongols. However, following China's conquest of the region in 1949, the Chinese population increased rapidly. According to China's Seventh National Population Census in November 2021, East Turkistan's current population is 25,852,345 people, including 10,920,098 members of the Han ethnic group, or 42.24%. In contrast, the population of the Uyghur ethnic group was 11,624,257, or 44.96%, while the remainder comprised other ethnic groups.[1]

Currently, the international community recognizes East Turkistan as a Chinese region of "Xinjiang." As historical documents incontrovertibly prove, there were empires and states representing the people of East Turkistan prior to the Qing and Chinese conquests. The name "Xinjiang" was given by the Manchu Qing empire's (1644–1911) Han Chinese general Zuo Zongtang in 1877, during the empire's attempt to change East Turkistan from a more independent territory into a Chinese province. The name was enshrined again in 1955 with the founding of the Xinjiang Uyghur Autonomous Region, after the People's Republic of China (PRC, 1949–present) had colonized the region and established a system of constitutionally guaranteed regional autonomy for non-Han groups.

The name "Xinjiang" is offensive to the native peoples of East Turkistan because it reflects a long history of colonialism. Manchu Qing imperialism began in the 1750s when the Qing conquered East Turkistan, after which the region was still ruled separately from the Chinese part of the empire for a century. In 1864, the peoples of East Turkistan rebelled against the Manchu empire and established the emirate of Kashgaria (*Yette Sheher*). Later, after 1877, Qing colonialism emerged from certain Confucian traditions.[2] While Qing colonialism had different origins from Euro-American colonialism, its assimilatory, violent rule was aimed at territorial acquisition through sociopolitical reorganization and assimilating the people of the dominated territory, specifically to the norms of Confucianism.[3] However, Islam is the religion of the majority of people in the region, and Confucianism was neither attractive nor superior to Islam. No matter how bloody the forced assimilation was, they had failed to transform East Turkistan into one of China's provinces.

Following the fall of the Manchu empire, the people of East Turkistan twice defeated Chinese warlords and established two independent republics that controlled most of the territory of East Turkistan. These were independent nation-states established by the people of East Turkistan and representing the people of East Turkistan. Unfortunately, the newly established PRC conquered East Turkistan with Stalin's help in 1949. Like any other classic colonizer, they aimed to maintain the superiority of Han Chinese colonizers over the colonized people of East Turkistan. Meanwhile, they also followed Manchu empire's Han Chinese general Zuo Zongtang's footsteps in pursuing coercive, assimilatory colonialism, imposing Chinese-style Communist ideology and even reviving Confucianism, which rapidly escalated after Xi Jinping came to power. The most significant difference between Communist China's colonialism and that of the Manchu Qing is that modern China's coercive assimilatory colonialism is facilitated through settler colonialism and intensified with genocide.

RELATIONSHIP BETWEEN CHINA AND EAST TURKISTAN

East Turkistan's Right to Choose Sovereignty mainly focuses on the relationship between the PRC and the people of East Turkistan, specifically between China's settler colonialism and genocidal nation-building and East Turkistan's independence movement. Settler colonialism, which is a replacement of autochthonous people with outsiders, is being implemented through the Chinese central government's total control of every level of administration, from local affairs to natural resources and to the region's legal, educational, religious, and cultural institutions. The PRC has established a distinct settler apparatus, the Xinjiang Production and Construction Corps (or "Bingtuan"), and directs millions of Han settlers to the region every year. However, the Chinese government is not satisfied with its total power in East Turkistan. The identity of the Turkic Muslim peoples of East Turkistan, particularly the Uyghurs, presents a challenge for the Chinese government, as they are highly resistant to assimilation and racially, culturally, religiously, and linguistically distinct from Han Chinese. That difference makes it very apparent that East Turkistan is not part of China or is like a Chinese province, which makes it difficult for China to hide its colonialism. It also causes insecurity in Chinese leaders as they ambitiously expand through the New Silk Road project, in which East Turkistan plays the role of the main geographical gateway to the world.

China's nation-building project could have recreated its country by providing equal rights to Uyghurs and other Turkic Muslims. Instead, China's nation-building has led to genocide. In order to achieve an unchallenged settler state and ethnic Han Chinese nation-building in its colonized territory, China has committed to eliminating the challenges posed by the identity of East Turkistan's people. It has manipulated history to advance its false claim that there was never any such state as East Turkistan, so as to claim that it was *terra nullius*—without a people or a nation-state—when they occupied it and justify their legal ownership of it.

This plan has been implemented through various genocidal policies since 2017. Under the guise of "education" and "vocational training," China has undertaken a massive program of torture, execution, imprisonment, and forced labor against these people. According to survivors' testimonies and leaked documents, the program began in 2014, and at least 1 million people were incarcerated in the camp system. Genocidal policies referred to euphemistically as "family planning" and "labor transfer" are leading to the destruction of East Turkistan's people. The global community, despite the threat that genocide poses to the international system, has been slow to respond. Presently, the world has bought into China's rhetoric about "stability" and "fighting extremism," and international organizations accept China's presentation of Uyghurs and other people as "minorities" within a postcolonial Chinese nation-state.

This book analyzes the cause and provides the tools and the argument to understand East Turkistan's actual status in the international community and advocate for its future. It is based on detailed studies of East Turkistan's political and territorial history, as well as international self-determination law and Genocide Convention law, which it takes up as a legal theoretical framework. I have studied hundreds of articles in various languages, including English, Uyghur, Turkish, and Chinese. Primary sources include official documents related to the two East Turkistan Republics (1933–1934 and 1944–1949), Western and Chinese media sources, and a variety of historical documents, ranging from the diaries of nineteenth-century Chinese leaders to declassified US intelligence files. Moreover, I have interviewed Uyghur concentration camp survivors, refugees, parents whose children were taken away, and women who experienced sterilization, forced abortion, and rape. I also interviewed leaders of Uyghur organizations and collected original documents, photos, and videos to analyze current Chinese policy in East Turkistan.

CHAPTER OUTLINE

The book divides the discussion of East Turkistan's right to self-determination into two parts. Part I, consisting of three chapters, focuses on East Turkistan's relationship to decolonization and law. Chapter 1 lays out debates over the meanings of sovereignty, indigeneity, and self-determination and relates them, point by point, to key aspects of East Turkistan's history that are explained in detail in subsequent chapters. Chapter 2 demonstrates the existence of independent states in East Turkistan prior to 1949, advancing detailed historical evidence to push back against Chinese assertions that Uyghurs and other Turkic Muslims have never been independent. It shows a long history of territorial and national independence going back long before the Manchu Qing and Communist Chinese conquests.

Chapter 3 shows that the Chinese state's absorption of East Turkistan after 1949, by all reasonable definitions, is a conquest of an independent state and people and that it was understood and acknowledged as such at the time. This is contrary to China's claims of "peaceful reunification." This chapter explains how China uses and distorts international legal principles for its own benefit. Moreover, it discusses how UN Member States recognize China's authority to colonize East Turkistan, Tibet, and Mongolia while condemning European colonization in other parts of the world.

Part II builds on part I by exploring the question of China's legal right to rule East Turkistan. Looking beyond decolonization means focusing on China's failure to recognize East Turkistan's internal self-determination and highlighting China's genocide vis-à-vis its "nation-building" strategies. Moreover, this part of the book argues that asserting East Turkistan's right to sovereignty is the most effective way to end crimes against humanity and genocide according to the remedial secession theory. This part of the book includes six chapters. The first three (chapters 4, 5, and 6) illustrate how China's rejection of political, territorial, and economic rights of the people in the so-called Xinjiang region contradicts China's official propaganda of "China's national unity" (*Zhongguo minzu yiti hua*), "the shared consciousness of the Chinese nation" (*Zhonghua minzu gongtongti yishi*), and the assertion that "Xinjiang is an inseparable part of China." Chapter 4 establishes the intent to commit genocide through a close examination of party and state rhetoric and policies at multiple levels. It focuses on dehumanizing rhetoric. Chapter 5 shifts from discourse into action through a thorough account of genocidal acts and policies, each one related to a matter of international law. It emphasizes the process of settler colonialism. Chapter 6 approaches genocide and colonization from a broader perspective, demonstrating how the Chinese state has made East Turkistan a site of resource of extraction and Han settlement at the expense of Turkic Muslim people.

Chapter 7 is a history of resistance movements after 1949 that shows how Turkic Muslim people have consistently sought to restore their independence and self-rule. This establishes a long history of a struggle for independence on multiple levels. Chapter 8 challenges China on its own ground by showing how the PRC has failed to honor its own laws on ethnic and regional autonomy.[4] The conclusion chapter returns to the question of self-determination in international law and internal and external factors of the meaning of independence of East Turkistan. It argues that there are both legal and ethical grounds for East Turkistan's self-determination and, as a last resort, independence.

NOTES

1. Consulate General of the People's Republic of China in Toronto, "Main Data [1] of Xinjiang Uygur Autonomous Region from the Seventh National Population Census," June 6, 2021, accessed February 21, 2022, https://www.fmprc.gov.cn/ce/cgtrt/eng/news/t1884310.htm.

2. Eric Schluessel, *Land of Strangers* (New York: Columbia University Press, 2020), 6.

3. Ibid.

4. This book expands on the ideas presented in my self-published draft essay, *Right to Self-Determination of East Turkistan*. The essay provided some of the content for chapter 8. See for the sources: Rukiye Turdush, "Right to Self- Determination for East Turkistan," *Grin*, October 26, 2020.

I

SELF-DETERMINATION IN INTERNATIONAL LAW AND THE COLONIAL HISTORY OF EAST TURKISTAN

1

The People of East Turkistan

An Illegally Occupied Nation

THE PRINCIPLE OF SELF-DETERMINATION

A fundamental principle of United Nations (UN) law is the right to self-determination, which is described both in customary law and in international conventions. This right has been articulated in several international instruments, including the "Declaration on Principles of International Law Concerning Friendly Relations and Co-operation among States" within the UN Charter of 1970, the Helsinki Final Act adopted by the Conference on Security and Co-operation in Europe of 1975, the Vienna Declaration, the Programme of Action of 1993, among others. Articles 1 and 55 of the UN Charter both mention the right to self-determination.[1] Resolution 1514 of the General Assembly states, "All peoples have the right to self-determination; by virtue of that right they freely determine their political status and freely pursue their economic, social and cultural development."[2] Similarly, the principle of equal rights and self-determination of people in the 1970 "Declaration on Friendly Relations" is articulated in this expanded form:

> By virtue of the principle of equal rights and self-determination of peoples enshrined in the *Charter of the United Nations*, all peoples have the right to freely determine, without external interference, their political status and to pursue their economic, social and cultural development, and every State has the duty to respect this right in accordance with the provisions of the Charter.[3]

This resolution clarified the purpose of self-determination as a means to "a speedy end to colonialism" and to ensure peaceful and friendly relations between states.[4] These resolutions and articles of the UN Charter universally state that "all peoples" have the right to self-determination.

The General Assembly Resolution 3103 (XXVIII) of 1974 also solemnly proclaimed the following:

> The struggle of peoples under colonial and alien domination and racist régimes for the implementation of their right to self-determination and independence is legitimate and in full accordance with the principles of international law.[5]

As many commentators have argued, none of these articles or resolutions offer a clear definition of what "all people" means, and therefore it remains an unsettled question. Does "all people" refer to religious and ethnic minorities, as well as indigenous people? Or does it only indicate the nationhood of colonized nation-states? What is the definition of these distinct groups?

This book explores in detail the position of the people of East Turkistan with regard to claims to self-determination in international law. As one may ascertain from the fraught international discourse around the issue of East Turkistan's independence and the rights of its people to self-determination, there is considerable misunderstanding surrounding the basic terminology, categories, and definitions that are necessary to understand the situation and to articulate a legal case. In order to approach the problem of definition, this introduction must begin by addressing a deceptively simple question: How should one categorize the people of East Turkistan?

DEFINING THE PEOPLE AND
TERRITORY OF EAST TURKISTAN

There are several ways to categorize groups of people in the context of international law and conventions. Even the superficially obvious notion of "a people" is contested and has required definition at the UN. Aureliu Cristescu, special rapporteur for the Sub-Commission on Prevention of Discrimination and Protection of Minorities, defined "people" thusly in 1981:

(a) The term "people" denotes a social entity possessing a clear identity and its own characteristics;
(b) It implies a relationship with a territory, even if the people in question has been wrongfully expelled from it and artificially replaced by another population;
(c) A people should not be confused with ethnic, religious or linguistic minorities, whose existence and rights are recognized in article 27 of the International Covenant on Civil and Political Rights.[6]

The issues of identity, characteristics, and territory will be useful to keep in mind as we explore the broader issue of definition.

Joshua Castellino offers a clear and simple typology of different groups of people under international law, which will be useful for discussing the status of the people of East Turkistan. His categories are as follows:[7]

(a) Peoples, also referred to as "nations" or "submerged nations";
(b) Indigenous peoples, also referred to as First Nations or "Indians," and usually considered to subsume "Tribal Peoples";
(c) Minorities, also referred to as "ethnic, linguistic, or religious minorities" or, more problematically in Europe, as "national minorities."

An official definition of "indigenous" has not been adopted by any UN system. Instead, on account of the diversity of indigenous peoples and the history of indigenous issues at the UN, there is considerable debate on the definition of "indigenous people." The most widely accepted description was provided by Jose R. Martinez Cobo, special rapporteur of the Sub-Commission on Prevention of Discrimination and Protection of Minorities, in his "Study of the Problem of Discrimination against Indigenous Populations." His definition of an indigenous person or people was mainly studied by the following criteria:[8]

• Self-identification as an indigenous person and group consciousness
• Acceptance by the indigenous community as an indigenous person
• Autochthonous inhabitants of their lands
• Distinct culture, language, religion (Some indigenous people have diverse traditional forms of religion)
• Common ancestors
• Disadvantaged and nondominant groups of society
• Resolution to maintain and reproduce ancestral environments and systems as distinctive peoples and communities

Although the people of East Turkistan are indigenous to the territory of East Turkistan and possess a language, culture, and set of religious beliefs that are distinct from those of their colonizers, they are nevertheless not fit to the "indigenous people" as listed or categorized by the United Nations. Even though the Chinese government rejects Uyghurs and other Turkic groups' indigeneity to the illegally occupied territory of East Turkistan and defines them as "minorities" within China, Uyghurs do not self-identify themselves as indigenous people. Instead, with regard to the history of Uyghur nation-states and the present status of the Uyghur homeland as a colonized territory, East Turkistan fits more closely into the category of an "illegally occupied nation," which we will discuss further in this chapter.

A broader concept of "minorities" was advanced at the UN in 1977 by Francesco Capotorti, special rapporteur of the United Nations Sub-Commission on

Prevention of Discrimination and Protection of Minorities, according to whom a minority is

> a group numerically inferior to the rest of the population of a State, in a non-dominant position, whose members—being nationals of the State—possess ethnic, religious or linguistic characteristics differing from those of the rest of the population and show, if only implicitly, a sense of solidarity, directed towards preserving their culture, traditions, religion or language.[9]

The people of East Turkistan are currently numerically inferior to the Chinese settlers in East Turkistan, because of China's genocide and the enormous scale of Han Chinese migration into the region. The people of East Turkistan are also in a nondominant position, as the Chinese government deprives them of their political and economic rights. They possess ethnic, religious, and linguistic characteristics differing from those of their colonizers. However, as the UN document "Minorities Under International Law" clarifies, a minority group will not always be a numerical minority, and a numerical majority may also define itself as being in a nondominant position, such as that of the blacks under the Apartheid regime in South Africa.[10] Even though the people of East Turkistan have been turned into a numerical and nondominant minority in their own homeland, they are not merely struggling to preserve their language, culture, traditions, and religion.

Rather, the struggle of the people of East Turkistan against China's control has passed through three stages of history, which will be discussed in this book: first, the struggle for liberation from the Chinese invaders to regain their independent state; second, the search for equal rights and genuine autonomy; and finally, the shift back to seeking full independence as a response to China's ongoing genocide. The people of East Turkistan differ from many stateless minorities around the world who have never possessed a nation-state or are not indigenous to their land. The people of East Turkistan do not fit the definition of an ethnic, linguistic, or religious minority living in someone else's country, nor are they a stateless tribal group. Rather, they comprise a national group of people who have a common language, religion, and ethnicity, as well as a common territory where they established a nation-state and nationhood before the invasion of the People's Republic of China (PRC) in 1949. Uyghurs, Kazaks, and other Turkic people were historically and continue to be the main populations in East Turkistan. Both groups believe in Islam, speak different varieties of Turkish, and are indigenous to East Turkistan, while both the Uyghurs and Kazaks each have their own ethnic cultures.

Many commentators have tried to answer the question of which people are entitled to self-determination. Those analyses link a "people" to a colonial territory based on history in the context of self-determination law. For example, at the United Nations, Resolution 1514, "Declaration on Granting of Independence to Colonial Countries and Peoples," was adopted by the General Assembly in 1960 as part of a process aiming at global decolonization and the liberation of "colonial people."[11] The following paragraphs state the aim of the resolution, referring to a "people" as those who are yearning for independence from colonization:

> Recognizing the passionate yearning for freedom in all dependent peoples and the decisive role of such peoples in the attainment of their independence, Welcoming the emergence in recent years of a large number of dependent territories into freedom and independence, and recognizing the increasingly powerful trends towards freedom in such territories which have not yet attained independence, Convinced that all peoples have an inalienable right to complete freedom, the exercise of their sovereignty and the integrity of their national territory, Solemnly proclaims the necessity of bringing to a speedy and unconditional end colonialism in all its forms and manifestations.

General Assembly Resolution 2625 Principle V (1970) also states the following regarding the full consideration of who should be entitled to self-determination:

> The establishment of a sovereign and independent State, the free association or integration with an independent State or the emergence into any other political status freely determined by a people constitute modes of implementing the right of self-determination by that people.[12]

Any of these three scenarios is viable under self-determination law. They are often referred to as forms of "external self-determination," indicating that self-determination is possible on the basis of the international status of a territory and its people, not the relationship between the people and its government within the state.[13] This distinction will be discussed shortly. As will be explained in more detail in chapter 2, the relationship between the people of East Turkistan and the Chinese state has never been one between the state and its people since the people of East Turkistan are not treated equally as Chinese citizens, nor is the Chinese government qualified to represent the people of East Turkistan.

Even though, in many cases, minority ethnic groups or indigenous people also claim the freedom to establish an independent state, self-determination law refers to decolonization, and people who are colonized are entitled to independence. Contrary to self-determination law, this has not been the case when the question comes to the independence of East Turkistan. The international community has linked East Turkistan's self-determination instead to the territorial integrity of China, and from this perspective, Uyghurs and Kazaks are merely considered minority people in Chinese territory. However, this ignores the fact that the territory of East Turkistan was colonized by China. Therefore, as this book argues, the people of East Turkistan are legally entitled to independence from their colonization by China.

In this respect, the "Convention on the Elimination of All forms of Racial Discrimination" adopted general recommendations concerning the right to self-determination in 1996. General Assembly documents, unlike UN Security Council resolutions, have no binding effect on all member states.[14] However, the recommendations adopted did provide a comprehensive explanation of the legal principles of self-determination. According to the view of the committee in this general recommendation "International law has not recognized the general right of peoples unilaterally to declare secession from a state."[15] They also made a distinction between internal and external self-determination. The internal aspect of self-determination defines, for example, "the rights of all peoples to pursue freely their economic, social and cultural development without outside interference."[16] The external aspect is defined thus:

> The external aspect of self-determination implies that all peoples have the right to determine freely their political status and their place in the international community based upon the principle of equal rights. Thus, the concept of external self-determination provides the legal framework necessary to the liberation of peoples from colonialism and also the prohibition of the subjugation of peoples to systems of domination and exploitation.[17]

The definition of external self-determination is clearly linked to independence from colonization, while internal self-determination develops as a "people's" rights and autonomy within an existing state.

The principle of territorial integrity referred to in the UN Charter, Article 2(4), does not mention whether it is applicable to nonmember states or "independent" actors that have not yet been recognized as a state:

> All Members shall refrain in their international relations from the threat or use of force against the territorial integrity or political independence of any state, or in any other manner inconsistent with the Purposes of the United Nations.[18]

What, then, about the relations between a state and such independent actors? The case of Kosovo demonstrates that the court has not limited the prohibition on the use of force to interstate relations.[19] The independence of Kosovo did not conflict with state integrity law, nor did it violate general international law or UN Security Council Resolution 1244.[20] The current situation of the people of East Turkistan is no less dramatic than that of the people of Kosovo, even if China is not conducting mass killings openly in front of the world. The conjunction of both China's totalitarian state policies in East Turkistan and its intention to destroy the national group or ethnic population of the people of East Turkistan in whole or in part does not comply with state integrity law, or, to put it another way, East Turkistan's independence should not be hampered by state integrity law if we consider East Turkistan's occupied and oppressed situation. I will discuss further in the next chapter of this book, how state integrity law is not applicable to the situation of East Turkistan.

Although UN General Assembly Resolution 1514 grants the right of self-determination to colonial peoples, Resolution 1514 guides member states in determining whether they are obliged to inform colonized populations of their rights under the UN Charter (specifically, Article 73[e]), especially groups in territories that are not self-governing. Principle IV of Resolution 1541 (XV) defines non-self-governing territories as those that are geographically separate and ethnically and culturally distinct from the countries controlling them.[21] However, General Assembly Resolution 637, commonly known as the "salty water thesis," argues that one prerequisite to decolonization of non-self-governing territories is geographical separation from the colonizer's territory by blue water or by the borders of independent states.[22] Consequently, self-determination has generally been reserved for colonies across the sea from their colonizers. Nevertheless, Principle IV never mentions the salty water thesis, and Resolution 637 is simply irrelevant to the case of East Turkistan since neither water nor the borders of another state separate East Turkistan from China. However, East Turkistan is separated from China by the Gobi Desert, which is beyond China's traditional border, as defined by the Great Wall, although both China and Mongolia lay claim to parts of the desert. The people of East Turkistan are in fact culturally and ethnically distinct from the Han Chinese. Moreover, tracing the development of the status of other self-determination cases in the UN reveals that the salty water condition is not always relevant. For example, the exclusion of colonized territories such as Hawaii from decolonization shows that this "thesis" has not been applied universally.

The case of East Timor and the Indonesian occupation is also worthy of mention here. When the Portuguese left East Timor in August 1975, Indonesia claimed that East Timor was supposed to merge with West Timor, which was part of Indonesia. However, East Timor was strongly opposed to joining Indonesia, which nonetheless began to invade East Timor in late 1975. The international community strongly opposed Indonesia's occupation of East Timor and considered it a violation of the right to self-determination. After years of East Timorese resistance—and the deaths of more than 100,000 East Timorese—the ouster of Indonesian dictator Suharto in 1998 made it possible for East Timor to aspire to independence. In a referendum the next year, East Timor voted overwhelmingly for independence, and it held its first elections two years later. The Indonesian occupation of East Timor was even considered a violation of the right to self-determination. Eventually, Indonesia asked to hold a referendum, and the referendum's result was in favor of the independence of East Timor. Applying the right of self-determination under Resolution 1514 to the case of East Turkistan is probably less complicated than it was in the East Timor case because East Turkistan continues to have a clear boundary with China and had an independent government before 1949. However, the law of the right to self-determination almost always works in favor of big, influential powers, and China's invasion of East Turkistan has never been recognized as an illegal occupation by the UN Member States.

Instead, the international principle of uti possidetis has been used to determine how the territory of a new state emerged from a previous empire. According to uti possidetis juris, a new state's territory can be recognized on the basis of preceding dependent territory and colonial administrative lines.[23] If such colonial administrative lines formed a clear and definite border at the moment of independence, the territory within these boundaries would serve the new state, even though the new state had never possessed the territory.[24] Obviously, uti possidetis juris developed to apply to postcolonial and post-Mandate situations, as in the formal transfer of the territory of India from the British to the newly independent state of India. In the case of East Turkistan, while the newly independent state of China never possessed

the territory of East Turkistan before its invasion in 1949, the principle of uti possidetis seems to imply China's territorial continuity with the Qing, which fell in
1912. Besides, China is not the sole successor of the Manchu Empire: both East
Turkistan and China were successors of previous colonial administrations within
their separate territories. Moreover, there is no parallel to a post-Mandate situation,
in that the Manchu Empire did not transfer its entire colonized territory to communist China. In this case, uti possidetis juris should be applicable to the independent
territory of East Turkistan, while China should not have territorial sovereignty over
East Turkistan and is instead in violation of the same uti possidetis juris doctrine.

Regardless of the legal status of territorial claims, the essence of decolonization is
not only about the colonized region's geographic separation but whether the colonized people are oppressed and their human rights are grossly violated.[25] The UN's
"Declaration on Friendly Relations" defines "the well-being of the inhabitants of the
Non-Self Governing Territories," in Article 73(a) and (b) Chapter XI, as follows:

> Members of the United Nations which have or assume responsibilities for the
> administration of territories whose peoples have not yet attained a full measure of
> self-government recognize the principle that the interests of the inhabitants of these
> territories are paramount, and accept as a sacred trust the obligation to promote to the
> utmost, within the system of international peace and security established by the present
> Charter, the well-being of the inhabitants of these territories, and, to this end:
>
> a. to ensure, with due respect for the culture of the peoples concerned, their
>   political, economic, social, and educational advancement, their just treatment,
>   and their protection against abuses;
> b. to develop self-government, to take due account of the political aspirations of
>   the peoples, and to assist them in the progressive development of their free
>   political institutions, according to the particular circumstances of each terri-
>   tory and its peoples and their varying stages of advancement;[26]

Nevertheless, it should be noted again here that in General Assembly Resolution
2625 (XXV), Principle V, the principle of equal rights and self-determination of
peoples does not mention that self-determination law is only limited to "colonial
people." Rather, it refers to "all people":

> By virtue of the principle of equal rights and self-determination of peoples enshrined in
> the Charter of the United Nations, all peoples have the right freely to determine, with-
> out external interference, their political status and to pursue their economic, social and
> cultural development, and every State has the duty to respect this right in accordance
> with the provisions of the Charter.[27]

Self-determination law was developed and has been practiced based on the context
of decolonization, not solely limited to contexts of geographic separation. In this
regard, "all people" in self-determination law refers to the people of the colonized
territory.[28] However, in most cases, the oppression and gross violations of the human

rights of territorially defined people have emerged because these people were treated as aliens. In this case, these "aliens" become "people," making them no different from the people of a colonized country.

Many minority groups do not qualify for external self-determination because they equally benefit from the rights and obligations of the existing nation-state and therefore are not treated as aliens. While those minority groups may exercise their right to internal self-determination, their secession movements are generally not supported by international law. Previous cases, such as those of Kosovo, Quebec, northern Iraq, and Catalonia, each had specific characteristics qualifying them for international support. When analyzed collectively, they can provide a clearer understanding of the circumstances under which the right to external or internal self-determination may be claimed according to international law. In this book, I will look closely at East Turkistan to analyze the question of its right to self-determination, both in terms of decolonization and beyond, and also examine whether East Turkistan can justify its claim to external self-determination under international law.

COLONIAL HISTORY OF EAST TURKISTAN

Claims regarding the legal status of peoples and territories, and of the legality of their struggles for self-determination, are closely bound up with history. It will be instructive to review the history of East Turkistan here in terms of its relationship to the maintenance and violations of its territorial integrity.

East Turkistan has natural boundaries as well as a constructed border formed by the Great Wall. In the past, long before the Mongol invasions of the thirteenth century and the Manchu invasions in the eighteenth, Uyghurs established their own kingdoms and states, such as the Idiqut Kingdom of Qocho (840–1370s) and the Qarakhanid state (840–1212).[29] Many other independent polities followed, including the Kingdom of Moghulistan (1347–1514) and the long-lived Yarkand Khanate (1514–1705), not to mention a key period of independence under the government of Sufi leaders (1705–1759). The territory of East Turkistan has been under Chinese rule only since the fall of 1949.[30]

Today, the Chinese government asserts instead that East Turkistan was part of the Western Han dynasty (202 BCE–9 CE), one of many states that China now claims as part of its own historical territory. A recent Chinese government white paper entitled *Historical Matters Concerning Xinjiang* states that "since the Western Han Dynasty [Xinjiang] has been an inseparable part of the multi-ethnic Chinese nation."[31] However, this claim remains unfounded: the Han dynasty only captured the Turpan area, a minute portion of the vast region of East Turkistan, for a short period. Others pointed to the Tang (618–907) dynasty's brief domination in East Turkistan during the eighth century.[32] However, it must be remembered that the Tang ruling house was not originally Han Chinese but came from the steppe, much like the later Mongol conquerors.

The Manchu Qing invasion of East Turkistan was part of a longer process of empire-building. Manchus from what is now called Manchuria invaded China in

1644. They seized Beijing, which was the capital of the Chinese Ming dynasty, and henceforth referred to the Ming dynasty's territory as "China," and the Han people as "Chinese."[33] The Manchu Qing conquest of China was a century earlier than their conquest of East Turkistan, and East Turkistan, Tibet, and Mongolia were not part of Ming China.[34] To be sure, Manchu rulers identified their empire as "China" after they conquered the Ming, and they often interchangeably used "Manchu" or "Qing" to mean "China." However, the territory of the Manchu Empire was not solely home to Han Chinese people, and the Manchu court envisioned the empire as a multiethnic entity. To be clear, that meant that Qing rulers saw a general equivalence between their empire and "China," and it does not mean that the empire's territory belonged to Han Chinese people.

Though the Manchu Qing empire conquered the region in the 1750s, the territory was administratively, legally, and culturally separate from the Han-majority areas in "China proper."[35] It began to be called "Xinjiang," meaning "new territory" in Chinese, indicating simply that it was the latest in a series of imperial conquests. As Rian Thum, Gardner Bovingdon, and other experts on Uyghur history explain, at that point in time, East Turkistan was governed by a Manchu-dominated military, not by ethnic Chinese.[36] In 1864, the peoples of East Turkistan rebelled against the Manchu Empire and established the emirate of Kashgaria (*Yette Sheher*) under the leadership of the military officer Ya'qūb Beg.[37] In 1876, the Manchu Empire invaded East Turkistan again. The Manchu Qing finished reconquering the region in 1878 and in 1884 transformed it into a province, now formally called "Xinjiang." As James Millward has persuasively argued, this shift in the region's status to "Xinjiang" was conducted by the Qing empire, and not by China, which is a distinct historical entity.[38]

China's white paper also insists that the main population (Uyghurs) were migrants from the Selenga and Orkhon river basin in 840s who integrated and assimilated with the locals.[39] However, what this paper ignores is that the Uyghur people belonged to distinct polities, the Eastern Turkic Khaganate, and Western Turkic Khaganate. The leaders of those polities were all Turkic-speaking tribes belonging to the same Turkic land or empire. The "Turks," as they called themselves collectively, overthrew the Ruanruan Proto-Mongol rulers of the region and established the Turkic empire.[40] In 583, this empire was divided into the Eastern Turkic Khaghanate centered around present-day Mongolia and the Western Turkic Khaganate, which encompassed today's Zungharia, the Ferghana Valley, the western Tarim Basin, and parts of Afghanistan and northern India.[41] By 744, the Eastern Turks were ruled by an Uyghur Turk Khaganate to which even China paid large sums of gold as tribute for many years.[42] During the 840s, the Uyghur Turks from Eastern Turkic Khaganate moved to the territory of the Western Turkic Khaganate regions (sources indicate it was because of Kyrgyz invasions and or natural disaster) and formed a new Khaganate—the Uyghur Idiqut Kingdom in the Turfan Basin. It extended to Kumul and Kucha. The Uyghur Idiqut state submitted to Chinggis Khan's Mongol empire in 1209.[43]

The white paper does not deny that one of the Uyghur subgroups moved to today's Turpan region in 844 and established the Idiqut Kingdom, also known as Gaochang or Qocho. Other Turkic tribes, such as the Qarluq and Yaghma, moved to today's southern East Turkistan, where they established the Qarakhanid empire extending from Kashgaria to Transoxiana—almost all of today's Central Asia—prior to the Mongol invasions.[44] However, despite this acknowledgment, the white paper still claims that the Uyghurs and other Turks should not be considered indigenous to the region. Today's Uyghurs originate from the Uyghur Turks of the Idiqut Uyghur state, the Qarluq and Yaghma Turks of the Qarakhanid Empire, most likely other local tribes, such as the Sogdians (Persian, Central Asian merchants), and Islamic converts among the Mongols from Chinggis Khan's invasion. It is ignorant to simply state that the Uyghurs are a totally distinct people from those of East Turkistan and that they came from the Selenga and Orkhon River Basin. China's white paper's groundless claims also fail to explain whether or not Chinese settlers ruled the region before the people of East Turkistan, nor how or why the Uyghur and other Turkic ethnic groups became the main population in the region in the first place. That is because, in reality, the sole historical instance of their control over the region was a period of partial rule lasting a short period of time, during the Han dynasty. Even with a more modern setting, the white paper avoids explaining the independent Uyghur state of Kashgaria (*Yette Sheher*) of the mid-nineteenth century, and how the fledgling Chinese Communist state cooperated with the Soviet Union to invade the region in the mid-twentieth century.

After the end of Manchu rule in the revolution of 1911–1912, Han Chinese people and rulers began to claim and often invade the territories that the Manchu Empire had once colonized in the name of establishing a so-called multiethnic state. However, no Han-dominated state was able to rule East Turkistan until after 1949.[45] Yuan Shikai (1859–1916), who briefly turned China's nascent republic into a revived empire and ushered in an era of warlordism, appointed a monarchist governor to rule East Turkistan, Yang Zengxin (1864–1928). Yang nominally remained loyal to the Chinese Republic yet detached himself from it, for example, by printing money, controlling external trade, and establishing independent diplomatic relations with neighboring states. However, he never declared East Turkistan, which was effectively his personal fiefdom, to be an independent state.[46] His independent rule and detachment from the new Chinese Republic further exemplify that, after the fall of the Manchu Empire, the territory of East Turkistan was not transferred to the new Chinese Republic.

The people of East Turkistan fought against Yang's rule, as well as that of his successor, Jin Shuren (1883–1941). In 1932, Uyghurs, Hui Muslims, Kazaks, Kyrgyz, and Mongols rebelled and overthrew Jin's government in southern East Turkistan. On November 12, 1933, the people of East Turkistan established an independent East Turkistan Islamic Republic in the south of the region. However, the Soviet Union actively opposed the establishment of a new Islamic Republic just across the border from its own Central Asian territory. There is a commonly held view that the Soviets may have feared Japan's interest in the new state. Subsequently, the Soviets sent troops to attack Hui Muslim forces in the northern part of East Turkistan, who then fled to the south and entered the city of Kashgar, which was the republic's newly established capital city. Those Hui forces had agreed to cooperate with the Nanjing government, which was dominated by the Chinese Nationalist

Party (Guomindang, often called KMT). They slaughtered the Uyghur population and ultimately destroyed the East Turkistan Islamic Republic.[47] The late Manchu Empire then appointed another Han Chinese governor, Sheng Shicai (1895–1970), to rule East Turkistan. Yet Sheng Shicai, like Yang Zengxin, was only nominally loyal to the Chinese Republic and in actuality ruled as a puppet of the Soviets. His loyalties later changed to the Nationalists (KMT) again and then to the Communists, before he finally fled the region to join the Nationalist government in Taiwan. Later, in November 1944, the northern region of East Turkistan was liberated again by the people of East Turkistan, and the East Turkistan Republic was officially and successfully established second time with the help of the Soviet Union. The significance of an independent Kashgaria or *Yette Sheher* state under Yaʻqūb Beg and of the establishment of two East Turkistan Republics prior to Communist China's invasion will be discussed in the next chapter.

NOTES

1. U.N. Charter art.1, ¶ 2; U.N. Charter art. 55.
2. G.A. Res. 1514 (XV), Declaration on the Granting of Independence to Colonial Countries and Peoples, at 67 (Dec.14, 1960), https://www.sfu.ca/~palys/UN-Resolution%201514.pdf.
3. G.A. Res. 2625 (XXV), Declaration on Principles of International Law Concerning Friendly Relations and Cooperation Among States in Accordance with the Charter of the United Nations, A/RES/2625(XXV), at 123 (October 24, 1970).
4. G.A. Res. 2625 (XXV), at 124 (October 24, 1970).
5. G.A. Res. 3103 (XXVIII), Basic Principles of the Legal Status of the Combatants Struggling Against Colonial and Alien Domination and Racist Regimes, at 142 (December 12, 1973), https://digitallibrary.un.org/record/191382?ln=en.
6. Aureliu Cristescu (Special Rapporteur on the Righ to Self-determination), *The Right to Self Determination: Historical and Current Development on the Basis of United Nations*, 41, ¶ 279, UN Doc. E/CN.4/Sub.2/404/Rev.1(1981).
7. Joshua Castellino, "Peoples, Indigenous Peoples and Minorities" in *Self-Determination and Secession Law* (Oxford: Oxford University Press, 2014), 32.
8. Jose R. Martinez Cobo (Special Rapporteur of the Sub-Commission on Prevention of Discrimination and Protection of Minorities), *Study of the Problem of Discrimination Against the Indigenous Populations*, UN Doc. E/CN.4/Sub.2/1982/2/ Add .6.
9. Francesco Capotorti (Special Rapporteur of the Sub-Commission on Prevention of Discrimination and Protection of Minorities), *Study on the Rights of Persons Belonging to Ethnic, Religious and Linguistic Minorities*, ¶ 568, UN Doc. 1/E/CN.4/Sub.2/384/Rev.1(1979).
10. Britannica, T. Editors of Encyclopaedia, "Minority," *Encyclopedia Britannica*, September 18, 2019, accessed November 3, 2021, https://www.britannica.com/topic/minority.
11. G.A. Res. 1514 (XV) (December 14, 1960).
12. G.A. Res. 2625(XXV), at 124, Principle V, ¶ 4 (October 24, 1970).
13. David Raic, *Statehood and Law of Self-Determination*, vol. 43 (The Hague: Kluwer Law International, 2002), 206.
14. U.N. Charter art. 25 ¶ 2 and art. 12. See also United Nations, Power and Function of General Assembly, accessed October 9, 2020, https://www.un.org/en/ga/about/background.shtml.

15. Comm, on the Elimination of Racial Discrimination (CERD), General Recommendation 21, on Its Forty-eight Session, U.N. Doc. A/51/18, annex VIII at 125 (1996).

16. *Id.* at para. 4.

17. *Id.*

18. U.N. Charter art. 4, ¶ 2.

19. Christian Walter, "Kosovo Advisory Opinion: What It Says and What It Does Not Say" in *Self-Determination and Secession Law*, ed. Christian Walter, Antje Von Ungern- Sternberg and Kavus Abushov (Oxford: Oxford University Press, 2014), 21.

20. S.C.R. 1244 (June 10, 1999).

21. G.A. Res. 1541(XV), Annex, Principle IV and V (December 15, 1960).

22. G.A. Res. 637 (II), at 26-27 (December 16, 1952).

23. Fozia Lone, "Uti Possidetis Iuris," *Obo in International Law*, March 23, 2012, https://www.oxfordbibliographies.com/view/document/obo-9780199796953/obo-9780199796953-0065.xml.

24. Abraham Bell and Eugene Kontorovich, "Palestine, *Uti Possidetis Juris,* and the Borders of Israel," *Arizona Law Review* 58 (2016): 633–92, 643.

25. David Raič, *Statehood and the Law of Self-Determination*, 328.

26. U.N. Charter art. 73.

27. G.A. Res. 2625(XXV), at 123 (October 24, 1970).

28. David Raič, *Statehood and the Law of Self-Determination*, 208.

29. James Millward, *Eurasian Crossroads* (New York: Columbia University Press, 2007), 47–88.

30. Linda Benson, *The Ili Rebellion: The Moslem Challenge to Chinese Authority in Xinjiang, 1944–1949* (Armonk: M. E. Sharpe, 1990), 10.

31. China, The State Council Information Office, *Historical Matters Concerning Xinjiang* (Beijing: Foreign Languages Press Co. Ltd., 2019), http://english.www.gov.cn/archive/whitepaper/201907/21/content_WS5d33fed5c6d00d362f668a0a.html.

32. Millward, *Eurasian Crossroads*, 34–37.

33. Frederic Wakeman, Jr, *The Fall of Imperial China* (New York: The Free Press, 1975), 81.

34. Zhao Gang, "Reinventing China: Imperial Qing Ideology and the Rise of Modern Chinese National Identity in the Early Twentieth Century," *Modern China* 32, no. 1 (January 2006): 5–12.

35. Güljanat Kurmangaliyeva Ercilasun and Konuralp Ercilasun, eds., *The Uyghur Community: Diaspora, Identity, and Geopolitics* (New York: Palgrave Macmillan, 2018), 6.

36. Rian Thum, "The Uyghurs in Modern China," in *Oxford Encyclopedia of Asian History* (Oxford: Oxford University Press, 2018), 4.

37. David Brophy, *Uyghur Nation: Reform and Revolution on the Russia-China Frontier* (Cambridge: Harvard University Press, 2016), 72; Millward, *Eurasian Crossroads,* 124.

38. Millward, *Eurasian Crossroads*, 138.

39. China, The State Council Information Office, *Historical Matters Concerning Xinjiang*.

40. Millward, *Eurasian Crossroads*, 31; Turghun Almas, *Uyghurs* (Munchen: World Uyghur Congress, 2010), 18.

41. Ibid., Millward, 31.

42. Ibid., Millward, 45.

43. Ibid., Millward, 47.

44. Muhammed Imin Bugra, *History of East Turkistan* (Ankara: Ankara Publishing, 1987), 117.

45. Millward, *Eurasian Crossroads*, 24.

46. Ibid., 181–85.

47. Ibid., 198–200.

2

East Turkistan Was Not Terra Nullius

EAST TURKISTAN'S STATEHOOD
BEFORE CHINA'S INVASION (1877–1933)

The Manchu colonization of East Turkistan in 1877 was not the colonization of stateless land but the invasion of Kashgaria, an independent state. Kashgaria had trade relations with Russia, while its head of the state, Ya'qūb Beg, was recognized by the Ottomans as the sultan and by the British as "The Ruler of the territory of Kashgar and Yarkand."[1] The Ottomans sent military officers and instructors, while the British appointed representatives to Kashgaria's government, which was allowed to purchase weapons from India.[2]

Similarly, although the East Turkistan Republic (1933–1934) established during the Chinese warlords' occupation of East Turkistan did not survive long, nevertheless it published its own constitution, organized its own military, distributed coinage, and printed banknotes. To this day, November 12, the day of its founding, is celebrated as East Turkistan's Independence Day, on which the people of East Turkistan raise their national East Turkistan Islamic Republic flag, which features a crescent moon on a blue background. Students and soldiers paraded on that day in 1933, and the East Turkistan Islamic Republic's national anthem was adopted, the song "On the Road to Freedom" (*Qurtulush yolida*). As figure 2.1 shows, East Turkistani passports were issued as official travel documents. The Constitution of the East Turkistan Islamic Republic, a full translation of which is added at the end of the book, reflected both Islamic law and the state's modern civic national ideology.[3] Its clauses emphasized not only the guidance of the Quran but also the central roles of populism—according to which everything is for the people's benefit—free speech, and the democratic election of parliamentary representatives.

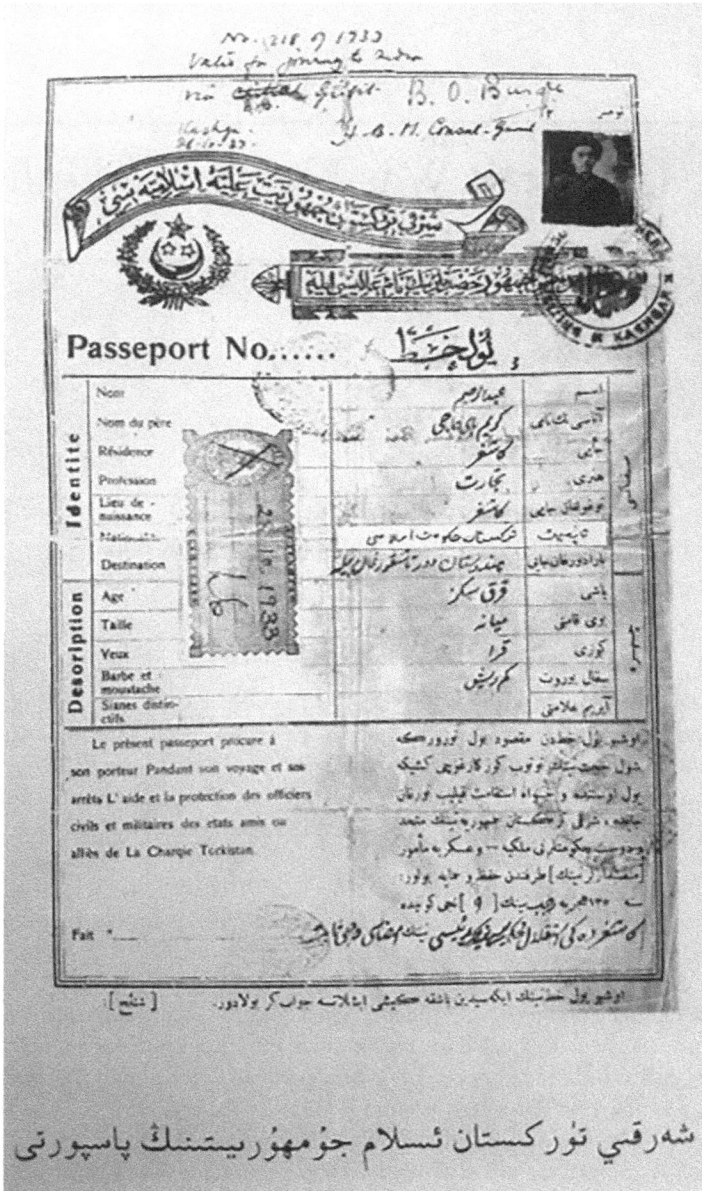

Figure 2.1   Passport of Islamic Republic of East Turkistan in 1933. *Source:* Bughra, Muhemmed Emin. *History of East Turkistan*, Last edition. Ankara: Ankara Publishing, 1987.

EAST TURKISTAN'S STATEHOOD BEFORE
CHINA'S INVASION (1944–1949)

Declaration of Independence

As a result of the people of East Turkistan's unceasing resistance, in November 1944, the Second East Turkistan Republic was officially and successfully established five years before the People's Republic of China's (PRC) invasion. While this republic liberated the northern part of East Turkistan, its army and the people of East Turkistan continued to wage war against their colonial Han warlords in the South. On January 5, 1945, the nine precepts of the "Declaration of Independence of East Turkistan" were announced.[4] These precepts demonstrated the aspiration of establishing a government that represented civic liberal nationhood in East Turkistan. They specifically delineated the equality of all ethnic groups in East Turkistan, as well as fair elections, and fundamental human rights and freedoms as follows:

1. The Chinese killers [warlords] in the East Turkistan national territory must be eliminated.
2. All East Turkistanis must be treated equally in the creation of a genuinely free and independent republic.
3. The economy of East Turkistan, including agriculture, farming, industry, transportation, private commerce and handcrafts, shall be developed, to improve the economic well-being and quality of living of the people of East Turkistan;
4. Because Muslims constitute the vast majority of the people in East Turkestan, religion of Islam will be given special emphasis. Other religion's freedom to practice must also be guaranteed.
5. Governmental public health infrastructure and governmental bodies administering education shall be developed;
6. Peaceful diplomatic relationships with all democratic nations worldwide shall be established, particularly with the Soviet Union and other states neighboring on East Turkistan including China.
7. To defend East Turkestan and preserve peace, a robust army must be established from members of all racial and ethnic groupings;
8. The government of East Turkistan is responsible for providing postal services, regulating financial institutions, establishing government ownership and government-led natural resource management, including forestry, and establishing government-owned energy industries, including oil and coal;
9. Ethnonationalism, bureaucratism and bribery shall be banned countrywide.[5]

Elihan Tore Shakirov was elected president, Hakimbeg Hoja vice president, Abdureup Mehsum secretary-general, and Zirip Kari Haji the judge of the East Turkistan People's Court on November 12, 1944.[6] Aslihan Tore, Elihan Tore's son, later recalled the president's speech on the day the East Turkistan Republic established its independence:

> The territory of East Turkistan belongs to people of East Turkistan. This land belonged to the Turkic king Oghuzhan back in the days of prophet Abraham. . . . We will eliminate the invaders in the south of our territory. . . . On the day of independence of all East Turkistan, on the day the election is nationwide, we will elect the president of East Turkistan again.[7]

Government Structure

The government council was the legislative branch of the government, which is similar to a congress. The primary function of the council was to create and modify laws, and it was established to control state affairs and the social and legal order. The government had a State Bank of East Turkistan, Ministry of Finance, Ministry of Education, Ministry of Agriculture, Ministry of Land and Water Systems, judicial system including the Supreme Court of East Turkistan, Ministry of Religious Affairs, Ministry of Internal Affairs, Office of State Media, Ministry of Health, Head Command of Partisans, East Turkistan National Army, and many prefectural, county, and village-level government offices.[8] The table 2.1 shows the members of the council of the East Turkistan Republic as recorded in official documents. It demonstrates the multiethnic but fundamentally Turkic and Muslim character of the East Turkestan Republic as well as its complex political organization.[9]

In mid-January 1945, the East Turkistan Republic announced the Declaration of the Political Functions of Government as follows:

1. Eliminate all policies of the colonizers of East Turkistan.
2. Establish a democratic body of the government of East Turkistan.
3. Military of East Turkistan belongs to the people of East Turkistan or East Turkistan nation.
4. All ethnic groups in East Turkistan are equal before the constitution
5. East Turkistan government respects religion and religious freedom.
6. Government officials must be elected by the people of East Turkistan.
7. The government of East Turkistan will maintain a close relationship with the Soviet Union.
8. The government of East Turkistan will regulate and develop an educational administration.
9. The government of East Turkistan recognizes the Uyghur language as an official language at the national level.[10]

On May 13, 1945, the East Turkistan Republic released two important regulations: the Provisional Regulations on Criminal Procedure of the East Turkistan Republic and the Provisional Penal Code of the East Turkistan Republic. These regulations codified the status of the "Nine Political Precepts" as the supreme law of

Table 2.1   Members of the Council of the East Turkistan Republic

Name	Ethnicity	Position	Background
Elihan Tore	Uzbek	President of the Interim Government	Chairman of the Ghulja National Liberation Group
Abdulkerim Abbasov	Uyghur	Minister of Internal Affairs; later served as Ministery of Propaganda and Director of the Political Department of the National Army	Leader of the Ghulja National Liberation Group
Mehmetjan Mehsum	Uyghur	Chief Justice of the Supreme Court	Leader of the Ghulja National Liberation Group
Jani Yoldashov	Uyghur	Director of the Supervisory Committee	Leader of the Ghulja National Liberation Group
Abdureup Mehsum	Uyghur	Secretary-General of the Interim Government	Leader of the Ghulja National Liberation Group
Rahimjan Sabir Khoja	Uyghur	Vice Minister of Military Affairs, later served as Minister of Military Affairs and Minister of Internal Affairs	Leader of the Ghulja National Liberation Group
Salman Bay	Uzbek	Minister of Agriculture	Leader of the Ghulja National Liberation Group
Zunun Tayof	Tatar	Assistant Director of the Supervisory Committee; later served as Minister of Military Affairs and Deputy Commander of the National Army	Leader of the Ghulja National Liberation Group
Hakimbeg Khoja	Uyghur	Vice President of the Interim Government	Son-in-law of the last Qing-era Uyghur administrator of Ili
Enver Musabayov	Uyghur	Minister of Finance	Member of the famous Musabayov commercial family
Ablimit Eli Khelpe	Uyghur	Minister of Religious Affairs	Religious figure
Abdulla Gheni	Uyghur	Chief Judge of the Military Tribunal	Leader of the Nilka Guerillas
Habib Yuqi	Tatar	Minister of Education	Intellectual with a history of study in the Soviet Union
Ubulhari Tora	Kazak	Minister of Nomadic Pasturing	
Piotr Alexandrov	Russian	Commander-in-Chief of the National Army, Minister of Military Affairs	Soviet commander of the Ghulja uprising

(continued)

Table 2.1   (Continued)

Name	Ethnicity	Position	Background
Povel Maskolyov	Russian	Minister of Internal Affairs; later served as Chief of Staff of the National Army	White Russian residing in Ghulja
Puja Abal	Mongolian		Elite member of the Mongolian community

Source: Adapted from Wang Ke, *The East Turkistan Independence Movement 1930s–1940s.*

the country, declaring that observance of the precepts was the duty of every citizen of the republic.[11] The interim government also introduced many resolutions related to finance and the military. For example, provisions on matters related to taxation in Resolution No. 1 established charges of 5% sales and goods tax and 3% agricultural tax with no discrimination between Muslims and non-Muslims.[12] All of this evidence establishes that the East Turkistan Republic was a functioning state with complete political and financial institutions that also represented a distinct group of people.

The East Turkistan Republic Represents the Whole Territory and People of East Turkistan

The East Turkistan Republic of 1944 was the resurrection of the East Turkistan Islamic Republic of 1933. Prior to the foundation of the republic, the National Revolutionary Committee published a document entitled "Why Are We Fighting?" that demonstrates this point clearly. Clauses in the document clarified that the objective of the East Turkistan Republic was to bring freedom to the whole territory of East Turkistan and that East Turkistan belonged to the people of East Turkistan, not to Han Chinese settlers or Manchus:

(1) East Turkistan is our homeland; [Uyghurs, kazaks and other ethnic people]
(4) Since 1937, under the oppressive rule of Sheng Shicai, many ethnic leaders have been assassinated, chief among them being Hoja Niyaz and Sharif Khan;
(5) The Chinese rulers have sent a total of 1 million Chinese and Manchurian emigrants to the Xinjiang colony.[13]

Clause 2 of this document also stated the aim of establishing a multiethnic, civic nation-state:

(2) The Turkic inhabitants of Kazakhstan, Kyrgyzstan, Uzbekistan, and Tatarstan are our compatriots.

According to these facts, the East Turkistan Republics of 1933 and 1944 met the essential criteria to be categorized as sovereign nation-states outlined in Article 1 of the Montevideo Convention on the Rights and Duties of States of 1933.[14] According to this article, a sovereign state should have a permanent population, a defined territory, a government, and the capacity to enter into relations with other states. State territory is usually defined by the government that represents the people who live in that territory. The East Turkistan Republics of 1933 and 1944 fully met the four criteria of the Montevideo Convention, even though either government only exercised its power over the North or the South of East Turkistan. The South of East Turkistan legally did not belong to any state in 1944, while the North of East Turkistan did not legally belong to any state in 1933. The permanent population of East Turkistan were ethnically Uyghurs as well as other Turkic Muslims, Hui Muslims, and Mongols. The participation of all these ethnicities constituted the government and army of East Turkistan. At that time, the Han Chinese population of the region did not exceed 4%, many of whom came with Manchu soldiers from inner China.

Relations with the East Turkistan Republic and Other States

The East Turkistan Republics of 1933 and 1944 both entered into relations with other states. Sabit Damolla, the head of the first East Turkistan Republic, wrote to the British consulate in Kashgar asking protection from the Soviets and expressing his willingness to cooperate with the British.[15] In September 1933, the president and commander-in-chief of the republic also sent a letter and diplomats to the British consulate in Kashgar to request recognition. They described the situation of East Turkistan in detail and requested help from the Parliament of Great Britain in exchange for silk, wool, and other products.[16] The state of East Turkistan established in the North in 1944 also entered into relations with other states. They had trade relations with the Soviet Union, to which they exported wool, animal skins, and leather products and imported tractors, farm vehicles, and other heavy and light industrial products.[17] The president of East Turkistan, Elihan Tore, sent a letter to the Soviet Union on behalf of the people of East Turkistan and demanded continuous aid from Stalin to expel all colonizers from East Turkistan.[18] This letter was written while the East Turkistan army was engaged in battle with Chinese Nationalist colonizers who had not been expelled from the South. Regardless, the letter shows wartime diplomatic exchanges between the two states. The Montevideo Convention, in its definition of sovereign states, requires that such a state possess the capacity to establish relations with other states, and the East Turkistan Republics clearly possessed that capacity. Although many states, undermining the legal norms of the international community, did not recognize the statehood of East Turkistan because of their own political interests, nevertheless, this "non-recognition" is immaterial to the legal status of a state, as "recognition" is a political act. As the Montevideo Convention, Article 3 provides:

> The political existence of the state is independent of recognition by other states. Even before recognition, the state has the right to defend its integrity and independence, to provide for its conservation and prosperity, and consequently to organize itself as it sees fit, to legislate upon its interests, administer its services, and to define the jurisdiction

and competence of its courts. The exercise of these rights has no other limitation than the exercise of the rights of other states according to international law.[19]

CHINA'S ILLEGAL SOVEREIGNTY
OVER EAST TURKISTAN

It should be noted here that, since a state is a territorial entity, the state has to exercise its power over a specific territory. However, to be clear, that does not mean that securing territory guarantees the colonizer's claim to rightful sovereignty. In this respect, the four criteria of the Montevideo Convention cannot apply to the PRC's claims on colonial territory, and the Chinese government cannot represent the permanent population of East Turkistan simply because it has conquered their territory. The territory of East Turkistan that the Manchu Empire had colonized was not Han Chinese territory, either. Today, China is recognized as a nation-state capable of engaging in relations with other states, but its exercise of sovereignty over East Turkistan does not make that exercise legal or just if we consider the above reasons.

Claims to self-determination to gain independence historically rely on the constitution of the state currently exercising sovereignty over the territory. This is known from several cases. For example, in 1994, Ethiopia's constitution included the right to self-determination for every nation or distinct people in its territory in order to ensure the unconditional right to self-determination, including the right to secession.[20] The Union of Burma also constitutionally established self-determination in 1947.[21] Even if self-determination is not included in the existing state's constitution, people may still be entitled to independence if this existing state's government agrees. The PRC never provided the secession through right to self-determination to the people in East Turkistan in its own constitution when they invaded them, despite the fact that the people of East Turkistan share a common culture, identity, language, religion, values, and belief and predominantly inhabit an identifiable territory, all of which makes them very distinct from the Chinese nation. However, their constitution guaranteed national autonomy for East Turkistan which is never actually provided.

So much is clear from statements by Chinese leaders. The founder of the Chinese Nationalist Party Sun Yat-sen opposed the Manchu Empire. In 1923, he explained in his manifesto how, in his view, the independence of Chinese people from colonization by Manchus resembled the freedom that the Chinese had secured after long domination by the Mongols, when ethnically Han Chinese people established the Ming state. The term "Chinese" in his manifesto clearly refers to the Han Chinese ethnicity, which Sun associated with the territory and state of the Ming, not the ethnically distinct people of East Turkistan, Tibet, or Mongolia:

> During the periods when their political and military prowess declined, they could not escape for the time from the fate of a conquered nation, but they could eventually

vigorously reassert themselves. Thus, the Mongol rule of China . . . was finally over-
thrown by Tai Tse of the Ming dynasty and his loyal follower. So in our own time was
the Manchu yoke thrown off by the Chinese.[22]

In his manifesto, Sun Yat-sen expressed his intention to annex territories not
belonging to China by declaring that the "five nations"—referring to the five regions
of the Manchu Empire—belonged under a single flag.[23] This merely represented the
rhetorical transformation of an imperial system into a nation-state without a real
change to its structure. Mikhail Borodin, a Russian advisor to Sun Yat-sen, drafted
Sun's original Nationalist Party Congress Manifesto on the basis of Lenin's "Theses
on National and Colonial Questions." The manifesto called for self-determination
of colonized nations, with the pledge of guaranteeing national self-determination,
including the right of political secession of non-Han territories colonized by the
Manchu Empire before their eventual reunion with the Chinese state. However,
Nationalist Party members had strongly opposed Borodin's draft, as they believed
that it distorted Sun's "three great principles."[24] As a result, Sun Yat-sen convinced
Borodin to replace the disputed text with his own "Outline for National Reconstruction." The new outline removed anything related to the independence of non-Han
nations, including East Turkistan, Mongolia, Tibet, and Manchuria. Outlines of the
text emphasized the superior nationality of the ethnic Han Chinese that could foster
and cultivate other non-Chinese "small domestic ethnicities."[25] The constitution of
Chinese Communist Party in 1931 recognized independence of non Chinese people,
but this promise was not kept.[26]

However, the people of East Turkistan rose up, and they successfully established
the first and second East Turkistan Republics in 1933 and 1944, respectively.[27] In
fact, both republics were established before the PRC was even formally founded and
before the idea of a "Chinese nation" had fully taken hold in most of China itself.[28]
Though the first East Turkistan Republic soon fell to Soviet and Chinese attacks
in 1933, this Republic represented East Turkistan's first attempt at establishing an
independent nation-state without the support of outside forces. After ten years of
struggle, the Second East Turkistan Republic was established in 1944 and received
military aid from the Soviet Union through trade but was betrayed by the Soviet
Union shortly after. Stalin showed his full support to the Chinese Communist Party
(CCP) and encouraged them not to delay the occupation of East Turkistan as he
worried about Western influence in the region. During a discussion between Stalin
and a CCP delegation in June 1949, Stalin said,

> One should not put off occupation of Xinjiang, because a delay may lead to the interfer-
> ence by the English in the affairs of Xinjiang. They can activate the Muslims, including
> the Indian ones, to continue the civil war against the communists, which is undesirable,
> for there are large deposits of oil and cotton in Xinjiang, which China needs badly.[29]

After two months of discussion, in August 1949, the leaders of the second East
Turkistan Republic were invited to Moscow for negotiations. However, it was
announced that the East Turkistan delegates were killed in an airplane accident on

their way to Beijing to participate in diplomatic meetings.[30] Many Uyghurs suspect that the accident was an assassination purposefully planned by Mao Zedong and Stalin because, soon after following the crash, in October 1949, the newly established Chinese state's People's Liberation Army invaded East Turkistan.[31] This incident has since served as part of the basis upon which Chinese Communist leaders have claimed East Turkistan as an integral part of China and peacefully liberated by the Chinese People's Liberation Army.

In fact, between 1950 and 1955, the East Turkistan Republic's army was disarmed, demobilized, and brought under the control of the CCP.[32] At the Bandung Conference in April 1955, Zhou Enlai, the head of the Chinese delegation, gave a speech at the plenary session of the Asian-African Conference, which criticized colonization of African countries and called upon African and Asian countries to stand together to support decolonization. Ironically, he avoided mentioning China's colonization of East Turkistan, Mongolia, and Tibet.[33] Only five months after the conference, China established a colonial administration and in October 1955 proclaimed the so-called "Xinjiang Uyghur Autonomous Region" (XUAR).[34] Within a few years, anyone who opposed the Chinese invasion or had a negative opinion about the Chinese army or participated in the resistance guerilla movements in East Turkistan was sentenced to death or life imprisonment.[35]

That "autonomy" has never been implemented. Chinese scholars today argue that the concept of modern Chinese identity is not limited to ethnic Han Chinese identity and Chinese territory, but that it includes the vast territory of the old Manchu Empire and a unified, multiethnic identity.[36] However, more than seventy years of Chinese oppression and China's genocide in East Turkistan have proven that today's China is not a civic nation-state and that the modern Chinese state's national identity is not multiethnic, but built around a single ethnic identity, that of Han Chinese. The second part of this book will discuss how China's nation-building process achieved this identity and laid the solid foundation for the recent Uyghur genocide to eliminate the right to independence of the people in East Turkistan.

NOTES

1. Qin Hancai 秦翰才, "*Zuo Zongtang quanzhuan*" 左宗棠全传 [The Complete Biography of Zuo Zongtang] loc. 925–949 (2016) Apple books.
2. Adeeb Khalid, *Central Asia: A New History from the Imperial Conquests to the Present* (Princeton: Princeton University Press, 2021), 88–90.
3. "Qanun-i asasiy," [Constitution] *Istiqlal Mejmuesi* 1, no. 2 (1933): 21–41.
4. Nebijan Tursun, *General History of Uyghurs*, Uyghur edition, Vol. 7 (Ankara: Uyghur Research Institute, 2020), 300–307. The precepts had been shortened from the thirty-point Declaration of Independence of the first East Turkistan Republic, and from the nineteen points of the "Manifesto of the East Turkistan Liberation Organization" that had been published in July 1943 in Ghulja's *Freedom Spark* newspaper [authors translation].
5. "Resolution No. 4 of the Interim Government Council of the East Turkestan Republic," dated January 5, 1945, contains the "Nine Political Precepts," along with other content.

Cited in Nebijan Tursun, *General History of Uyghurs*, Uyghur edition, Vol. 7 (Ankara: Uyghur Research Institute, 2020), 300–307. Translated by author from Uyghur to English.

6. Tursun, *General History*, vol. 7, 275, 318.

7. Ibid., 277.

8. Ibid., 315–19.

9. According to Uyghur historian Nebijan Tursun and numerous other Uyghur historians, the word "Interim Government of the East Turkistan Republic" appears only in the nine precepts of the "Declaration of Independence of East Turkistan." The term "interim" was not used in any of the remaining government documents.

10. Ibid., 310.

11. Wang Ke, *The East Turkistan Independence Movement 1930s–1940s*, trans. Carissa Fletcher (Hong Kong: The Chinese University of Hong Kong Press, 2019), 146.

12. Ibid., 148.

13. Ibid., 110.

14. The Montevideo Convention on the Rights and Duties of States was signed at Montevideo, Uruguay, on 26 December 1933, during the Seventh International Conference of American States. Even if the convention was signed only by nineteen states, it has been almost universally accepted as the main reference in order to identify the constitutive elements of states. online at: https://www.jus.uio.no/english/services/library/treaties/01/1-02/rights-duties-states.xml. See also: Montevideo Convention, art. 1. December 26, 1933, Treaty Doc. 165 LNTS 19.

15. Jamil Hasanli, *Soviet Policy in Xinjiang: Stalin and the National Movement in Eastern Turkistan* (Lexington: Lexington Books, 2021), 28.

16. "Sinkiang Internal Situation," September 1933, BL, FO India/ IOR/L/PS/12/2364 cited in Joy R. Lee, "The Islamic Republic of Eastern Turkistan and the Formation of Modern Uyghur Identity in Xinjiang" (master's thesis, Manhattan University, 2005), 91–92, https://apps.dtic.mil/sti/citations/ADA455923.

17. Tursun, *General History*, vol. 10, 492.

18. "Letter from L. Beria to Cde. I.V. Stalin, May 11, 1945, GARF, Fond R-9401ss, Opis' 2, Delo 95, ll. 352-359," obtained by Jamil Hasanli and translated by Gary Goldberg, China and Soviet Union in Xinjiang 1934-1949 Collection, History and Public Policy Program Digital Archive, Wilson Center, Washington, DC, https://digitalarchive.wilsoncenter.org/document/121725

I reproduce the full text of the letter here:

Dear Commander-in-Chief

Marshal Stalin

I send ardent greetings to the creator of the culture and equal rights of all peoples, the great leader of the Soviet Union.

I, and the peoples of East Turkestan recently liberated from oppression, hope in you, Chief Marshal, that the peoples of East Turkestan will be liberated only with the aid of the Great Soviet Union, which is giving us comprehensive aid in this cause. Millions of people of East Turkestan constantly look to you as their leader, protecting the interests of oppressed peoples. We are deeply confident that we will always receive the legitimate and necessary assistance from you. We will thereby be able to expel all our oppressors from our homeland. I hope that the colonizers will be expelled if we have the aid we need from the Soviet Union.

I greet the Red Army and its heroes, which have finally defeated the enemies of freedom-loving peoples of the world, the fascists.

I have sent all our remaining wishes to dear Petr Andreyevich.

I remain expectant of favorable results of our conversation with him.

I also impatiently await the return to us of dear Vladimir Stepanovich, who will give us the necessary aid.

Head of the East Turkestan Government - ALIHAN TORE [SHAKIRJAN]

22 April 1945
Ghulja [Yining]
Authenticated by: V. Popova
19. Montevideo Convention, art. 3.
20. CONST.(FDRE.) art. 39, ¶ 1.
21. CONST. OF BURMA (1947), TTN.47, Chap I, § 1.
22. Sun Yat-sen, *Fundamentals of National Reconstruction* (Taipei: China Cultural Service, 1953), 76–83.
23. Sun Yat-sen, "Sanminzhuyi" [Three Principles of the People], in *The Complete Works of Sun Yat-sen* loc.1194 (2016) Apple Books.
24. James Leibold, *Reconfiguring Chinese Nationalism* (New York: Palgrave Macmillan, 2007), 55–57.
25. "Fundamentals of National Reconstruction," *China Copy Right and Media Blog* (blog), ed. Rogier Creemers, April 12, 1924, accessed March 21, 2022 https://chinacopyrightandmedia.wordpress.com/1924/04/12/fundamentals-of-national-reconstruction/.
26. Magnus Fiskesjo, "Rescuing The Empire: Chinese Nation-Building in The Twentieth Century," *European Journal of East Asian Studies* 5, no. 1 (2006): 15–44.
27. Justin M. Jacobs, *Xinjiang and the Modern Chinese State* (Seattle: University of Washington Press, 2016), 133–35; Millward, *Eurasian Crossroads*, 201–203, 216; Sean Roberts, *The War on the Uyghurs* (Princeton: Princeton University Press, 2020), 36.
28. Gardner Bovingdon, *Strangers in Their Own Land* (New York: Colombia University Press, 1983), 26. See also William C. Kirby, "When Did China Become China?: Thoughts on the Twentieth Century" in *The Telegony of the Modern Nation State: Japan and China*, ed. Joshua A. Fogel (Philadelphia: University of Pennsylvania Press, 2004); 105–14; Victor H. Mair, "The North Western Peoples and Recurrent Origins of the 'Chinese' State" in *The Telegony of the Modern Nation State: Japan and China*, ed. Joshua A. Fogel (Philadelphia: University of Pennsylvania Press, 2005); 46–48.
29. "Memorandum of Conversation Between Stalin and CCP Delegation, 27 June 1949, APRF: F. 45, Op.1, D.329, LI.1-7." trans. Sergey Radchenko, Sino-Soviet Relations Collection, History and Public Policy Program Digital Archive, Wilson Center, Washington, DC, https://digitalarchive.wilsoncenter.org/document/113380.
30. "Cable No. 3582 from Flilippov [Stalin] to Cde. Mao Zedong, 2 September 1949, RGASPI, f. 558, op. 11, d. 332, l. 8." trans. Gary Goldberg, China-Soviet Relations Collection, History and Public Policy Program Digital Archive, Wilson Center, Washington DC, https://digitalarchive.wilsoncenter.org/document/176340.
31. "Cable, Mao Zedong to Comrade Filippov [Stalin], 25 October 1949," Sino- Soviet Relations Collection, History and Public Policy Program Digital Archive, Wilson Center, Washington, DC, https://digitalarchive.wilsoncenter.org/document/176641.

32. Gardner Bovingdon, "Autonomy in Xinjiang: Han Nationalist Imperatives and Uyghur Discontent," *Policy Studies*, no. 11 (2004): 15.

33. "Main Speech by Premier Chou En-lai [Zhou Enlai], Head of the Delegation of the People's Republic of China, Distributed at the Plenary Session of the Asian-African Conference," April 19, 1955, History and Public Policy Program Digital Archive, Wilson Center, Washington, DC, http://digitalarchive.wilsoncenter.org/document/121623.

34. Bovingdon, *Autonomy in Xinjiang*, 16.

35. Central Intelligence Agency Electronic Reading Room, "Chinese Communist Regime in Sinkiang Province," 29 October 2009, CIA-RDP80-00810A001400020009-5, https://www.cia.gov/readingroom/document/cia-rdp80-00810a001400020009-5.

36. Zhao Gang, "Reinventing China: Imperial Qing Ideology and the Rise of Modern Chinese National Identity in the Early Twentieth Century," *Modern China* 32, no. 1 (2006): 3.

3

Counterargument against China's State Integrity Claim

PEACEFUL LIBERATION OR ARMED INVASION?

Did China invade and forcefully colonize East Turkistan, or was it "peaceful unification" as China claims? Historical facts and definitions from international law are helpful in cutting through China's rhetoric and establishing a clear picture of East Turkistan's status. I will demonstrate here that East Turkistan is an "occupied territory" as defined in Article 42 of the 1907 Hague Regulations, which states that "Territory is considered occupied when it is actually placed under the authority of the hostile army. The occupation extends only to the territory where such authority has been established and can be exercised."[1]

There neither was a "peaceful liberation" of East Turkistan as China claims, nor has there been any voluntary unification of the people of East Turkistan through a referendum with China. There was an illegal armed occupation of East Turkistan by the People's Republic of China's (PRC) army, and a subsequent armed resistance against it, in 1949. In September 1949, Mao Zedong sent a letter to Stalin requesting thirty to forty Soviet aircraft to transport 500,000 troops to East Turkistan. He stated in his request that China needed to send troops before the harsh winter weather set in, or else they would need to postpone until spring.[2] Stalin sent one division to aid the Chinese invasion and shipped aviation fuel to facilitate the transportation of soldiers.[3]

They were met with desperate armed resistance. One of the most prominent resistance forces in East Turkistan against the Chinese invasion was that of Osman Batur (1899–1951), a local Kazak leader. However, he was defeated by the more advanced armed forces of China, backed by Stalin.[4] Nevertheless, the people of East Turkistan continued scattered resistance movements. According to an Urumchi Radio report dated January 1, 1952, the Chinese army killed a total of 120,000 resistance fighters as enemies of the state.[5] The same radio station reported that, in March 1954, the army eliminated 30,000 resistance fighters, according to several witnesses.[6] In four years, China defeated and eradicated East Turkistan's resistance forces and gained total military control of East Turkistan. The legendary heroism of Osman Batur and his forces is still remembered by every Uyghur and Kazak today, and the independence movement continues overseas. Rebellions against China's colonialism continued to occur periodically. More than forty riots joined by several thousand Uyghurs occurred in Khotan alone between late 1954 and May 1956.[7] An underground East Turkistan Party led by Muhammet Sayidin, established in Turpan, organized many riots and rebellions in Turpan, Koktokay in the North, and Kumul, which took place between 1950 and 1960 and were violently crushed by Chinese forces. Around 1,423 people were arrested from Ghulja city alone between February and March 1958.[8]

It is essential to note here that the independence movement of East Turkistan is not merely ethnic or religious in nature but is in fact primarily territorial in nature. The resistance fighters of East Turkistan did not derive from a single ethnic group. Rather, it was the cause of a multiethnic national group of people who originated to land of East Turkistan. Historical documents and eyewitness testimonies contradict Chinese claims of the so-called "peaceful liberation of Xinjiang." The Uyghur leader Ahmet Igemberdy, who witnessed the Chinese army's entrance into East Turkistan, recalled that the people of East Turkistan grieved over their reoccupation. He said:

> I was a school kid. We were angry when we were forced to line up and welcome the Chinese Communist army through the streets. None of the Uyghurs went to the streets voluntarily to welcome the Chinese army. How could we? We fought with Nationalist Chinese warlords and kicked them out, and we did not expect Chinese Communist soldiers to enter our land afterward. No nation in this world could welcome a stranger's invasion. I saw Chinese immigrants valutarily go to the streets to celebrate the Chinese Communist occupation, but not Uyghurs and other Turks.[9]

Igemberdy's testimony is only one of the countless eyewitness reports detailing the violence of the Chinese occupation, which involved not only hunting down armed resistors but executing other "enemies of the state" en masse.

UN General Assembly Resolution 2625 (XXV) reiterates:

> The principle that States shall refrain in their international relations from the threat or use of force against the territorial integrity or political independence of any State or in any other manner inconsistent with the purposes of the United Nations.[10]

On the basis of this principle, China's invasion of the East Turkistan Republic in 1949 was a serious violation of the UN Charter, Article 2(4)'s prohibition of the use of force in interstate relations,[11] because China used force to destroy the political independence and territorial integrity of East Turkistan. Despite the fact that China used excessive force against the territorial integrity of East Turkistan even during the era of decolonization, the Chinese government strictly denies that this was actually a form of colonization. It claims instead that it was preserving its state integrity as if the separation of East Turkistan were a violation of China's territorial wholeness or national sovereignty. In reality, it was the forceful invasion of a territory previously held in fact by a non-Chinese empire.

IS IT LAWFUL FOR CHINA TO REJECT EAST TURKISTAN'S PEACEFUL DEMAND FOR INDEPENDENCE?

The Chinese state has continued for more than seventy years to reject East Turkistan's peaceful demands for independence. China has justified this by claiming that any support of East Turkistan's independence is actually a violation of China's own state sovereignty. A recent Chinese government white paper reaffirmed the longstanding assertion that "Xinjiang is an inseparable part of China."[12] To the contrary, this territorial acquisition was a result of the use of force and illegal occupation of East Turkistan and the Chinese state's aggressive, violent oppression of the native populations living there. UN General Assembly Resolution 3314 (XXIX), Article 5(3), on the "Definition of Aggression," provides that "No territorial acquisition or special advantage resulting from aggression is or shall be recognized as lawful."[13] Resolution 3314, Article 7, further states the right to self-determination, freedom, and peaceful independence for peoples under aggressive alien colonization:

> Nothing in this Definition, and in particular article 3, could in any way prejudice the right to self-determination, freedom and independence, as derived from the Charter, of peoples forcibly deprived of that right and referred to in the Declaration on Principles of International Law concerning Friendly Relations and Cooperation among States in accordance with the Charter of the United Nations, particularly peoples under colonial and racist regimes or other forms of alien domination: nor the right of these peoples to struggle to that end and to seek and receive support, in accordance with the principles of the Charter and in conformity with the above-mentioned Declaration.

China's claim of legal ownership of the region, which they refer to as Xinjiang, is by their insistence that there is no East Turkistan and that the new region of Xinjiang is an inseparable part of China. However, on the basis of Resolution 3314 and of two further points to be discussed in this chapter, this is clearly illegal. First, China executed an armed invasion to conquer and occupy East Turkistan in August 1949. According to Resolution 3314, Article 5(3), territorial acquisition by means of aggression is considered unlawful. Therefore, the Chinese state cannot be the legal owner of the region. Second, China has aggressively and violently rejected any peaceful demands for self-determination by the people of East Turkistan for more than seventy years and continuously rejects them today on the pretext of Chinese state integrity.

The UN's Colonial Declaration, paragraph 6, served the interest of China, as if China was recognized as a sovereign state, but not East Turkistan.[14] Based on paragraph 6, any action by an East Turkistan independence movement has been seen as a disruption of China's national unity, despite the fact that East Turkistan and its people are historically not part of China. Neither do the people of East Turkistan have a sense of belonging that allows them to perceive themselves as members of the Chinese nation, nor does China afford rights and protection of the law or guarantee the freedoms that the nation-state should afford to its citizens. In spite of that, the international community has recognized and legitimized Chinese state integrity exclusively on the basis of state integrity and of the claims to national unity made in Chinese discourse. Those claims include China's "one-China policy" and self-serving historical account of the "peaceful liberation of Xinjiang," including the historical assertion that "Xinjiang is an inseparable part of China," which preclude any discussion of the original history of East Turkistan and Chinese colonialism. The international community's one-sided interpretation of paragraph 6, and its recognition instead of China's claim to sovereignty over East Turkistan, legitimized the current status of East Turkistan as a Chinese province by denying and ignoring its history of colonization and of state integrity.

Conquering an opponent's territory does not constitute the legal right or basis for a title to that land under international law.[15] Therefore, according to international law, the territory of East Turkistan remains subject to the legal title of the defeated nation (i.e., the East Turkistan Republic), as disputes continue until today. China's claim of "state integrity" is established on the premise of colonization and violent oppression against peaceful demands for self-determination by the people of East Turkistan. Moreover, the peaceful independence movement of East Turkistan that has risen both inside and outside of East Turkistan in recent years, which we will discuss later in this book, justifies that there is no threat of the use of force against China currently. Furthermore, the people of East Turkistan are not receiving or seeking any armed external support for their struggle for independence.

WHO IS BREACHING INTERNATIONAL PEACE?

Nearly seventy years after China's violent and illegal invasion of East Turkistan, it has become clear to part of the international community that the Chinese state is breaching international peace and conducting genocide against the people of East Turkistan. China's historical and current policies and treatment of the people of East Turkistan are serious violations of the UN Charter, Chapter VII, Article 39.[16] As is stated in General Assembly Resolution 1514 (XV), "The subjection of peoples to alien subjugation, domination and exploitation constitutes a denial of fundamental human rights, is contrary to the Charter of the United Nations and is an impediment to the promotion of world peace and co-operation."[17]

How China is breaching world peace through genocide will be discussed in detail in chapters 4 and 5. However, it is worthwhile to outline a few reasons here, as the Chinese government and Chinese commentators have adamantly rebuffed every attempt by the international community to address human rights violations in East Turkistan by claiming that the region is their own internal issue and that it has no relation to the concept of "international peace." China's claim has no substantial basis for the following reasons: first of all, the people of East Turkistan are part of the international community. Therefore, the destruction of the Uyghur and other Turkic Muslims in East Turkistan in whole or in part is necessarily an issue of international peace. Second, it is apparent that China's genocidal policies in East Turkistan could be an effective tactic or model to crack down on others opposed to the autocratic regime, or who present peaceful demands for secession from China's autocratic international partners. Consequently, many autocratic countries, including Egypt and Zimbabwe, export the methods and technologies employed by China to create their own "surveillance states" against their citizens.[18] Furthermore, there is already evidence of China encouraging replication of its policies elsewhere. For example, China uses its veto power as a member of the United National Security Council to support the Ethiopian government's gross violations of human rights, including crimes against humanity against the Tigray people.[19]

SHOULD CHINA HAVE THE LEGAL TITLE OVER EAST TURKISTAN?

China has rejected the facts of the history of East Turkistan and its colonization by the Manchu empire. Furthermore, they have ignored the fact that the people of East Turkistan are indigenous to that territory and instead construe East Turkistan as having been a Chinese territory under the Manchu government. In so doing, they claim that the territory of East Turkistan is a legitimate territory of China on the principle of uti possidetis juris.

Uti possidetis juris is a valuable principle of international law, but one that can easily be manipulated through the selective presentation and willful misinterpretation of facts. As we argued earlier, the principles of decolonization, self-determination, and state integrity provide that newly independent states will maintain the same borders they had when a former colonial power colonized them.[20] If one credulously accepts the idea that the Manchu empire was territorially equivalent to the modern Chinese nation-state, or that the territory of an empire in whole belongs to one of its former subject communities, then one could assume that anything the Manchus conquered is rightly the inheritance of a communist state. In fact, the overthrow of the Manchu empire and the foundation of the Republic of China in 1912, let alone the founding of the Chinese Communist Party (CCP) in 1921, had little to do with the continuity of any claim on East Turkistan. There was no peaceful or legal transfer of East Turkistan's territory from the Qing to the Chinese Republic, nor of course between the Qing and the Chinese Communists, whose state was founded forty-seven years after the fall of Manchu power. It should also be pointed out that the Communists were not the sole successors of the Manchus who claimed the legal title of East Turkistan based on the United Nations general principle uti possidetis—not only did the Chinese Nationalists make a weak claim to it, so of course did the people of East Turkistan, as the Declaration of Independence of East

Turkistan preceded the formation of the PRC in 1949. In this regard, especially as the territorial boundaries of East Turkistan were already evident at the moment of decolonization from the Manchu empire, the East Turkistan Republic's territorial claim conforms correctly to the principle of uti possidetis juris. Furthermore, East Turkistan did not attempt to *secede from* Chinese territory but, conversely, attempted to *drive China out* of East Turkistan's territory. East Turkistan's attempt to re-establish and legally actualize its independence is based on preexisting colonial boundaries that should be respected in their exercise of self-determination. Thus, the United Nations' recognition of Communist China's claim over East Turkistan violated its legal principle of self-determination.

Under the traditional conceptual framework of international law, only a state can acquire the title of a territory, not a people, because a "people" is relative and fluid.[21] Once a new state emerges in a particular territory, international law should accept the reality of independence as an ownership of legal title to that territory. However, China and the Soviet Union rejected and actively worked to end the reality of East Turkistan's independence. China inaccurately characterizes the territory of East Turkistan as having been terra nullius prior to its invasion, in part through a very selective presentation of history. Following the collapse of the Manchu empire, East Turkistan was controlled by nominally Nationalist-aligned warlords from 1912 onward.[22] The people of East Turkistan defeated the warlord Sheng Shicai and his successors, and they rebuilt the second East Turkistan Republic in 1944.[23] The PRC rejects the legitimacy of the East Turkistan Republic as a state, on the pretense that the East Turkistani army did not fully liberate the whole territory of East Turkistan from those Nationalist-aligned warlord regimes. China plays both sides: it simultaneously rejects the warlords as illegitimate tyrants and claims that any East Turkistani struggle was in fact part of a broader process of national liberation taking place across all of China, while also embracing the warlords as legitimate representatives of the Chinese government who protected China from the "separatism" of East Turkistanis whom China alternatively characterizes as Soviet agents sent to destabilize China. Either way, the narrative denies the independence and legitimacy of the struggles of the people of East Turkistan.

There are several strong arguments against such a characterization. First of all, the warlords who controlled parts of East Turkistan did not represent Communist China. Yang and Jin, as described earlier, were highly independent of any central Chinese government. Famously, Sheng Shicai switched sides between the Chinese Communists and Chinese Nationalists, while in fact being mainly a puppet of the Soviets. In early 1943, having recently thrown in with the Axis, he tried to prove his loyalty to Stalin and the Communists, but by the sipring of 1942 he had returned to his Nationalist patrons.[24] Although the Chinese Nationalist government was internationally recognized as a successor of the Manchu empire, the warlords in East Turkistan did not fully control East Turkistan nor were they fully loyal to any Chinese Nationalist government. Later, in 1946, with the pressure of the Soviet Union, the government of the East Turkistan Republic negotiated with Chinese Nationalists and established a coalition government in East Turkistan. However, it quickly fell apart and only existed on paper. The Chinese Nationalist Party (Kuomintang) never implemented the negotiated agreement.[25] Most of the territory of East Turkistan had already been liberated from Chinese Nationalist forces by the East Turkistan army. Even the Communist Chinese government itself characterizes these Nationalists as having governed illegally in China, and not representing a true Chinese state. After the founding of the PRC, Chinese premier and Foreign Minister Zhou Enlai sent telegrams to both the secretary general of the United Nations and the president of the UN General Assembly calling for the expulsion of the illegal representative of the Nationalist Party and demanding that a representative of the PRCreplace him at the United Nations.[26] Only the East Turkistan Republic, which actually owned the land and established an independent nation-state during that time, was in the true, legal sense eligible to acquire the legal title to East Turkistan.

Second, neither the Chinese Nationalist nor Communist government held effective control over the territory of East Turkistan. Maps from the period illustrating the actual extent of either party's control universally excluded East Turkistan, which the international community recognized as a de facto independent territory, and one that was only peripherally involved in Chinese politics. For example, a 1932 map from the *North China Herald* in figure 3.1 showing the extent of Communist and Nationalist control does not even include East Turkistan.

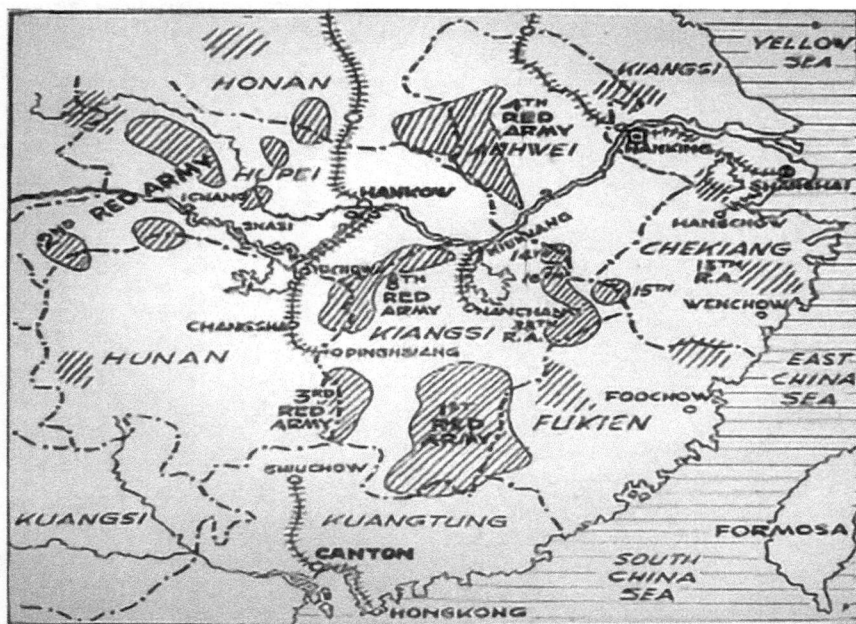

Figure 3.1 Map of Communist Base Areas. *Source: North China Herald,* October 19, 1932, 93.

The American magazine *China Today* published a map of China in November 1934, after the fall of the first East Turkistan Republic, when Sheng Shicai was nominally loyal to the Nationalists but de facto aligned with the Soviets. This map, in figure 3.2, given that it was produced by supporters of the Nationalist regime, ought to have shown the globally recognized armed Communist presence in that region, or else made a clear claim to Nationalist control. It does neither, but instead presents East Turkistan as a country similar to its neighbor, the People's Republic of Outer Mongolia.

Another foreign map of Nationalist territory in 1930, shown in figure 3.3, this one produced in Japan, frankly notes that they were only "nominally ruling over entire China," entirely excluding the regions of East Turkistan, Tibet, and Mongolia.

The Chinese Communists led by Mao Zedong defeated the Chinese Nationalists in the Chinese provinces, while the East Turkistani army defeated the Chinese Nationalists in East Turkistani territory. Mao then established the PRC with the help of Stalin and invited the leaders of the East Turkistan government leaders to participate in China's National People's Consultative Congress.[27] The Soviet Union pressured those leaders to accept the invitation. Shockingly, the entire East Turkistan delegation was killed in a mysterious plane crash in August on their way to Beijing. In October, the PRC strategically invaded East Turkistan. Clearly, East Turkistan was not terra nullius—there was a nation-state there. Furthermore, even in a hypothetical scenario in which China could have conquered the region violently prior to the establishment of the second Republic, it would have been illegal to do so. Consequently, Communist China's acquisition of this territory is clearly an invasion of the state integrity and sovereignty of East Turkistan.

Figure 3.2 **Map of China**. *Source: China Today,* November 1934, 39.

Figure 3.3 Map of Nationalist Territory. *Source*: Courtesy Norman B. Leventhal Map & Education Center at the Boston Public Library.

SUMMARY

According to Article 1 of the Montevideo Convention on the Rights and Duties of States in 1933, a sovereign state should have a permanent population, a defined territory, a government, and the capacity to enter into relations with other states. The land of East Turkistan was neither terra nullius nor res communes before the Chinese invasion of 1949. The independent East Turkistan Republic has its own defined territory, people, and government. Even though states did not recognize the East Turkistan Republic, it had a government, it represented the people of East Turkistan, and it had the capacity to enter into relations with other states. East Turkistan did in fact adhere to the definition of a sovereign state. Therefore, the people of East Turkistan will continue to argue legally for their sovereignty over the territory of East Turkistan.

NOTES

1. Hague Convention (IV) Respecting the Laws and Customs of War on Land and Its Annex: Regulations Concerning the Laws and Customs of War on Land art. 42, October 18, 1907, AJIL Supp. 90-117 (1908).

2. "Cable with Message from Mao Zedong to Stalin, 26 September 1949, RGASPI, f. 558, op. 11, d. 332, ll. 54-56," trans. Gary Goldberg, China and Soviet Union 1934-1949

Collection, History and Public Policy Program Digital Archive, Wilson Center, Washington, DC, https://digitalarchive.wilsoncenter.org/document/176341.

3. "Ciphered Telegram No. 4159 from Filipov [Stalin] to Kovalev, 14 October 1949, RGASPI, f. 558, op. 11, d. 332, I,116," trans. Gary Goldberg, Sino- Soviet Relations Collection, History and Public Policy Program Digital Archive, Wilson Center, Washington, DC, https://digitalarchive.wilsoncenter.org/document/176342.

4. James Millward, *Eurasian Crossroads: A History of Xinjiang* (New York: Columbia University Press, 2007), 232.

5. *Central Asian Review*, 7:1 (1959), 95. Quoted in Donald Hugh McMillen, "Chinese Communist Power and Policy in Sinkiang, 1949-73: Revolutionary Integration vs. Regionalism" (master thesis, Colorado University, 1967), 55.

6. Gulemhan Dawut, Osman Haji, Abdukadir Yasinbay, in discussion with the author, March 1998, Ghulja. These elderly Uyghurs, including the author's grandfather, who had listened to Urumchi Radio broadcast confirmed that 150,000 Uyghurs and Kazaks had been killed.

7. Zhe Wu, "Caught between Opposing Han Chauvinism and Opposing Local Nationalism: The Drift Toward Ethnic Antagonism in Xinjiang Society, 1952–1963," in *Maoism at the Grassroots: Everyday Life in China's Era of High Socialism*, ed. Jeremy Brown and Matthew D. Johnson (Cambridge, MA and London: Harvard University Press, 2015), 307–14.

8. Ibid., 320–21.

9. Ehmet Igemberdi (former president of East Turkistan Government in Exile), Phone interview, March 2, 2021.

10. G.A. Res. 2625 (XXV), Declaration on Principles of International Law Concerning Friendly Relations and Cooperation Among States in Accordance with the Charter of the United Nations, A/RES/2625(XXV), Principle 1 (October 24, 1970).

11. U.N. Charter art. 2, ¶ 4.

12. The State Council Information Office of the People's Republic of China, *Historical Matters Concerning Xinjiang* (Beijing: Foreign Languages Press Co. Ltd., 2019), http://english.www.gov.cn/archive/whitepaper/201907/21/content_WS5d33fed5c6d00d362f668a0a.html.

13. G.A. Res, 3314 (XXIX), Definition of Aggression, A/RES/3314, art. 5, ¶ 3 (December 14, 1974).

14. G.A. Res, Declaration on the Granting of Independence to Colonial Countries and Peoples, A/RES/1514(XV), ¶ 6 (December 14, 1960); Note: People's Republic of Communist China was not recognized as the legitimate representative of China to the United Nations until October 25, 1971.

15. Malcolm N. Shaw, *International Law* (New York: Cambridge University Press, 2017), 371.

16. U.N. Charter, Ch. VII, art. 39.

17. G.A. Res. 1514 (XV), ¶ 1 (December 14, 1960).

18. Amy Hawkins, "Beijing's Big Brother Tech Needs African Faces," *Foreign Policy*, July 24, 2018, https://foreignpolicy.com/2018/07/24/beijings-big-brother-tech-needs-african-faces/.

19. "UN Scrapped Plans to Issue a Statement Calling for an End to Violence in Ethiopia's Tigray Region," *AFP*, March 5, 2021, https://www.justiceinfo.net/en/74599-un-scraps-plans-for-statement-on-ethiopias-tigray-region-diplomats.html.

20. Anne Peters, "The Principle of Uti Possidetis Juris: How Relevant Is It for Issues of Secession?" in *Self-Determination and Secession in International Law*, ed. Christian Walter,

Antje von Ungern-Sternberg, and Kavus Abushov, (Oxford: Oxford University Press, 2014), 105.

Malcolm N. Shawt, "The Heritage of States: The Principle of *Uti Possidetis Juris* Today," *British Yearbook of International Law* 67, no. 1 (1996): 97. doi: 10.1093/bybil/67.1.75.

21. J.G. Starke, "The Acquisition of Territorial Sovereignty by Newly Emerged States," *The Australian Year Book of International Law* 2, no. 1 (1968): 13. doi: 10.1163/26660229-002-01-900000003.

22. Michael E. Clarke, *Xinjiang and China's Rise in Central Asia: A History*, (New York: Routledge, 2011), 28.

23. Millward, *Eurasian Crossroads*, 209–12.

24. Millward, *Eurasian Crossroads*, 211.

25. "Letter from Ahmetjan Qasimi and Rahim Jan Sabri to Mr. Savel'yev, Consul General of the USSR in Urumqi, 12 July 1947, RGASPI F. 17, Op. 128, D. 391, ll. 115-119," obtained by Jamil Hasanli and translated by Gary Goldberg, China and Soviet Union in Xinjiang 1934-1949 Collection, History and Public Policy Program Digital Archive, Wilson Center, Washington, DC, https://digitalarchive.wilsoncenter.org/document/121803.

26. "Telegram, Mao Zedong to [Liu] Shaoqi and [Zhou] Enlai, 7 January 1950," China at the United Nations Collection, History and Public Policy Program Digital Archive, Wilson Center, Washington, DC, https://digitalarchive.wilsoncenter.org/document/112681.

27. Millward, *Eurasian Crossroads*, 234–37.

II

THE RIGHT TO CHOOSE SOVEREIGNTY BEYOND DECOLONIZATION

The Political, Territorial, and Economic Status of the People of East Turkistan

General Assembly Resolution 2625 (XXV) states: "The use of force to deprive peoples of their national identity constitutes a violation of their inalienable rights and of the principle of non-intervention."[1] China's historical use of force and invasion in East Turkistan, as outlined in the previous chapter, and current attempts to commit genocide against the people of East Turkistan indicate serious violations of the above principles.

According to Section 2 of the Vienna Declaration of 1993, all people have the right to self-determination. However, the declaration refers only to governments of states representing entire peoples:

> In accordance with the Declaration on Principles of International Law concerning Friendly Relations and Cooperation Among States in accordance with the Charter of the United Nations, this shall not be construed as authorizing or encouraging any action which would dismember or impair, totally or in part, the territorial integrity or political unity of sovereign and independent States conducting themselves in compliance with the principle of equal rights and self-determination of peoples and thus possessed of a Government representing the whole people belonging to the territory without distinction of any kind.[2]

If the people of East Turkistan were to belong to the "whole people" within the territory of China, and if the Chinese government were representative of them, then, on the basis of Section 2 of the Vienna Declaration, the territorial integrity of that state would not be dismembered. At the same time, it is also understood that people have a remedy for gaining independence through dismembering the state if the government cannot represent the whole people and instead denies their rights. Consequently, if East Turkistan is an inseparable part of China, then Turkic Muslims must be treated as equal citizens. However, does the Chinese government represent them and protect their rights and security? Are they treated as part of the nation of China? This part of the book tries to answer these questions by examining the status of East Turkistan's people under China's nation-building project and settler colonialism.

In defining the right to self-determination under international law, UNESCO notes that the "people" attempting secession should be distinct from the nation of the existing state.[3] Different qualities, such as language, religion, cultural homogeneity, and racial and ethnic identity, ideological affiliation, and territorial connection, help determine whether or not a people should be considered distinct. In the case of Quebec, Canada, for example, the Supreme Court of Canada clearly distinguishes the term "people" from the term "nation" in reference to the existing state.[4] The people of Quebec have equal rights and are treated as part of the Canadian nation. They are not referred to as a "people" despite possessing a distinct historical territory, language, and culture. However, the Supreme Court has recognized the constitutional obligation for parties to negotiate Quebec's independence if the people of Quebec decide they no longer wish to remain a part of Canada.[5] The case of the people of East Turkistan is very different. They consider themselves to be illegally occupied by China and reject the suggestion that they belong to the nation of China. They also argue that they are not treated as an equal nation within the Chinese state. The people of East Turkistan understand themselves to be distinct from the Han Chinese. Furthermore, the cruel treatment that Uyghurs and other Turkic Muslims have faced under the Chinese state has intensified this distinctiveness, thereby defining the status of Uyghurs and other ethnic Muslims in international law.

In East Turkistan today, Uyghur and other Turkic Muslims outside of China's mass detention camps are forced to sing "red" songs, raise Chinese flags every morning, and participate in public denunciation sessions of their religion and identity. They are forced to swear oaths of loyalty, participate in hours-long propaganda lectures, praise Xi Jinping, and declare, "I am a member of the Chinese nation." Videos related to these campaigns are widely distributed on China's social media as part of China's nation-building propaganda. Why is China's national identity imposed on Uyghurs and other Turkic Muslims, and why is it accompanied by genocidal policies, including sterilization, mass incarceration, and forced labor? The answer is closely related to China's settler colonialism since its genocidal targeting of these people is not only because of who they are but also because of the territory they belong to. Chinese scholars of ethnic policy such as Hu An'gang and Hu Lianhe call these policies "second-generation" ethnic policies.[6] In reality, they are more accurately understood as a "genocide project," illustrating China's fake and failed nation-building.

One of the founders and most prominent members of the interdisciplinary field of nationalism studies, Anthony Smith, identified fundamental features of national identity. According to Smith, national identities have both internal and external functions, which enable groups and individuals to locate themselves as nations and members of nations in relation to a state.[7] In many states, a homogenous, standardized, compulsory educational system is intended to bring internal coherence to the nation by creating a shared national culture. This is the case in China, where the government may succeed in creating an artificial Chinese nation in East Turkistan by imposing this internal process on Uyghurs and other Turkic Muslims. Nevertheless, such assimilation cannot last without external dynamics. The external functions of a nation, according to Smith, are legal-political, territorial, and economic. He argues that legal-political functions can be effective when the legal and political rights and obligations of the members protected by the government represent the nation's national will. He also argues that governments also provide territory, usually historically determined, within which members can live and work, fulfilling their territorial function. Economically, nations use various means to allocate economic resources between members. Under the rule of the Chinese colonizers, the people of East Turkistan do not have access to any of these rights.

As discussed in chapter 1, the historical territory of East Turkistan should belong to the people of East Turkistan, not China. As a result of China's colonization, the historical, territorial rights of Uyghurs and other Turkic Muslims as a nation of East Turkistan have been denied. They are also not allowed to equally enjoy such rights of the Chinese nation after they had been annexed and claimed by China as a Chinese nation. Unlike Han Chinese people, who can enjoy the privileges of Chinese national status, the private land ownership rights of Uyghurs and other Turkic Muslims are violated and their political and legal rights as a citizen are not protected by either domestic or international law. The following chapter will discuss how China's historically developed nation-building project is actually an act of genocide against the people of East Turkistan.

NOTES

1. G.A. Res. 2625 (XXV), Declaration on Principles of International Law concerning Friendly Relations and Cooperation among States in accordance with the Charter of the United Nations, Principle 3, ¶ 3 (Oct. 24, 1970).

2. World Conference on Human Rights, *Vienna Declaration and Program of Action* ¶ 2, U.N. Doc. A/CONF.157/23 (June 25, 1993).

3. UNESCO, SHS.89/CONF.602/7, ¶ 22 (February 22, 1990).

4. *Reference re Secession of Quebec*, [1998] 2 S.C.R. 217, 1998 CanLII 793 (SCC) ¶ 124, 153, 154.

5. Id. ¶ 153.

6. Rukiye Turdush, "Genocide as Nation Building: China's Historically Evolving Policy in East Turkistan," *The Journal of Political Risk* 7, No.8 (2019), https://www.jpolrisk.com/genocide-as-nation-building-chinas-historically-evolving-policy-in-east-turkistan/ ; See also: Hu, A. and Hu, L, "第二代民族政策:促进民族交融一体和繁荣一体" (*The Second Generation of Ethnic Policy: Promoting National Integration and Prosperity*). 新华文摘 (*Xinhua Digest*), [online] 24, (2011): 6, available at: https://www.sinoss.net/uploadfile/2011/1229/20111229100022433.pdf [Accessed 24 Aug. 2019].

7. Anthony D. Smith, *National Identity* (London: Penguin Group, 1991), 15–17.

4

China's Nation-Building

Specific Intent to Destroy

CRIMINALIZATION OF UYGHURS: PRECONDITION OF GENOCIDE

Much as Jews were racialized in Germany during the Holocaust, the Chinese government has purposefully defined the Uyghurs as so-called "savage people" (*yeman ren*) and encouraged anti-Uyghur sentiment in the form of myths and stereotypes, creating a lack of trust and tolerance between Chinese settlers and Turkic Muslims. According to Dr. Stanton's ten stages of genocide, this is the third stage, the process of discrimination.[1] This discrimination was widely ignored both by Uyghurs themselves and in the international community. No one predicted that China would rapidly shift into other stages of genocide against the Uyghurs and other Turkic Muslims with sophisticated state policy. Nevertheless, as we will see, discrimination and dehumanization have deep historical roots in the modern Chinese state.

The Chinese government has labeled the people of East Turkistan with many derogatory terms in order to justify their oppression and elimination. In the 1950s and 1960s, right after China colonized East Turkistan, its people were labeled "feudal elements," "ethnic nationalists," "landowners," and "rich people," all of which terms indicated enemies of the proletariat. People who secretly supported independence fighters' resistance against Chinese colonialism were arrested and killed. In the 1970s and 1980s, many Uyghur elites were imprisoned, tortured, and eliminated as "counterrevolutionaries." In the 1990s, following the Baren uprising, Uyghurs were labeled "separatists." It was also not uncommon for gangs from inner China to kidnap and traffic Uyghur children, as the Chinese government purposefully ignored, even implicitly supported, such crimes. In the early 1990s, it was not uncommon to see underage Uyghur kids being violently beaten to death by Chinese people on the streets of Chinese cities. In fact, people know that these children were "pickpockets" abused and controlled by adult gangs in cooperation with the Chinese police. Stereo-typing Uyghurs as "pickpockets" and "wild outsiders" created hate and dehumanized Uyghurs. Depicting Uyghurs as an "untrustworthy" and "backward nation" (*luohou minzu*) and subjecting them to economic segregation conditioned ordinary Chinese civilians to accept the oppression of Uyghurs and other Turkic Muslims as a means to demonstrate the dominance and superiority of the Han Chinese.

Consequently, anti-Uyghur sentiments become a motif of Han Chinese nation-alism and superiority. Many organizations in East Turkistan owned by Chinese settlers post signs on their door saying "we do not hire Uyghurs," regardless of how talented or educated their potential employees are, or fluent in the Chinese language. As a result, the unemployment rate of Uyghurs is significant. Some Uyghurs vol-untarily sent their children to Chinese schools despite the risk of losing the Uyghur language and culture even before China banned Uyghur schools. However, those children were still perceived as "others" or "strangers" in their land and were not granted access to employment opportunities on an equal basis with Han Chinese. Meanwhile, perception of Uyghurs as "savage people," "separatists," and "terrorists" is common, and animosity and hostile feelings are the norms. Taxi drivers in China refuse to take Uyghurs as passengers. It is no secret that Uyghurs are not allowed to stay in hotels or motels in inner China, while millions of Han Chinese settlers pour into East Turkistan every year. Police have ordered hotel owners not to allow Uyghurs to stay in hotels in Chinese cities, regardless of their legal documents. Uyghurs and other Turkic Muslims who are admitted to universities in Chinese cit-ies are also categorized as "Xinjiang students" and put in restricted subjects for study.

Starting in 2007, the Chinese state addressed the high unemployment rate by instituting forced labor instead of providing job opportunities. According to a Chinese white paper published in 2020, 2.76 million people, over 60% of them from southern East Turkistan, were removed from their homes and relocated to factories annually.[2] The tensions between Uyghurs and Han Chinese escalated more than ever before. The huge psychological, economic, and political gap between Han Chinese and Turkic Muslims created by these policies left people in East Turkistan extremely vulnerable. Male Uyghur youths were arrested from each family, tortured, disappeared, and eliminated. Following the attacks on the World Trade Center in the United States on September 11, 2001, China manipulated the global "war on terror" to label Uyghurs as "terrorists" to justify its destruction of Uyghurs and other Turkic Muslims. Some Uyghur resistance fighters fled to Afghanistan, as Afghani-stan was the only place that did not require a visa, and where Uyghurs were able to escape from Chinese oppression at that time. That created a favorable climate for China to label Uyghurs as "terrorists." The Chinese government opportunistically linked Uyghurs to Al-Qaeda, the international terrorist group. A document sub-mitted by the Chinese government to the United Nations indicated forty Uyghur organizations around the world as terrorist threats, even though most of the named groups are human rights organizations.[3] China further claimed the so-called East Turkistan Islamic Movement (ETIM) was a dangerous threat to China's national security and asked the United States to list ETIM as a terrorist organization. Despite the fact that there is no physical evidence of such an organization, the United States agreed to designate ETIM as a terrorist organization in 2002. Finally, in 2021, the US government removed ETIM from the list and confirmed that there is no such organization.[4] China also claimed that more than 200 terrorist incidents in East Turkistan killed 162 people and injured 440 between 1990 to 2001.[5] Some incidents did apparently target civilians, and this has led some observers to believe that this could be the main cause or motivation of China's recent genocidal policies in East Turkistan.

However, the majority of these incidents require independent verification because these were sourced from the unreliable Chinese government, some of these incidents are politically motivated as they targeted Chinese police stations and government officials therefore don't qualify to be framed as terrorism.[6] Clearly, even though a few terrorist incidents did occur, it is difficult to conclude there is an actual threat of terrorism that could motivate the massive genocide now targeting millions of innocent people. Terrorism rather serves as an excuse or pretext for genocide.

China's genocidal intent is reflected in a series of policies enacted over time. China's policy of regulating all Turkic Muslims' religious activities was first implemented in 2000,[7] and then broadened and intensified when the Xinjiang Religious Affairs Regulation took effect in March 2017[8] as a legal justification for the mass detainment that began that year. Since these regulations were instituted, between 1 and 3 million Turkic Muslims have been incarcerated in concentration camps.[9] This number is based on estimates of camp capacity and expansion as seen in satellite images, as well as on the reported proportions of people seized from different areas. Because of the extreme secrecy enforced by Chinese authorities, the number does not include those held in detention centers, those sentenced to life or long-term imprisonment, those sentenced to death in prisons, or Uyghur villagers who are deported to forced labor camps and factories. Men and women are sent to inner China, where they find themselves separated from their families and their society, religion, language, and other cultural practices inside forced labor camps.[10] Children, too, are separated from their families and sent to either Chinese boarding schools or children's concentration camps.[11] In addition, 80% of Uyghur women have been sterilized or otherwise forced to accept birth prevention measures.[12]

While the Chinese constitution claims that the fifty-six ethnicities in its country all belong to the Chinese nation, the question remains: Do the people of East Turkistan fit the definition of being a nation of China, and are they one of China's fifty-six ethnicities as China claims? In other words, has China granted them with the same legal, political, and economic rights that a nation would have in its own nation-state? The straightforward answer is no. Because China is committing genocide by imposing so-called "nation-building" policies in East Turkistan in order to create a single ethnic Han Chinese empire. As a result, "nation-building" policies became both pretext and effective instruments of genocide. The following section will examine the main characteristics of China's nation-building by focusing on how China forcibly dissolves the "people of East Turkistan" in part and destroys the rest.

ANNEXATION, COLONIZATION,
AND EARLY NATION-BUILDING

Such early Chinese nationalist thinkers and leaders as Liang Qichao and Sun Yat-sen, China's founding father and leader of the Nationalist Party, proposed the total assimilation of every non-Han people to a Han Chinese identity as a major technique of nation-building. This idea was advanced in Sun's "Plan for National Reconstruction" (*jianguo dagang*) of 1924 and has remained part of the Chinese toolkit ever since. Sun Yat-sen was influenced by the single nation-state ideology of Japan and the civic nation-state ideology of the United States. His idea was to construct a single Han Chinese nation-state as a melting pot into which all non-Han nations were to be included.[13] It was impossible to build a single "pure" Japanese-style nation-state because he wanted to annex East Turkistan, Tibet, and Inner Mongolia into Chinese territory. It was also impossible to establish an American-style civic nation-state since his ideology was to assimilate all these non-Chinese nations and establish an ethnic Chinese state. In his famous "Three Principles of the People" (*san min zhuyi*), he argued that Chinese people should sacrifice the biological ethnic purity of the Han Chinese to support Chinese imperialism and colonization of the territories, "boiling together" to create a Chinese nation.[14] This could be the reason why he preferred the term "Republic of the Chinese people" and refused to use the term "Republic of China" during that time.[15] Another leading Han Chinese nationalist, Zhang Binglin, criticized Sun Yat-sen for this ideology of annexing and assimilating alien nations into the Han Chinese. He believed that the Han Chinese are the direct descendants of the Huangdi, the first Chinese ancestors from the yellow river, and that assimilating others will contaminate the common biological blood lineage of the Han race.[16] Both positions remain prominent in Chinese thought concerning non-Chinese groups.

Following the rising of China in the twenty-first century, Chinese scholars and the Communist Party came strongly to believe that it was time for China to create a single Han Chinese nation-state, thus avoiding the tragedy of the collapse of the Soviet Union. This idea emerges from a historical ideology of "absorb others and grow" as articulated in the Chinese scholar Fei Xiaotong's book *The Pluralistic Unity of the Chinese Nation* (*Zhonghua minzu duoyuan yiti geju*). In his book, Fei praises the Han Chinese nation's expansion and imperialism, finding that it manifests the historical tradition of "great unity" (*da yi tong*). He presents an oversimplified version of early Chinese history as a story of assimilation, in which over 3,000 tiny states were gradually reduced to ten, most of which were established by non-Han people who were defeated and absorbed by the Chinese state.[17] Though Fei did not directly advocate eradicating or forcibly assimilating other nations or explicitly compare current Chinese ethnicity with ancient times, he gave implicit support for forcibly assimilating other nations into Han Chinese culture. He strongly believed that the integration of multiple nations should remain at the core of Han Chinese. In a lecture at the University of Hong Kong in 1988, he stated, "If all these former non-Han people should track down their blood lineages and find out their respective groups of origin, and denounce their current Han identity, then Hans would lose a sizable part of their population."[18] Fei's statement reveals how, while China uses the terminology of "state" (*guojia*) and "nation of the state" (*guojia minzu*), to describe its citizens, not all of them are seen as belonging to this "nation of the state." China claims that the state-building that began with the Chinese revolution successfully transformed the Manchu empire's colonial territories into a sovereign nation-state. That ignores how in the transformation of the empire the new Chinese nation-state invaded and recolonized the border territories that had already liberated themselves from the Manchu empire. Only a few years after 1949, China's first National People's Congress drafted a constitution that rejected the people of East Turkistan's right to self-determination, stating that "Xinjiang's provincial system are replaced with regional autonomy" as if the region was a part of China or Chinese province since People's Republic of China (PRC) was born.[19] The political structure of the Chinese nation-state aimed to control each institution of East Turkistan and implemented centralized governance from Beijing.

Seventy years of colonization in East Turkistan, which provided abundant wealth and power to China, along with Western support for China's integration into an international market, established the aggressive ideology of the "China Dream." Put simply, one can characterize the Chinese state as a nationalistic, ethnocentric political community with dreams of becoming a hegemonic superpower, motivated by geostrategic expansion into the world, and a nation determined to assimilate or exterminate its multiethnic colonial states to create a single, homogenous empire, even at the cost of committing genocide.

Unlike Risorgimento nationalism in Europe, which promotes liberty, equality, and independence, Chinese nationalism is centered on the promotion and expansion of ethnic Han Chinese. Mao Zedong stressed the Chinese Communist Party (CCP)'s rhetorical notion of combining internationalism and patriotism, defeating imperialism, and achieving national liberation.[20] Contrary to internationalism, he argued that building a greater and more expansive China could be achieved by expanding into natural resource-rich lands, while he characterized the people of East Turkistan, the people of Tibet, and the Mongols as minority nations within Chinese territory. This was written in 1939, ten years before his country invaded those territories.[21] As we can see from Mao's understanding of patriotism, Chinese elites did not differentiate the nationalism of great Han Chinese and patriotism; for them, it was inseparable from the power of the size of the territory and the size of the population. Like Hitler's nationalism, which focused on aggressively expanding into others' territory, Mao harbored a desire to eradicate the Uyghurs and other Turkic Muslims by forcing them to assimilate as he strongly believed that Marxist nationality theory of nationality differences among people would be disappeared. Further, he emphasized in his essays that Han Chinese nation is a great nation and the most civilized nation. The intention of genocide thus predated the Chinese invasion.

The difference between Hitler's nationalism and that of the Chinese Han lies in the idea of sacrificing the purity of the race discussed earlier. Hitler insisted on the purity of the German bloodline and race, whereas Chinese leaders thought blood was not necessarily important as long as ethnic Han Chinese become strong and superior by absorbing others' power. We can see Mao's strong support of Liang Qichao and Sun Yat-sen's idea of balancing the cost and benefit between expanding to other regions and establishing an ethnic Han Chinese state. In the end, they argued that the benefits outweigh the costs because the non-Han peoples held lands with rich natural resources but populations are tiny in comparison to the vast ethnic Han Chinese population. These demographic imbalances would make it easy to conquer and absorb those populations. It even motivated an intent to commit genocide in order to prepare living space for Han settlers. In March 1958, Mao wrote about so-called "national minorities" in a way that reflected Liang Qichao, Sun Yat-sen, and Fei Xiaotong's ideas:

> To begin with, the Han was not a big race, but a mixture of a great number of races. The Han people have conquered many minority nations in history and driven them to the highlands. [We] must take a historical view of our nationality question and find out that we either depend on minority nationalism or on communism. Of course, we depend on communism. We need our regions but not regionalism.[22]

Mao's statement "We need communism" indicates that he does not want to persecute the so-called "minority nationality" (*shaoshu minzu*) as long as they become communist. This viewpoint, however, also contradictorily indicated his intentions that those conquered nationalities as enemies, particularly Muslims of East Turkistan, are opponents since they are not communists, and communism does not tolerate religion. Evidently, the means of creating a "Chinese Nation" (*Zhonghua minzu*) is found in transforming colonized peoples into ethnic Han. Following Sun Yat-sen's idea, Mao Zedong's Sinification, Deng Xiaoping's doctrine of Chinese characteristics, and Xi Jinping's China dream all share the same ideology that promoted Chinese-style new world order led by ethnic Chinese people.[23]

The people of East Turkistan suffered greatly under Mao's Cultural Revolution. Religious leaders, elites, writers, poets, professors, and anyone else who spoke out against Mao were arrested, executed, or sentenced to long-term imprisonment. Muslims were forced to denounce Islam, and many mosques and religious historical sites were destroyed. One witness to the Cultural Revolution I spoke with said:

> We had to bow to Mao's photo before going to work in the fields, bow again when the work was done, and ask his permission to go home. His photo could not talk, but the head of the village or sometimes a Red Guard would stand beside Mao's photo and said: "Our great leader and father Chairman Mao permits you to go home." Sometimes they would say "The great leader does not permit you to go home" and force us to work overtime.

Uyghurs who survived the Cultural Revolution argue that Xi Jinping's policies in East Turkistan today resemble that period of political violence: Uyghurs in concentration camps are forced to praise Xi Jinping before receiving food and sing "red songs" about Xi Jinping and the CCP. Unlike Mao and other Chinese leaders, however, Xi Jinping's words have explicitly demonstrated his intent to destroy a national group, the people of East Turkistan. In his report to the 19th Party Congress, Xi Jinping stated that "we should do more to foster a Chinese spirit, Chinese values, and Chinese strength, to provide moral guidance to our people."[24] Those "Chinese" things do not refer to civic belonging to the PRC, but to the Han Chinese national group. The CCP sees East Turkistan as an inseparable part of China, despite its colonial history, and claims that it belongs only to Han Chinese, and so, "others" in this colonial land must be absorbed into the Han Chinese ethnic group.

NATION-BUILDING AS GENOCIDE IN THE XI ERA

According to the definitions of genocide law, China under Xi Jinping's leadership has both engaged in physical actions (actus reus) and displayed the state of mind to commit a crime (mens rea).

Special Intent: Derogatory Words

China's special intent is closely linked with Chinese colonialism in East Turkistan, which we can see in Mao Zedong and Sun Yat-sen's statements about how to absorb and assimilate non-Han Chinese people. This section brings us to the discourse of dehumanization and nationalism in the words of current Chinese leaders and how these words are reflected in policy.

"Transformation and extermination," cultural and biological genocide, has been at the core of the CCP's ideas about non-Han peoples for many years. We can trace it to the early 2000s, as when Chinese professor Ai Yuejin said at Nankai University in 2003: "Our great culture can assimilate any other nation or culture—we can change and absorb good ones, and torture and kill bad ones."[25] The idea of the superiority of the Han Chinese and their right to dominate, absorb, and eliminate any other race is applied first, particularly with the conception of a superior "self" versus an inferior "other," which many Han Chinese have cultivated toward the Turkic peoples in the colony. Once the idea of the Turkic peoples as an "enemy" was established, the intention to eliminate them soon followed. Meanwhile, a discourse of Uyghurs and other Turkic Muslims as internal enemies emerged. Once, the Nazis described the Jews as both master "Bolsheviks" and the masters of "international capitalism" and linked them together as a threat to the Nazi regime. Similarly, Uyghurs were also linked with both international terrorism and Western democratic ideology.[26]

Discourse turned into policy and action. In April 2014, Xi Jinping visited Urumchi police station where he examined weapons. "None of these weapons is an answer for their big machete blades, axe heads, and cold steel weapons," he is quoted as saying. "We must be as harsh as they, and show absolutely no mercy."[27] "Absolutely no mercy" was clearly meant and interpreted as an order to instigate violence against the civilians using the language of warfare. Starting in 2017, Xinjiang Party secretary Chen Quanguo encouraged officials to "round up everyone who should be rounded up."[28] This order appears repeatedly in internal documents from 2017 following Xi

Jinping's call for "absolutely no mercy," through mass detention, torture, and extermination. The Chinese government did not select people for concentration camps or forced labor camps randomly but systematically, in order to destroy them in whole or in part on the basis of race, ethnicity, culture, and religion. No other intent could explain the overwhelming selection of people from specific ethnic, religious, and racial groups rather than genocidal intent. Xi Jinping's role as the "core leader" of the Chinese Party and state means that his words can be understood and applied literally with extreme cruelty and implemented in the most heartless manner imaginable by lower-level officials. Therefore, Xi could give the green light for the killings and physical violence or actus reus described in Article 2 of the Genocide Convention. Concentration camp survivor Tursunay Ziyawudun and several other camp survivors confirmed that the guards in the camps informed the prisoners that no one could rescue their lives or even care about what was happening to them because they were unworthy of life and may be executed at any time for disobedience.[29] As we can see, the torture and killing of Turkic Muslims are not prohibited in East Turkistan—rather, Xi's orders have engendered a culture of perpetrators willingly implementing state policy on a genocidal level.

There is an undeniable similarity between the derogatory words used against Turkic Muslims and Nazi anti-Semitic doctrines. For instance, in 1938, the Nazi newspaper *Der Stuermer*'s leading article "The Germ" described "the Jew" as a "germ and pest, not human being" and "an enemy, a spreader of diseases who must be exterminated."[30] Uyghurs are described by Chinese officials in similar terms, with words such as "a cancerous tumor" and "weeds," not as human beings with a right to maintain their distinct culture, language, and religion but as an evil "three evil forces" that must be eliminated. Chinese propaganda claiming that "re-education camps" will "cure" people widely cites Xi Jinping's descriptive words "cancer cell" in 2017:

> When the devil appears, it pretends to be an angel. Similarly, religious extremism is like a powerful psychedelic drug, which poisons people, causing mental madness to make them murderous devils. If religious extremism is not eradicated, it will grow like a cancer cell![31]

Following this, on October 11, 2017, the Xinjiang Uyghur Autonomous Region (XUAR) Party Youth League recording "What Kind of Place is the Educational Transformation Center," published on the WeChat social media network by Request/Offer Salon, also echoed Xi Jinping's words, characterizing Uyghurs who had been sent for political "re-education" as "infected by an ideological illness and cancerous tumor"—like a disease that must be treated at a hospital:

> Members of the public who have been chosen for re-education have been infected by an ideological illness. They have been infected with religious extremism and violent terrorist ideology, and therefore they must seek treatment from a hospital as an inpatient.[32]
> There is always a risk that the illness will manifest itself at any moment, which would cause serious harm to the public. That is why they must be admitted to a re-education

hospital in time to treat and cleanse the virus from their brain and restore their normal mind. . . . Being infected by religious extremism and violent terrorist ideology and not seeking treatment is like being infected by a disease that has not been treated in time, or like taking toxic drugs. . . . There is no guarantee that it will not trigger and affect you in the future.[33]

Even though these cancerous tumors are affiliated with religious extremism and terrorism in the recordings, the discourse conflates this extremism with all Turkic Muslims' religious beliefs and identities. Two to three million Uyghur and other Turks are incarcerated and dehumanized because they are perceived as "having a cancerous tumor." The Youth League represents the CCP; their words echo the party's words. So, these words also represent the party's plan to eliminate the entire Uyghur population and their values, ideologies, and religious beliefs. The Chinese Party and state believe that these people's ideology is cancer and this belief also led to the intention to destroy the Turkic peoples in whole or in part.

The Chinese ambassador to the United States also dehumanized the people of East Turkistan when he responded to global criticism about the mass detention of Uyghurs and other Muslims in China's so-called "re-education camps," claiming "that it is to change Uyghurs into a normal person."[34] In this way, China differentiates Turkic Muslims from "normal" human beings—meaning Han Chinese—to justify their underlying intention. Local-level Chinese officials have also used derogatory words and dehumanized the Uyghurs and other Turkic people. For example, Yasinahun, the chief of police security for the Kashgar's Chasa township, informed RFA that one of the Han Chinese officials told them during a meeting, "You cannot uproot all the weeds hidden among the crops in the field one by one—you need to spray chemicals to kill them all." Yasinahun reported that his superior further explained "re-educating people is like spraying chemicals on crops."[35] It does not matter whether these derogatory words come from high-level or low-level Chinese officials. All of them represent the party, and the party represents the state, so it can reveal the special intent of genocide.

"Spray chemicals to kill the weeds" is a symbolically dehumanizing expression, but Uyghurs are literally treated as weeds. Camp survivor Zumret Dawut recalled her two-month experience in Chinese concentration camps, surprising which she saw a video of workers wearing entirely white protective gear as they disinfected the streets of Wuhan, China, when the Covid-19 pandemic broke out. She told me:

I saw these fully geared people in the camp too. It was my second day. Two of them came and sprayed chemicals on a bunch of women over their camp uniform. These women jumped and screamed like hell when they were sprayed with the chemicals; it must be immensely painful. I saw that these women's hands and necks were wounded and bleeding. Someone told me they had skin diseases because of poor hygiene in the camp, and that is how these geared-up workers were disinfecting them.[36]

There is thus a close connection between discourses of biological elimination and acts of biological genocide. Some may argue that the specific intent of Chinese leaders is not to destroy the national people of East Turkistan but to absorb them through colonization. That assumption is contradicted by well-documented practices of biological elimination, as illustrated in the next chapter and as hinted in this chapter by state discourses at every level: from Xi Jinping, to local officials, to guards within the camps.

SUMMARY

Every act to enforce these policies against the people of East Turkistan is planned and committed by individual actors who represent the party and act on behalf of the state. The 1996 Commentary of the International Law Commission on its draft Code of Crimes against the Peace and Security of Mankind addressed Article IV of Genocide Convention that explicitly recognized the responsibility of individual actors who implement state policies or plans that have genocidal aims:

> The extent of knowledge of the details of a plan or a policy to carry out the crime of genocide would vary depending on the position of the perpetrator in the governmental hierarchy or the military command structure. This does not mean that a subordinate who actually carries out the plan or policy cannot be held responsible for the crime of genocide simply because he did not possess the same degree of information concerning the overall plan or policy as his superiors. The definition of the crime of genocide requires a degree of knowledge of the ultimate objective of the criminal conduct rather than knowledge of every detail of a comprehensive plan or policy of genocide.[37]

In practice, when international criminal tribunals prosecute genocide cases and consider the role of the state, this involves identifying the state's plan or policy and then prosecuting those most responsible for planning and those most responsible for implementation.[38] Based on international laws related to the Genocide Convention and its practice, we can conclude that the systematic nature of the Chinese state's plan to eliminate Uyghurs and other Turkic Muslims in East Turkistan sufficiently demonstrates genocidal intent. Policies are planned by the Chinese state, or high-level government officials representing the Chinese state, and consciously target Uyghurs, the majority population and main racial group in East Turkistan. Officials, police, and workers who implement these policies have a general knowledge of the destructiveness of these policies and have been given leeway to implement them with cruelty. As a result, many of the Chinese government policies in East Turkistan are equal to or inseparable from specific genocidal intent.

NOTES

1. Gregory H. Stanton, "The Ten Stages of Genocide," *Genocide Watch,* 1996, accessed January 6, 2022, https://www.genocidewatch.com/tenstages.

2. China, The State Council Information Office, *Full Text: Employment and Labor Rights in Xinjiang* (Beijing: Foreign Languages Press Co. Ltd., 2020), http://www.xinhuanet.com/english/2020-09/17/c_139373591.htm.

3. Embassy of the Peoples Republic of China in the Republic of Estonia, "Terrorist Activities Perpetrated by 'Eastern Turkistan' Organizations and Their Links with Osama bin Laden and the Taliban," *Embassy of the Peoples Republic of China in the Republic of Estonia*, November 29, 2001, accessed September 10, 2020, http://ee.china-embassy.org/eng/ztlm/fdkbzy/t112733.htm.

4. Phelim Kine, "How China Hijacked the War on Terror," *Politico*, September 9, 2021, accessed in November 22, 2021, https://www.politico.com/news/2021/09/09/china-hijacked-war-on-terror-511032.

5. Sean R. Roberts, *The War on the Uyghurs* (Manchester: Manchester University Press, 2020), 72, Kindle.

6. Roberts, *The War on the Uyghurs*, 72.

7. Human Rights Watch, *Devastating Blows: Religious Repression of Uyghurs in Xinjiang* (New York: Human Rights Watch, 2005). https://www.hrw.org/report/2005/04/11/devastating-blows/religious-repression-uighurs-xinjiang.

8. China Law Translate, "Decision to Revise The 'Xinjiang Uighur Autonomous Region Regulation on De-Extremification'," *China Law Translate*, October 10, 2018, accessed May 19, 2020 https://www.chinalawtranslate.com/en/decision-to-revise-the-xinjiang-uighur-autonomous-region-regulation-on-de-extremification/.

9. U.S. Department of Defense, *Assistant Secretary of Defense for Indo-Pacific Security Affairs Schriver Press Briefing on the 2019 Report on Military and Security Developments in China* (Washington, DC: U.S. Department of Defense, 2019). https://www.defense.gov/News/Transcripts/Transcript/Article/1837011/assistant-secretary-of-defense-for-indo-pacific-security-affairs-schriver-press/.

See also Joshua Lipes, "Expert Says 1.8 Million Uyghurs, Muslim Minorities Held in Xinjiang's Internment Camps." *Radio Free Asia*, November 24, 2019, https://www.rfa.org/english/news/uyghur/detainees-11232019223242.html.

10. Vicky Xiuzhong Xu, et al., *Uyghurs for Sale* (Canberra: Australian Strategic Policy Institute, 2020), https://www.aspi.org.au/report/uyghurs-sale.

11. Amy Qin, "In China's Crackdown on Muslims, Children Have Not Been Spared," *New York Times*, December 28, 2019, https://www.nytimes.com/2019/12/28/world/asia/china-xinjiang-children-boarding-schools.html.

12. Adrian Zenz, *Sterilizations, IUDs, and Mandatory Birth Control: The CCP's Campaign to Suppress Uyghur Birthrates in Xinjiang* (Washington, DC: The Jamestown Foundation, 2020), 3. https://jamestown.org/product/sterilizations-iuds-and-mandatory-birth-control-the-ccps-campaign-to-suppress-uyghur-birthrates-in-xinjiang/.

13. Jiang Xian huan 蒋先欢, "'Minzu guo jia' keyi jian guo Zhong hua minzu?: Sun zhongshen de minzu tong hua sixiang ji qi shi dai nan ti zhong"民族国家"何以建构中华民族?--孙中山的民族同化思想及其时代难题中 [Is"Nation-state" Suitable for the Construction of Chinese Nation? ——Sun Yat-sen's Thought of Ethnic Assimilation and Its Dilemma], Lingdao kexue luntan, 领导科学论坛, 2017, no. 17 (2017): 42–54. doi: 10.19299/j.cnki.42-1837/C.2017.17.006.

14. Sun Yat-sen 孙中山, "Sanminzhuyi" 三民主義 [Three Principles of the People], *in Sun Zhongshan quanji* 孙中山全集 [*The Complete Works of Sun Yat-sen*], 5 (Beijing:

Zhonghua shuju, 1985), 187–88; See also: Sun Yat-sen, "Sanminzhuyi" [Three Principles of the People], in *The Complete Works of Sun Yat-sen* loc.1194 (2016) Apple Books.

15. Liu Ming fu, *China Dream: Great Power Thinking and Strategic Posture in the Post American Era* (New York: CN Times books Inc) loc.30 (2015) Apple books.

16. James Leibold, *Reconfiguring Chinese Nationalism: How the Qing Frontier and Its Indigenes Became Chinese* (London: Palgrave Macmillan, 2007), 31; Chow Kai-wing, "Imagining Boundaries of Blood: Zhang Binglin and the Invention of the Han 'Race' In Modern China," in *The Construction of Racial Identities in China and Japan,* ed. Frank Dikötter (Hong Kong: Hong Kong University Press, 1997), 34–52.

17. Fei Xiao tong 費孝通, "*Zhonghua minzu duoyuan yiti geju* 中華民族多元一題格局 [The Pattern of Plurality and Unity in the Chinese Nation], 2nd ed. (Beijing: Zhongyang minzu da xue chubanshe, 2003), 154–55.

18. Fei Xiao tong 費孝通, "Plurality and Unity in the Configuration of the Chinese" (lecture, University of Hongkong, November 15–18, 1998).

19. Resolution of the Standing Committee of the National People's Congress on the Establishment of the Xinjiang Uygur Autonomous Region and the Revocation of the Xinjiang Provincial System (Promulgated by Standing Comm. Nat'l People's Cong., SESS 21, September 13, 1955), chap. 1, art. 3, 1955 P.R.C. LAWS.

20. Mao Zedong, "The Role of the Chinese Communist Party in the National War," in Selected Works of Mao Tse-tung, vol. II, October 1938, Marxists Internet Archive, https://www.marxists.org/reference/archive/mao/works/red-book/ch18.htm.

21. Mao Zedong, "The Chinese Revolution and the Chinese Communist Party," in Selected Works of Mao Tse-tung, vol. II. December 1939, Marxists Internet Archive, accessed May 18, 2021, https://www.marxists.org/reference/archive/mao/selected-works/volume-2/mswv2_23.htm.

22. Mao Zedong, "National Minorities," in Selected Works of Mao Tse Tung Vol. VIII. March 1958, Marxists Internet Archive, accessed March 10, 2021, https://www.marxists.org/reference/archive/mao/selected-works/volume-8/mswv8_07.htm.

23. Liu Mingfu, *China Dream: Great Power Thinking and Strategic Posture in the Post American Era*, 33.

24. Xi Jinping, "Secure a Decisive Victory in Building a Moderately Prosperous Society in All Respects and Strive for the Great Success of Socialism with Chinese Characteristics for a New Era" (Speech, Beijing, delivered at the 19th National Congress of the Communist Party of China, October 18, 2017), accessed September 23, 2020, www.xinhuanet.com/english/download/Xi_Jinping's_report_at_19th_CPC_National_Congress.pdf.

25. Youku, "2013年南开大学艾跃进：中国国防政策的历史沿革 (二)" (The History of China's National Defence Policy), April 26, 2013.Youku video, 00:38, https://v.youku.com/v_show/id_XNTQ4Mjg5NTcy.html, accessed April 4, 2022. Author's translation, https://v.youku.com/v_show/id_XNTQ4Mjg5NTcy.html.

26. Human Rights Watch, *Eradicating Ideological Viruses: China's Campaign of Repression Against Xinjiang's Muslims, September* (New York: Human Rights Watch, 2018), 20–25. https://www.ecoi.net/en/file/local/1443021/4792_1536632022_china0918-web.pdf;

Note: Many Uyghurs have been imprisoned, tortured, convicted, or forcibly disappeared for talking to foreigners or for reading Western media in secret. I learned that on July 15, 2022, several Uyghur youths were arrested, accused of being infected by Western ideology, and tortured because they spoke a few times about very simple things in daily life with a European tourist in Urumchi who followed me on Twitter, despite the fact that these Uyghur youths were unaware of me or my Twitter account.

27. Austin Ramzy and Chris Buckley, "'Absolutely No Mercy': Leaked Files Expose How China Organized Mass Detentions of Muslims," *New York Times,* November 16, 2019, https://www.nytimes.com/interactive/2019/11/16/world/asia/china-xinjiang-documents .html.

28. Ibid.

29. Tursunay Ziyawudun (Chinese concentration camp survivor), phone interview with author, March 25, 2021.

30. Office of United States Chief of Counsel for Persecution of Axis Criminality, "Nazy Conspiracy and Aggression," September 1938 ("Red series"): Volume 8, Leading article in Der Stuermer, No 38. M-36, Military Legal Resources, Library of Congress, Washington, DC, https://www.loc.gov/rr/frd/Military_Law/pdf/NT_Nazi_Vol-VIII.pdf.

31. "Xuan jiang gao: dao jiaoyu zhuanhuaban xuexi shi dui sixi-ang shang huanbing qunzhong de yici mianfei zhuyuan zhiliao: 宣讲稿: 到教育转化班学习是对思想上患病群众的一次免费住院治疗" [Presentation: Studying in the Educational Transformation Facilities Is Free Hospitalization for Ideologically Ill Individuals]. *Yidu* 壹读, March 31, 2017, accessed September 24, 2021, http://web.archive.org /web/20211117160618/https:/read01.com/zh-sg/n3L6Do.html.

32. "Xinjiang Political 'Re-Education Camps' Treat Uyghurs 'Infected by Religious Extremism': CCP Youth League," *Radio Free Asia,* August 8, 2018, accessed September 2021, https://www.rfa.org/english/news/uyghur/infected-08082018173807.html. See: Eric Levitz, "China Declared Islam a Contagious Disease—and Quarantined 1 Million Muslims**,"** *Intelligencer,* August 28, 2018, accessed September 2021, https://nymag.com/intelligencer/2018 /08/china-muslims-camps-uighur-communist-party-islam-mental-illness.html?gtm=bottom &gtm=top.

33. Ibid.; "Xinjiang Political 'Re-Education Camps' Treat Uyghurs 'Infected by Religious Extremism': CCP Youth League," *Radio Free Asia.*

34. Alexandra Ma, "Chinese Ambassador to the US Says Mass Surveillance and Oppression of Muslim Minority Is to Make Them 'Normal Persons'," *Insider,* November 28, 2018, accessed September 24, 2021, https://www.businessinsider.com/china-ambassador-muslim -uighur-crackdown-make-normal-persons-2018-11.

35. Shohret Hoshur, "Chinese Authorities Jail Four Wealthiest Uyghurs in Xinjiang's Kashgar in New Purge," *Radio Free Asia,* January 5, 2018, accessed September 24, 2021, https://www.rfa.org/english/news/uyghur/wealthiest-01052018144327.html.

36. Zumret Dawut (Chinese Concentration Camp Survivor, Currently Awaiting Political Asylum in US), Phone Interview with Author, September 3, 2021. This testimony also provided to Uyghur Tribunal.

37. Arthur Watts, *The International Law Commission 1949-1998,* Vol. 3 (New York: Oxford University Press, 1999), 1743.

38. William A. Schabas, "State Policy as an Element of International Crimes," *Journal of Criminal Law and Criminology* 98, no. 3 (2008): 981.

5

Sophisticated Genocidal State Policies

GENOCIDE: INTENT AND ACTS

Article II of the 1948 United Nations Convention on the Prevention and Punishment of the Crime of Genocide presents a clear and widely accepted definition of genocide:

> In the present Convention, genocide refers to any of the following acts committed with intent to destroy, in whole or in part, a national, ethnical, racial or religious group:
>
> (a) Killing members of the group;
> (b) Causing serious bodily or mental harm to members of the group;
> (c) Deliberately inflicting on the group conditions of life calculated to bring about its physical destruction in whole or in part;
> (d) Imposing measures intended to prevent births within the group;
> (e) Forcibly transferring children of the group to another group.[1]

Despite what some have asserted, this definition does not refer solely to the intent to "kill" but clearly states "intent to destroy, in whole or in part." In other words, destroying a nation is not limited to the act of physically killing people. We cannot present physical evidence of hundreds of thousands of dead bodies, the remains of those believed to have been killed by the Chinese government, because this genocide is hidden by sophisticated state propaganda. However, the evidence that we have gathered proves how China's colonial policy in East Turkistan meets all the criteria that used to define genocide, including killings.

Violation of Article II(a): Killing Members of the Group

Killings during the Uyghur Protests

Over the past seventy years, each uprising of the people of East Turkistan against Chinese colonialism has resulted in the killing of hundreds of thousands of Turkic Muslims. The Uyghur Research Institute's report on genocide in East Turkistan cited Chinese state media, who estimated that between 1949 and 1954 alone, 150,000 people from East Turkestan were eliminated after China's invasion.[2]

According to one official Chinese document, during the Baren Uprising of 1990, which was a rebellion by Uyghur farmers against China's birth control policies and forced labor, 3,000 Uyghurs were arrested and 200 executed. However, according to unofficial sources, people from neighboring villages reported that the original population of Baren, around 10,000 people, was completely eliminated, and it took three years for the Chinese government to repopulate Baren with people from nearby.[3] Even though these killings were prompted by an Uyghur uprising against the Chinese government, violent Chinese repression during and after this and other uprisings, regardless of whether Uyghurs had participated or not, strongly suggests a Chinese intent to destroy the Uyghur people as an ethnicity—and not merely for political reasons. For example, one of the Chinese soldiers who participated in the crackdown at Baren stated: "That time was very entertaining, we shot anybody human in that Uyghur village."[4]

There are dozens of eyewitness video testimonies from people who experienced the July 5, 2009, uprising in Urumchi. In one account, a witness explains:

> A bunch of Chinese mobs attacked my friend Gulshan's brother at Urumchi's Youhaolu bridge when he was walking back from his work, stabbed and killed him just because he is Uyghur, despite him begging them to "please stop, I have a six-month-old baby."[5]

Killings in Concentration Camps

Following the introduction of the new "de-extremification" policy in 2017, China launched a massive campaign to detain Uyghurs and other Turkic Muslims, forcing possibly as many as 3 million into concentration camps.[6] The leak of Chinese government records revealed high-level Chinese officers' speeches and thousands of mugshots from two concentration camps in Tikes county in Ghulja and Kona-Sheher county in Kashgar include children under ten and elderly women age seventy-three. All look scared and confused, many of them had their heads shaved and hands tied behind their back.[7] Zhaokeji, the highest-ranking civil government official of the People's Republic of China (PRC), praised their achievements in his secret speech on genocidal policies in East Turkistan. He summarized these so-called security achievements as "The ten Well-done" stating that the first well done is the "strike hard battle," which is a high-pressure attack on Uyghurs and other Turkic Muslims.[8]

He described their strike hard battle by using phrases like "digging, reducing, and shoveling" in the following remark:

> Xinjiang has two million people who have been influenced by pro-Xinjiang independence and "Double-Pan" [pan-Turkist and pan-Islamist] thinking. Southern Xinjiang has more than two million people who have been severely influenced by the infiltration of extremist religious thought. As the work of "Digging, Reducing, and Shoveling" continues to deepen, the living spaces for dangerous persons in Xinjiang have been continuously reduced.[9]

This implies that China will continue to eradicate the entire Uyghur and Turkic populations. Because Uyghurs and other Turkic populations are the original inhabitants of East Turkistan, and never desired to be part of China, and Chinese government views all of them as a separatist. Meanwhile, the majority of Uyghurs and Kazakhs are devout Muslims who are easily labelled as religious extremists and are continuously subjected to China's work of "Digging, Reducing, and Shoveling." Not surprisingly, China has continuously expanded detention centers and prison facilities in East Turkistan, which extensive international research has corroborated. The Australian Strategic Policy Institute has mapped 385 newly built detention sites since 2017.[10] The Intercept obtained the Chinese police database developed by the private company Landasoft that contains close to 250 million data rows. It confirmed and provided more detail about the mass scale arrests of Muslims in the region.[11] Though it remains extremely difficult to acquire accurate death statistics, many deaths in concentration camps have been reported with confidence, and these cases clearly demonstrate the violation of Article II(a) of the Genocide Convention.[12] In an unabashed evocative of Orwellian doublespeak, as International Consortium journalist Bethany Allen-Ebrahimian showed,[13] leaked Chinese government documents mention rules such as "Never allow abnormal deaths," in the concentration camps. Camp survivors have revealed that "Never allow abnormal death" means that inmates have no right to end their own life and must instead bear extreme torture to be killed. Many former prisoners and camp survivors believe that death by torture is permissible and normal in the camps and said: "You are extremely lucky if you are not killed or mentally and physically destroyed in the camp."

Camp survivor Mihrigul Tursun testified that she witnessed nine deaths in just three months among the sixty-eight women in her cell. She believes that all of these young and healthy women were killed by inhuman torture.[14] Testimonies from the Uyghur diaspora as well as news reports from Radio Free Asia have confirmed many deaths in the concentration camps, and a police officer at the Kuchar County police department confirmed at least 150 deaths in the No. 1 concentration camp in the Yengisheher district between June and December of 2018.[15] At the time of writing, the Xinjiang Victims Database has recorded 157 reported deaths in the camps between 2017 and 2021.[16] In reality, the real number could be much higher—it is very difficult to establish the actual death rates in concentration camps because the Chinese authorities use their utmost power to conceal it. However, what is clear is that there would be no mass scale, systematic arrest, torture, and killing of this targeted racial group without the intended destruction of that group.

Mass Killings

The murder of Uyghurs and other Turkic Muslims has not been limited to concentration camps or prison facilities; there is also a significant risk of mass killings outside of the camps. These populations have also been treated as experimental objects of murder exercises. The following is the testimony of two Chinese veteran soldiers interviewed by NTDTV (新唐人 Xin Tang Ren) on April 11, 2020:

> "That was in the summer of 2013. We secretly executed more than one hundred Xinjiang people in a mountainous area of a province," a retired soldier said. "Those people looked like Uighurs. Some were children. Senior leaders claimed the order was issued for the purpose of 'peacekeeping.' The Uighurs were unarmed. We fired with a ninety-five rifle [type 95 automatic rifle] and commanded an attack drone, and they died everywhere as they fled."[17]

This soldier expressed that it was a "nightmare" and that this operation in particular was conducted under tight secrecy. The soldiers had been told it was an exercise, only to be faced with the order to carry out the murders.

Another Fujian military veteran revealed the following story to the *Bitter Winter* magazine, as reported by NTDTV (新唐人 Xin Tang Ren):

> A few years ago, our captain was sent to a village in Xinjiang to slaughter Xinjiang people. Listening to our captain, the troops in the daytime wore plain clothes to inform the Han people there, "Cover your windows with newspaper. Stay asleep at night and lock the door. Don't listen to anything, don't look outside, don't turn on the lights in your house." The local Han people heard the bangs of gunshots in the night, and by first daybreak in the morning the Uyghurs had disappeared. Our captain said they were all killed, and even the blood was washed away.[18]

Targeting a specific racial and religious group with these mass murders proves that the Chinese government has authorized its forces to commit atrocities and worked to normalize the killings. There can be no question of the intent for destruction when whole Uyghur villages were targeted for killings.

Killings through Organ Harvesting

There is considerable circumstantial evidence that organ harvesting has also been part of China's program to exterminate the Uyghurs. For example, a report published in 2014 by the *BMC Medical Ethics Journal* revealed China's apparent falsification and manipulation of official organ donors' data sets.[19] The authors reported that between 2010 and 2018, annual voluntary deceased donors increased by a factor of 185 from 34 to 6,316 and between 2010 and 2016, kidney and liver transplants increased by a factor of 166, from 63 to 10,481. It is highly likely that most of these organs were from concentration camps or prisons, where up to 3 million Uyghurs were detained. A Chinese state newspaper attempted to reject these accusations on the grounds that organ transplants are best done near the patient in need. However, the disappearance of thousands of Uyghur inmates who were secretly transferred to inland Chinese cities suggests a possible correlation between organ transparency and forced disappearances.[20]

This effort might not be limited to prisoners: Chinese authorities collected DNA samples and the blood types of the entire Uyghur population, and people were forced to get blood tests and donate blood monthly.[21] Since blood tests are required for transplant and tissue matching, many Uyghurs believe those tests could be used for the purpose of organ harvesting or other biomedical experiments. According to the China Tribunal, led by the former prosecutor of the International Criminal Tribunal for the former Yugoslavia, Sir Goffrey Nice QC, the medical testing of Uyghurs on a massive scale indicates that they have become an "organ bank."[22] Apparently, Uyghurs and their organs have become a dehumanized product requisitioned by the state, and any individual Uyghur living in East Turkistan may be at risk of being killed at any time for organ harvesting.

The circumstantial evidence is thus considerable, and most if not all of these organ-harvesting deaths are likely to be intentional killings, not incidental or accidental. In the eyes of the Chinese state, these ethnic, religious, and linguistic people have no rights: their bodies have thus been degraded, dehumanized, and commodified by the Chinese government.

Aytursun Eli, thirty-five, a young healthy woman, was killed four days after she was called to the police station. Her mother testified as follows in a voice memo on the WeChat app and later gave a detailed interview to Radio Free Asia as well:

> Police called my daughter to visit the local police station in June 4, 2018. I was convinced she was taken into re-education camps like everyone else. After four days, the police called me to come to the front of the hospital. When I arrived two policemen were waiting for me. They told me to not cry or scream. I didn't understand. I asked them what happened? They didn't talk and escorted me to an office room in the hospital. There was one man sitting in front of the table. They made me sit between two policemen and the man said: "We will cut open your daughter's abdomen, should we?" I asked: "Why? What happened to her?" He didn't answer and gestured orders to the police. The police pulled my arm and forced me to sign some papers without letting me read it. I resisted. They said I couldn't see my daughter's face ever again if I refused. So I signed. They pulled to another room and pulled off a white sheet to show my daughter's face. I screamed and fainted.[23]

Because of the lack of international public awareness of China's organ harvesting, China's marketing of "halal organs," "young organs," and "quick delivery" has attracted many global and domestic clients, which has made China the most profitable site for organ harvesting and commerce.[24] In a recent interview, a Chinese woman told the host of Lude Press, a Chinese-language news channel on YouTube, that she had witnessed thirty-seven halal organ orders from Saudi patients in China's Tianjin Taida hospital, primarily obtained from ethnic Uyghurs.[25] Such hospitals in China quickly perform lung transplant operations: in less than a few days, a matching pair of donor lungs can be found.

This evidence is only circumstantial, but it is considerable. Some may argue that it is profit and economic benefit rather than "intended destruction" that may motivate China's organ market. However, the systematic selection of a specifically targeted group invalidates this argument. Moreover, in the eyes of the Chinese state, these ethnically, religiously, and linguistically distinct people have no rights: the bodies of these people have thus been degraded, dehumanized, and commodified. A specific intent to "destroy" easily follows.

Detention and Death Sentences for Uyghur Scholars

Hundreds of prominent Uyghur poets, artists, writers, storytellers, comedians, professors, medical doctors, religious figures, and other Uyghur scholars, intellectuals, and cultural icons have disappeared or been detained or imprisoned.[26] China attempts to cast these intellectuals as members of a "political group" by claiming that they have a separatist political ideology against China, but in actuality, they do not meet the legal definition of "political group" at all. The decision to attack Uyghur intellectuals was made by the Chinese state or high-level Chinese state officials as part of their policy of crackdown on so-called "two-faced officials" in East Turkistan, officials who supposedly harbor anti-party thoughts despite their outward loyalty.[27] In planning these policies, the Chinese state was fully aware that destroying Uyghur intellectuals could decapitate the whole nation, facilitating its destruction. Uyghur intellectuals, like in any other societies, bring fresh ideas, lead people with critical thoughts, shape the Uyghur community's mind, and play an indispensable role in the national survival of the people of East Turkistan. For example, Uyghur historians such as Turghun Almas and Muhammad Emin Bughra played a crucial role in educating people about East Turkistan's history and revealed China's distorted history about Uyghurs. Uyghur anthropologists, such as Rahile Dawut, are the critical forces in Uyghur society that could preserve Uyghur culture and identity by contributing so much substantial research. The Uyghur economist, Professor Ilham Tohti, or the writers such as Perhat Tursun and Yalkun Rozi, also contributed so much to the ideological development of Uyghur society that Uyghurs could question themselves and question Chinese colonizers' minds and policies with critical thinking. Medical doctor Halmurat Ghopur and Uyghur scholar Tashpolat Tiyip who reportedly sentenced to death by the Chinese government also played a leading role in the healthy development of Uyghur society, which could be an obstacle to China's genocidal plan. As William Schabas argues, when genocide is committed by state policy, it should be the case that the knowledge of the policy or plan determines the guilt or crime, not the intent of the individual perpetrator.[28] Leading individuals who engineer such policies also contribute intent to commit the crime. In the case of East Turkistan, a policy or plan and an individual policy maker's intent have combined to destroy part of a group that leads to the destruction of the whole group, which demonstrates institutional intent. This point was also emphasized by Lemkin, and this intent survives in the wording "in whole or in part," found in Article II.[29]

The Uyghur Human Rights Project report lists the names of 312 Uyghur, Kazakh, and Kyrgyz intellectuals and cultural elites whose detainment and imprisonment have been confirmed by the diaspora and other reliable sources in China as of late 2021.[30] Several of these intellectuals were either sentenced to death or disappeared from the Chinese prison. Among them, Halmurat Ghopur, the president of Xinjiang Medical University, has been given a two-year suspended death sentence for "separatism."[31] Tashpolat Tiyip, the head of Xinjiang University, was arrested and disappeared in 2017. His family heard that he was sentenced to death with two years' reprieve.[32] Religious scholar and academic translator Muhammad Salih Hajim was found dead shortly after his arrest in 2018.[33] The former director of Xinjiang's Education Department Sattar Sawut and his deputy Shirzat Bawudun were sentenced to death with two years' reprieve.[34] Many scholars sentenced to long-term imprisonment in the concentration camps, detention centers, or prisons are unknown.

It is not only educated elites who have been targeted for destruction but also important religious and cultural figures. China believes that any Uyghur or other Turkic Muslim in the region who possesses a strong sense of dignity cannot be loyal to the Communist Party and so has made such individuals targets of elimination. A reliable contact of mine in East Turkistan also confirmed the killings of these targets. The message in figure 5.1 is translated and summarized by the author as follows:

> Do not believe it when the Chinese state said they have released the people from the camp, they did not release religious and very intellectual ones. Only people who abandon their religion, are not talented, alcoholics, drug users, or people who are going to die soon because of torture or illness were released. My neighbour's religious, healthy young daughter was killed in 2018 in the camps within a few months, and they did not return her body.[35]

The killings of Uyghurs since China colonized the region as well as recent deaths and disappearances in concentration camps and public death sentences of Uyghur scholars should be taken seriously. We can conclude that these killings are committed with the intent to destroy, as this systematically targeted group has been subjected to hate, dehumanized, and killed, all facilitated by Chinese state policy.

Violations of Article II(b): Serious Bodily or Mental Harm

Article II(b) of the Genocide Convention prohibits serious bodily or mental harm directed against members of a group. Despite this prohibition, the Chinese government is enacting widespread physical and mental torture of Uyghurs and other ethnic Muslims in East Turkistan. China ratified the Convention against Torture and Other Cruel Inhuman or Degrading Treatment or Punishment on October 4, 1988.[36] However, it has violated this Convention through the use of rape and torture on a massive scale in women's concentration camps, tactics that must be understood as deliberate tools of extermination aimed at fulfilling the genocidal intent. Though

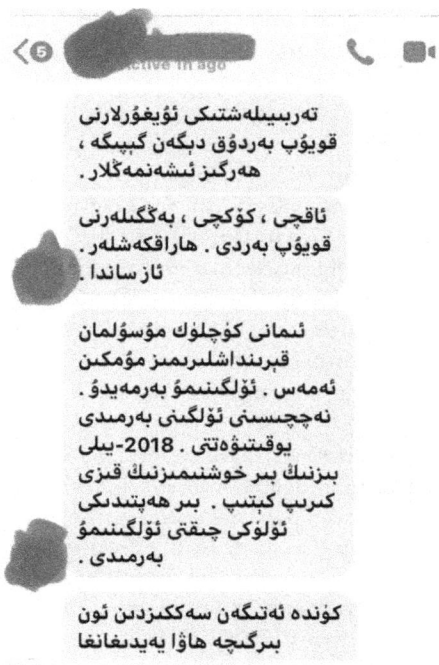

Figure 5.1   Private Chat Conversation with Worker at Neighborhood Committee in Aksu. The profile name was deleted to protect the identity of the interviewee.

China's arsenal of genocidal policies does not include a "rape policy," the policy of so-called "re-education camps," which incarcerated millions of Uyghur and other Turkic Muslims, in conjunction with Xi Jinping's order of "no mercy," created the conditions for the agents of the state to act with impunity, and rape and torture have long been the domain of war and genocide. This large-scale mental and physical harm to innocent civilians of a specific ethnic group can have no other imaginable end goal than the total destruction of that group. The severity of the systematically planned torture, which has often resulted in killings and physical and mental harm, would suggest that there is a genocidal intent.

Witness testimonies confirm that sexual violence in the camp is intended to destroy the victims and is implemented with extreme hatred. Ten female camp survivors were identified in the diaspora. I interviewed seven of them and relied on media interviews for the rest. All of the survivors confirmed mass sexual violence and torture in the camps. One of them had experienced rape and torture, and another experienced physical and verbal sexual assault. When other interviewees were asked if they had experienced rape and torture in the camp, one of them cried without words. Two of them said that they did not know and refused to answer.

Camp survivor Tursunay Ziyawudun suffered nine months of gang rape and inhuman torture before escaping from China. Her story explores how the body and spirit of Uyghur women are destroyed in China's systematic rape camps as well as the impossibility of recovery.[37] She was raped more than three times, each time by a tall, blue-suited man and three military-uniformed men. During the torture, they specifically attacked her womb, and their conversation confirmed their general intent, indicating knowledge of the consequences of their actions.[38] Attacking women to destroy their reproductive systems is evidence of their intent to destroy not only the dignity and spirit of the Uyghur population but their very existence.

Kalbinur Siddiq, a camp teacher who fled to Holland last year, also told me that the Han Chinese are proud of the culture of rape in the camps, and she often heard Chinese police talking about it. Another camp survivor, Gulbahar Jalilova, said,

> Every night, they chose young women and took them out. We could hear the terrible screams. Some of them returned with bruised bodies, looking terrified, and some of them never returned. When I asked them if they had been raped, because that is the worst thing that could happen to women that I could think of, they just cried, not saying a word. They cannot. How could they?

She also described how a beautiful young Uyghur woman around twenty years of age lost her mind after being interrogated for two nights:

> She was new. They called her out at night for two days. When she returned, she did not look at anyone. She looked awful and sat there frozen all night. In the morning, she suddenly ran to the toilet and made a beard of poop on her face and started laughing and screaming: "I am a man, not a woman, do not touch me!" Chinese guards dragged her out, and she never came back.[39]

The long-lasting damage of rape is not limited to the women in the camps. The effects of this torture are psychological and transgenerational, and they destroy the whole nation.

Every Uyghur individual was targeted for surveillance, indoctrination, arrest, torture, or execution because of their religious faith. Ruqiye Parhet, currently living in Holland, was arrested and tortured, naked, before she was released. Chinese police arrested her for the sole reason that she wore a hijab. She described the prison and torture during an interview with Istiqlal TV:

> Uyghur girls were naked and chained on one side of the big room, and Uyghur men were naked and chained on another side of the room. Our private places were exposed to one other. That is the XXX detention center in Ghulja. Most of the girls were raped by the Chinese police in front of the other prisoners. I witnessed a fourteen-year-old girl who kept banging her head on the wall; none of us stopped her because none of us had the energy to say anything to anyone. She lost her mind and then they released her to the street. I learned from other prisoners that she has no family because every one of her family was arrested.[40]

The sexual violence women faced was not limited to the camps either. Many Uyghur women faced systematic rape attacks organized by the Chinese government after their husbands were arrested. An Uyghur woman from Kashgar (for her safety I have not revealed her real name or specific place of origin) uploaded a TikTok video that criticized the actions of the Chinese state but deleted it quickly after people began posting comments such as "have you lost your mind," "you cannot talk about officials," "do not try to get yourself in trouble," "please delete the video," "you will get in big trouble," and so on. She said:

> I have three kids. A few days after my husband was arrested by government officials, police confiscated my motorcycle. When I went to their office to get my motorcycle back, they forced me to sign a letter saying that I was a prostitute, and I refused! Do you know what I mean? They forced me to confess and sign to something dirty and terrible that I never did. Since then, every day, many of them came and went from my home. When I refused, they said that they would detain me. Who will take care of my children then?[41]

There is also some second-hand evidence of sexual assault gathered from Chinese social media videos and testimonies of people who managed to escape. Even though it is very difficult to verify this evidence, it suggests that sexual assault was prevalent in Uyghur families following the establishment of a Chinese government policy to appoint more than 1.5 million Han Chinese men to become "relatives" of Uyghurs and sleepover regularly in Uyghur homes to spy on them. Uyghur camp survivor Zumret Dawut, who is currently living in Washington, said:

> The Chinese government purposefully matches Uyghur women to Han Chinese men and Uyghur men to Han Chinese women through their "family pair-up" policy, so these Han Chinese men not only spy on these women but also dominate them and sexually assault them. No one dares to resist; we have to be nice to these Han Chinese relatives appointed to sleep and eat with us in our homes for weeks out of every month. If not, they will give us a bad score and send the entire family to concentration camps to be tortured.[42]

There are many substantial eyewitness testimonies concerning the physical and mental torture of Uyghurs in the new Chinese concentration and detention camps. These accounts allude to food deprivation, lack of hygiene, rape, and torture, including restraint in "tiger chairs" that deliver electric shocks.[43] A former Chinese police officer in East Turkistan who is currently living in Europe confirmed the arbitrary detention and inhuman torture against Uyghurs and other Turkic Muslims in his interview with CNN.[44] This police officer confirmed that Chinese police forces would forcibly round up entire Uyghur villages overnight and subject every detainee including men, women, and children as young as fourteen to interrogation. Chinese police officers would step on detainees' faces to force them to confess and used various other torture methods as well:

> The methods included shackling people to a metal or wooden "tiger chair"—chairs designed to immobilize suspects, hang people from the ceiling, sexual violence, electrocutions, and waterboarding. Inmates were often forced to stay awake for days and were denied food and water.[45]

He also confirmed that these hundreds of Uyghur prisoners he was involved in arresting were ordinary people who had committed no crime.

TikTok has featured videos and information from Uyghurs in the diaspora who managed to contact their relatives, and these videos suggest that many of those who were "released" from these camps back into society have been rendered either physically disabled or mentally unstable. Some of the TikTok videos distributed by Uyghur youth on Chinese social media have mentioned their fathers' severe health conditions after being released. In the comments section of one such video, other Uyghur youth asked questions about why their fathers were not released or why their once-healthy fathers are very sick after their detention.[46] Another TikTok video posted in 2020 recounts the story of a thirty-five-year-old Uyghur man who became blind after three years in the concentration camps. He explains, "I lost my eyesight because I didn't see light for three years."[47]

The following cases represent only the tip of the iceberg, considering the millions of detained Uyghurs and other Muslims who have undergone debilitating torture, confinement, and malnutrition:

> Adile Kamran, a Uyghur Canadian woman, revealed that her 18-year-old brother was released from a detention camp after one year: "After a medical check-up he was diagnosed with an infertility-related disease," she said, requesting anonymity for herself and her brother due to her fear of reprisal. "He was very healthy before he was detained by the Chinese forces. Now he is skinny and looks very ill in the photo that my mother posted in WeChat after he was released. I don't know what is the exact name of his illness, but they told me it is a kind of disease related to infertility."[48]

Erkin Muhemmed, from Holland, told a woeful tale about his cousin but was afraid to provide his full name:

> "My cousin was released from the Chinese concentration camp recently, and they said he now has hepatitis B," said Erkin. "He was a very healthy young man before, but now he looks like a skeleton and his condition is deteriorating."[49]

Recent camp survivor Gulbahar Hatiwaji vividly explained China''s destruction of Uyghurs' memories and mental reprogramming as well as controlling their body movement in her book:

> Our exhausted bodies moved through the space in unison, back and forth, side to side, corner to corner. When the soldier bellowed "At ease!" in Mandarin, our regiment of prisoners froze. He ordered us to remain still. This could last half an hour, or just as often a whole hour, or even more. . . . The ones who'd been there longer looked down at their feet. They shuffled around in close ranks, like robots. They snapped to attention without batting an eye when a whistle was ordered to them. [50]

Depriving these people freedom of both body and soul goes far beyond harming their mental and physical health.

The systematic selection of people for concentration camps based on their nationality and religion demonstrates that the Chinese government is intent on destroying the people of East Turkistan with "absolutely no mercy." The serious bodily and mental harm to detainees in the camps is neither accidental nor the result of negligence; rather, it is the intended outcome of policies designed by those in power. Physical and sexual torture, food and sleep deprivation, and forced denunciations of cultural and religious beliefs are systematically implemented across all of the camps in East Turkistan. According to camp survivors' testimonies, every concentration camp operates the same way. Female camp survivors from different camps from different regions confirmed similar experiences of mass sexual assault. While it is true that, unlike Jews, who were exterminated in death camps, many Uyghurs are released and returned to their communities, however, many of those who are returned have suffered significant mental and physical hardships, and some have died within months of returning home. Because China will not allow independent investigations, it is very difficult to ascertain exact numbers, but Uyghurs in the diaspora have confirmed the severe mental and physical illnesses experienced by their released relatives. Starting in 2021, some of the Uyghurs who were released from so-called re-education camps and recovered from physical illness were arrested again and handed prison terms without any charges.[51]

The mental and physical health of Uyghurs outside of the camps is also severely harmed by China's unprecedented mass surveillance and monitoring of innocent people. Mass surveillance conducted with experimental AI technology, face and voice recognition cameras and phone spyware, the collection of blood and DNA samples from entire segments of the Uyghur population, the policy that sends more than a million Han Chinese male cadres into Uyghur homes as human spies every month, and monitoring the household members for possible infractions, all of this induces responses ranging from anxiety to outright terror, severely damaging Uyghurs' mental health.[52] As these policies have gradually become more genocidal, China's surveillance policy targeted and detected each individual ethnic Uyghur, strictly controlling their movement. Huawei, the world's largest maker of telecommunications equipment, has also contributed to these efforts, providing the servers, cameras, cloud-computing infrastructure, and other tools that support the technology of genocide. Huawei even developed technology that could send automated "Uyghur alarms" to Chinese authorities when its camera systems identify Uyghurs and other Turkic people in East Turkistan.[53]

Transferring Children

Since 2017, as many as more than 500,000 Uyghur children have been removed from their homes by the Chinese government and confined to Chinese orphanage camps, following the detention of their parents.[54] Even youth whose parents were not detained are locked up in residential schools, able to visit their families only once every two weeks. Data provided to the *Economist* by Adrian Zenz in 2020 indicates that 380,000 Uyghur children entered the residential schools between 2017 and 2019, demonstrating a mass separation of Uyghur children from their families and culture.[55] Thousands of social media videos distributed by Chinese workers in orphanage camps and residential schools, as well as the information I have collected directly from contacts in East Turkistan, confirm media reports. From this significant evidence, the following conclusions could be drawn about what is happening to Uyghur youths:

Uyghur Children Are Not Allowed to Speak Their Language or Practice
Their Culture and Religion and Face Severe Consequences If They Do So

Uyghur children are forced to speak in Mandarin Chinese, learn Confucian ideology and Han, Chinese culture, and sometimes even wear ancient Han Chinese clothing. There are thousands of social media videos speaking about how these kids are learning Chinese in these camps. In one of the videos, the Chinese teacher asked an Uyghur girl around the age of five or six to pronounce her brother's Uyghur name, and she said, "I do not remember my brother's Uyghur name, and I am ashamed to pronounce his Uyghur name. I feel a bit weird." And the Chinese teacher said: "Do not worry, just tell us his name" the girl said: "What if teachers curse me and hit me?"[56] Clearly, these children were punished if they spoke Uyghur. Another Uyghur child camp survivor who was released to Turkey because of his Turkish passport after spending a few years in a Chinese orphanage camp refused to speak to his parents in the Uyghur language until receiving many months of therapy in Turkey. He said the teachers would cut his skin if he spoke in Uyghur. His parents had a very difficult time convincing him that he is safe in Turkey and those Chinese teachers are far behind.[57] Another video posted on social media by a Chinese boarding school teacher demonstrated how Uyghur kids were forced to believe that they are Han Chinese, with black eyes, black hair, and yellow skin, despite the fact that many Uyghurs have diverse ancestry, with green, black, or brown eyes and brown or white skin. These children's identities are erased and then transformed into those of ethnic Han Chinese, and their self-respect is obliterated.

Uyghur Children Are Not Only Removed from Their Families
But Also from Their Communities and Culture

The research indicates that these children are not only deprived of their parents and family, they are also denied their cultural heritage. They are forced to eat pork, not allowed to speak their own language, and not allowed to practice their religion. Further, these children are isolated from the outside world; many so-called kindergartens and schools that lock up Uyghur children have implemented full-coverage surveillance systems, perimeter alarms, and 10,000-volt electric fences.[58] The following post, mentioned in figure 5.2 and figure 5.3 sent by a Chinese-speaking Uyghur worker who visited her friend who is working in an orphanage camp, is heartbreaking:

> They are never able to see their mom or any Uyghur. I had a chance to visit one of the orphanage camps, and kids ran toward me and cried and hugged me and did not want to

leave me because I am an Uyghur woman, and these kids think I am their mom. Boys and girls 3 to 5 years old, all have a short haircut and the same clothing, and you cannot differentiate them.[59]

Uyghur Youth Experience Mental and Physical Abuse in the Camps

It is difficult to know how poorly these kids are treated and how many are abused or killed while in these camps. However, what we do know is that separation from their parents and community creates long-term psychological and physical damage to developing brain cells. According to pediatric specialists, stress hormones created by the child's separation from their parents will kill dendrites—the little branches in brain cells that transmit messages. This separation will also kill neurons, disrupt the formation of children's brains, and cause dramatic psychological and physical damage.[60] It also falls within the scope of the Genocide Convention's Article II(b)—the prohibition against severe physical and mental harm. While it is very difficult to gather evidence about the kinds of mental and physical abuse that exists in these orphanage camps and boarding schools, it is not difficult to analyze their living condition through the social media videos posted by Chinese workers. For

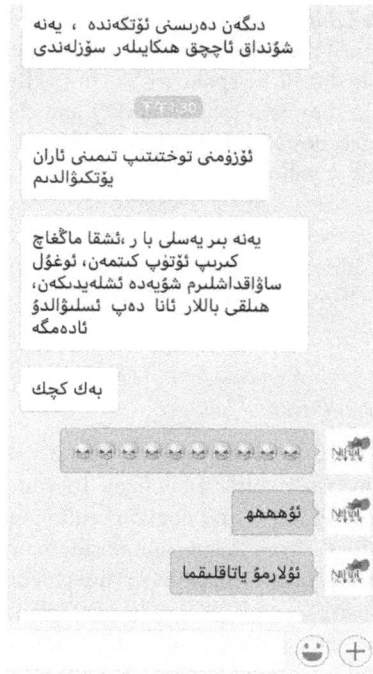

Figure 5.2 Private Chat Conversation with Author. The profile name was deleted to protect the identity of the interviewee.

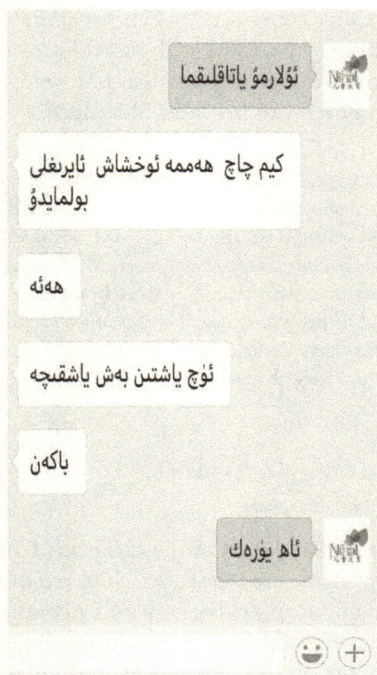

Figure 5.3 Private Chat Conversation with Author. The profile name was deleted to protect the identity of the interviewee.

example, videos show children crowded in orphanage camp beds, with three or four kids sleeping together in a tiny bed. Other videos show kids coughing, and both sick and healthy kids sleeping in the same bed, not separated. In some boarding schools, boys and girls are mixed in the same dormitory rooms. A worker at one of the Uyghur orphanage camps told Radio Free Asia about the terrible conditions there, reporting that the children, ranging from six months to twelve years of age, are incarcerated like farm animals.[61] According to a report from the Association for the Defense of Human Rights and Religious Freedom, a Chinese worker in an Uyghur children's camp in Korla stated that the children often asked teachers why they were imprisoned, and many attempted to commit suicide by drinking cleaning detergent.[62]

Children who have been released from the orphanage camps also have significant behavioral issues and terrible nightmares and are scared of everything. Often times these children do not want to talk to their parents and become extremely quiet. Elfira Nury's daughters were taken into a children's orphanage camp when she and her husband were arrested for having a twin for her third delivery, illegal within China's family planning policy. Her husband was not released, and she was released after three years. During the secret conversation with her friend in Europe, she said she was lucky enough to temporarily reunite with her children before they were sent to boarding school. However, she also said she does not want to live in this world and wants to commit suicide along with her kids. She added:

> Kids totally forgot how to speak in Uyghur language. The eldest one could not access school for three years when she was in orphanage camps. Now she has extreme difficulty catching up with her classes in boarding school. The youngest two of them did not recognize me. All my girls become incredibly quiet and often have nightmares at night. It is very difficult to convince them that they're at home and safe with me. They cry quietly and are very afraid of people, afraid of noises, even afraid of me. They repeatedly apologize for anything they have done, even if it is not wrong. Their behaviour becomes so strange, and they are no longer happy kids.[63]

Uyghur Children Are Not Allowed to Travel Out of China to Unite with Their Parents.

In fact, all of this is expressly outlawed in the Genocide Convention's Article II(e). While the Chinese government often describes child removal policies as protection of children, the principal aim is to deliberately inflict conditions of life that are calculated to bring about the physical destruction, in whole or in part, of the Uyghur people by destroying families and limiting population growth. If the Chinese government were really concerned about Uyghur children, removing them from their homes and placing them in orphanages for their own protection, as they claimed, then why are they tearing their families apart in the first place? The Chinese government's arrest of Uyghur parents is the sole reason for these children being orphans. Even when these parents are citizens or residents of other countries, the children are not allowed to leave and be reunited with their parents. Relatives are not allowed to visit them, and these children are not allowed to visit their homes or relatives. The figure 5.4 below depicts four Uyghur siblings who were forbidden to reunite with their parents in Italy.

Before China began its mass arrests and camp detentions, the parents of these children traveled to Turkey and then Italy for work, leaving the children with their grandparents. When the children were removed from their grandparents' home and locked in Kashgar Peyziwat children's camp, the parents tried desperately to return but were unable to because every Uyghur returning from overseas was arrested and disappeared. After the Italian government approved the family union visas for these siblings, the parents spent considerable amounts of money on their local Chinese contacts, and in November 2019, they managed to secretly release these children from the orphanage camp. On June 23, 2020, the children traveled to the Italian embassy in Shanghai to get their visas. However, Chinese police tracked them to their hotel in Shanghai and arrested all of them. The children disappeared and have not been heard of since.[64]

Figure 5.4   Home Town: Kashgar Peyziwat. Zumaira Ablikim was born on April 2, 2004 (Third from the Left). Yahya Ablikim was born on May 4, 2005 (First from the Left). Muhammet Ablikim was born on September 5, 2006 (Second from the Left). Xiayida Ablikim was born on October 15, 2008 (First from the Right). Siblings holding a paper sign writing a message saying they miss their parents. Photo provided by siblings cousin Araphat Ablimit who is currently resided in Canada.

Intentional Removal of the Younger Generation

Article 30 of the International Criminal Court (ICC) Statute defines the role of intent in international crime, including *dolus directus* and *dolus indirectus*:

1. Unless otherwise provided, a person shall be criminally responsible and liable for punishment for a crime within the jurisdiction of the Court only if the material elements are committed with intent and knowledge.
2. For the purposes of this article, a person has intent where:
   a.   In relation to conduct, that person means to engage in the conduct;
   b.   In relation to a consequence, that person means to cause that consequence or is aware that it will occur in the ordinary course of events.[65]

One form of intent, *dolus indirectus*—in which the perpetrator is aware of certain consequences of a criminal act, and the perpetrator means to cause those consequences—is applicable to China's crime of removing Uyghur children. Even if we cannot prove that China has the intent to destroy these children as a primary goal (*dolus directus*), their actions had fatal consequences. Although the removal of Uyghur children alone is not enough to prove China's specific genocidal intention of destroying the Uyghurs and other Turkic Muslims because of their race, religion ethnicity, culture, or nation, nevertheless, it is clear that, in the long term, this is the consequence of this policy. So, forcibly removing Uyghur and other Turkic children could establish *dolus indirectus* intent toward this racial group. The extermination or assimilation of one or two generations of Uyghur children will ensure that the next generation of children forget their Uyghur heritage and think of themselves as Chinese—thereby eliminating the Uyghur nation. Whether the children are assimilated and become Han Chinese or struggle with an identity crisis because they do not look Han Chinese, they will be unable to contribute to the survival of their ethnic community.

Potential Consequences of Child Separation

Uyghurs and Kazaks have a very diverse heritage. Many of them, however, especially populations from Turpan and Kumul, look Chinese or more broadly Asian. These children may forget their roots, they may be afraid to hold onto those roots, or they may learn to ignore their blood lineage and culture after their time in concentration camps or boarding schools. Some of these children may not experience any identity crisis and may come to identify themselves as Han Chinese.

Uyghur youths who do not look like Han Chinese, on the other hand, may struggle to discover their true identity and belongingness, even if their religion, culture, values, and ideology are assimilated into those of Han Chinese. They may still be rejected and racially discriminated against by the Han Chinese population because of their physical appearance. In this case, if they remember their childhood and what happened to them, they may hate both their original identities and the Han Chinese identity imposed on them. However, if the Han Chinese population accepts them, the following two scenarios may happen:

> First, since identity is also something that people can choose, not something fixed that people cannot change, it depends on how these kids identify themselves, even if they look different than Han Chinese. If they are not harshly rejected by mainstream Chinese society, then they may not experience an identity crisis when they speak Chinese and practice Chinese culture, values, and ideology. These children, who have been taught that their parents are criminals and terrorists, that their culture is backward, and that being a Uyghur or Kazak Muslim is shameful, may grow up loyal to China and hate their background and unique facial features.

I had the chance to research Uyghurs' identity crises before China's forced assimilation of the younger Uyghur generations started, and I share some of my findings in the two cases discussed next. These cases demonstrate the difficulty these assimilated kids have in returning to their original community and identifying themselves as Uyghur when they grow up, even if they were allowed to return.

Xiaoli, adopted by a Han Chinese family when she was a baby, struggled with her own identity. She was eighteen when I met with her. She has dark brown hair, big eyes, and a high-bridged nose. But she also has a Han Chinese name and identifies herself as Han Chinese. She said all her Chinese friends and the mirror always remind her that she is not Han Chinese. "My Chinese friends call me *Laowai* [alien] and *Zazhong* [impure/dirty race] whenever I have a dispute with them over some small issues, it is very hurtful," she said. "When I told them once that I am pure Uyghur, they said that how lucky I am for being raised by a Chinese family and speaking Chinese, but not lucky forever cannot be Chinese." She also explained that she did not know who she was, felt invisible and insignificant, and felt that she belonged nowhere. Even though everything about her is Chinese except her looks, she feels she can never be one of them. She feels that both communities reject her.

> But I cannot be Uyghur too. I have nothing in common with them. I do not identify myself as Uyghur. I hate this world. I am dreaming of going to somewhere that I could be accepted as myself only, not Han Chinese or Uyghur.[66]

A woman, who did not identify herself, from Aqsu had an Uyghur father and a Han Chinese mother. She said that she was totally rejected by the Chinese community despite her looking no different from Han Chinese. They also called her *zazhong* because her father was Uyghur, and paternal inheritance is important in China. This is one of the reasons China's forced marriage policy is aimed at Uyghur women marrying Han Chinese men, not at Uyghur men marrying Han Chinese women.

Another Uyghur girl, who identified herself only with the first name Miyesser, was taken into a boarding school in Tianjin from Urumchi when the boarding school system was partially implemented in East Turkistan in 2002. She told me about how she felt after her time in the school:

> I wanted to look Chinese. I always did makeup like the Chinese, so my Chinese classmates and teachers would treat me nicely. I expect they may think I am pretty if I look Chinese. But when I went home on summer vacation, my parents and grandparents gave me a disappointed look. My mom thinks I look ugly because of my Chinese hairstyle, my expression and my attitude. My parents and relatives, even close friends think almost everything about me looks like Han Chinese and I feel so sad about that.[67]

Xiaoli and Miyesser were among the Uyghur children who were removed from their cultural background before China's genocidal campaign started. They were not taught to hate their background and were not forced to be absolutely loyal to their new identity even if they were assimilated into Han Chinese. Their experiences show us that growing up in such circumstances leads them to feel confused about their identities. However, today, millions of Uyghur youths have been totally cut off from their roots, background, and community. They have experienced traumatizing childhood events and have been trained to be loyal to China and proud to be Han Chinese. Numerous Chinese social media videos published by Chinese journalists and Chinese teachers show that most primary school Uyghur kids in boarding schools want to be a soldier when they grow up to protect China. This indicates that these children cannot belong to the national people of East Turkistan, and, given the enforcement of these genocidal policies by Chinese police and military forces, they will most likely become enemies of their own nation.

Because the genocidal impact of these practices is reasonably foreseeable, it is sufficient to say that China intends—or at least has the indirect intent—to destroy the national people of East Turkistan. China's *dolus indirectus* is clear from the words of Chinese religious affairs official Maisumujiang Maimuer, spoken on August 10, 2017, on Chinese official social media *Xinhua Weibo*: "Break their lineage, break their roots, break their connections, and break their origins." This sentence was repeated in official document number 6 distributed by the Kashgar government administration office on March 6, 2018.[68] Later, *Xinjiang Police File* also revealed these guiding words were used by a Chinese high-level official, Minister of Public Security Zhao Keji, in his secret speech.[69]

Words of low-level Chinese officials who carried out the genocide clearly describe the Chinese government's genocidal policy and reflect statements made by high-level Chinese officials who represent the government's intention to commit genocide. This means, the specific intention of genocidal means of the words does not represent local Chinese official or individual himself who is responsible for implementation but represents the Chinese government and the Communist Party.

Violations of Article II(d): Birth Prevention, Forced Marriage, Forced Labor, and Deportation

The Chinese government has implemented various measures to prevent births within the Uyghur population in flagrant disregard of Article 2(d) of the Genocide Convention. These measures include sterilization and enforced abortions, forced marriages between Uyghur women and Han Chinese men, and concentration camps, deportations, and forced labor camps that segregate Uyghur women and men from each other and thus serve the same purpose.[70]

Prevention of Birth

Direct measures imposed by the Chinese government to restrict the number of births in the Uyghur population have worked in concert with a mass influx of Han Chinese into East Turkistan. The percentage of Han Chinese migration to East Turkistan was 67% in 1995, higher than any other interprovincial migration rate in China. Han Chinese migrants constituted 5.4% of the total population of East Turkistan in 1995, and in the intervening years, they have continued this influx into the area, ensuring significant Han Chinese population growth in the region.[71] In 2021, Han Chinese constituted more than 50% of the population of East Turkistan, a 46% increase compared to the 6% of the Han Chinese population represented in the region in 1949.

Meanwhile, the birth rate and natural population growth rate dropped from 19.74% and 12.81% in 1998[72] to 10.69% and 6.13% in 2019.[73] This indicates an almost 50% drop in population growth. The death rate also dropped in this time period to 4.56%. However, at the same time, the total population of East Turkistan increased from 17.47 million in 1998 to 24.87 million in 2019. How did the total population increase while the birth rate fell so dramatically?

German scholar Adrian Zenz gathered compelling evidence that the Chinese government began the campaign of eliminating the Uyghur population in part or in whole to make room for Han Chinese migrants to the south of East Turkistan, a region heavily populated by Uyghurs. Zenz calculated that natural ethnic minority population growth in southern Xinjiang would have reached 13.14 million by 2040 but that suppression measures could prevent up to 4.5 million births among Uyghurs and other ethnic minorities.[74] But why is China reducing the Uyghur population and diluting it with Han Chinese? Xi Jinping's top-secret speech, released in the "Xinjiang Papers" leaked in December 2021, stated that "population proportion and population security are important foundations for long term peace and stability."[75] Following Xi Jinping's speech, Han Chinese scholars linked the Uyghur population structure with China's national security issues and suggested "diluting the population" as a solution to China's national security problems because they saw the Uyghur population as a human threat.[76] China alleges that the people of East Turkistan are associated with the so-called "Three Evil Forces" of separatism, religious extremism, and terrorism. However, attacking an entire civilian population cannot possess any clear connection to any national security problem.

In reality, China's so-called "national security" excuse for its cruel policies reveals the historical fact of East Turkistan's status as an illegally occupied nation. Clearly, there must be a reason why China has singled out the people of East Turkistan as a security threat, and not the people of another region: because East Turkistani people are not an inseparable part of China. Furthermore, if the intention is not genocidal but to "dilute the population," why then has the Uyghur population been reduced through these genocidal methods instead of voluntary assimilation or relocation policies? Why is China also implementing sterilization policies even in northern East Turkistan where fewer Uyghur and other Turkic people live, and there is already a heavy influx of Han Chinese?

My own research comparing China's sterilization policy in the North and South of East Turkistan also confirmed this reality. I interviewed ten Uyghur women ages thirty-five to fifty-five in the Uyghur diaspora, six of whom were from the north, and four of whom were from the south, and all of whom escaped from East Turkistan between 2016 and 2017. These victims' experiences of forced sterilization are very similar. It is clear that China's intent to eliminate the Uyghur population through sterilization and other genocidal methods is to eliminate Uyghur population and create space for more Han Chinese settlers. So, genocide in East Turkistan is not only a matter of where the target is, but also who the target is. Having a different racial, religious, and national identity from Han Chinese is one reason, and East

Turkistan, their indigeneity to the territory where they live, is another reason for China's settler colonialism.

Most Uyghur women who live in East Turkistan and have had no children or only one child have directly experienced either IUD insertion or sterilization. Uyghur women who evade these rules and have more than two children been heavily punished.[77] Since 2015, this practice has intensified, even as it was relaxed for the Han Chinese population. The Uyghur woman Nurbiye Aisa was taken into the concentration camps at the beginning of 2018 for having twins after her second child and released in April 2021, while her husband, thirty-four-year-old Emet Turdi, was sentenced to life for having twin children. All of their children were taken into children's concentration camps during their incarceration. Nurbiye's parents and brother were also taken into a concentration camp for the sin of being related to a woman who did not obey China's birth prevention policy and did not abort her twins.[78] Like many other Uyghurs whose families have been ripped apart, three generations of Nurbiye's family were destroyed. The conditions of their life have been destroyed, they have been left homeless, and deprived of all of their assets. I have collected data of sixty-two Uyghur children from their relatives in the Uyghur diaspora. All of these children were removed from their homes by the Chinese government. Twenty-six of these children were taken to orphanage camps after their parents were arrested because of so-called "illegal" children born secretly in each of these families. A leaked document called the "Qaraqash List" also validated that having illegal children is the most common reason to detain Uyghurs in Qaraqash County.[79] The remaining thirty-six children in that data were sent to the camps after their parents were arrested because of their religion or ethnicity. There are also many cases of entire families being destroyed, such as Abdullah Tohti's family. His parents, siblings, wife, and children all were arrested and their houses confiscated by the Chinese government. These stories, which have been gathered directly from victims' direct family members and friends, are those that we have been able to verify—many, many more such stories exist.

"Forced Marriage" Policy

During World War II, Germans were banned from marrying Jewish people on the grounds that the German bloodline is pure and would be contaminated by Jewish blood. Unlike Nazi Germany, the Chinese state has sponsored Han Chinese men to marry Uyghur women with the intention of eliminating the bloodline of Uyghur Muslims. As noted earlier, the Han Chinese understand their empire to be created from diverse populations—they are not concerned about contaminating some pure bloodline, rather they are concerned about dominating the Uyghur population and incorporating them into the Chinese empire. Marrying Uyghur women is the domination of Uyghur women, which is the domination of the whole Uyghur nation.

Forced marriage was developed intentionally by the Chinese state with the goal of eliminating the population of Uyghurs and other Turkic Muslims, and it is enforced through both reward and threat; concentration camps are the punishment for non-compliance.[80] This policy contributes to the larger genocidal goal for two main reasons: first, Uyghur women who marry Han Chinese men cannot have Uyghur children since both communities belong to a patriarchal culture. Second, such women cannot contribute to Uyghur culture and religion, since they are dominated by the political and financial power of Han Chinese men. It is also well known that Muslim women are not to marry non-believers, so this policy, which forces them to do just that, also has the consequence of humiliating Uyghur and other Muslims and destroying their dignity and spirit.

While many Uyghur women were forced to marry Han Chinese men to save their families from concentration camps, there are also those who voluntarily inter-marry with Han Chinese. However, "voluntarily" can be a slippery word. My research indicates that these women have not made this choice out of love, but that they too have been coerced into marriage as a way of ensuring political and financial security. For example, some Uyghur women who married Han Chinese men have posted videos on Chinese social media displaying big smiles and saying: "I feel more secure marrying with Han Chinese"; "I love money, and Han Chinese men are not poor like Uyghur men"; and "I am happy to marry with Han Chinese, so what? I am not stupid like other Uyghurs end up in re-education camps."

Violations of Article II(c) and (d): Forced Labor and Deportation

To destroy the Uyghurs' economic livelihood completely, the Chinese government has arrested Uyghurs and sent them to concentration camps or to inland China where they are forced to work in factories. These forced laborers are known as "left-over labor supply" (*shengyu laodong*).[81] Depriving people in the colonies of all income sources has been a historical tactic of colonizing forces, as seen, for example, in the encomienda system in South America under Spanish colonial rule.[82] The conditions in China's forced labor camps in recent years have devastating consequences that reveal the CCP's genocidal intent. Some scholars argue that China may have no intent to destroy Uyghurs and other Turkic Muslims through forced labor and that the goal of forced labor is profit maximization. Indeed, China's intent to destroy is not immediately apparent. However, in the long term, forced labor disrupts Turkic Muslims' society, population growth, and conditions of survival as a cultural and national group.

In 2019 it was announced that the government transferred 526,600 people to inland China for the purposes of forced labor in the first quarter of the year.[83] This number could include people outside of concentration camps, though it does not include the 262,200 people sent from so-called "vocational training schools." Keeping all these women in inland China for many years also enforces a separation of the sexes and eliminates the possibility of marriage and family between these Uyghur women and the men from their own community.

Additionally, the Chinese government has forcibly sent 30,000 Uyghur workers from Khotan prefecture alone to join the workforce during the ongoing COVID-19 quarantine. China's Shenzhen city was targeted with 50,000 Uyghur forced labor-ers in 2021, and Guangdong's less developed areas are expecting another 50,000 Uyghur forced laborers in 2022.[84] Although we do not know precisely how many women have been sent to inland China in any given year, as official numbers may include both women and men, many local reports indicate that the goal is mainly to force Uyghur women into factory work in inland China as a form of modern slavery. There had been always Chinese social media advertisement related to selling Uyghur female workers such as "Supply Uyghur workers. government arranges teams for militarized management. no salaries," some of the screenshot images of those kinds of advertisements were published by Australian Strategic Policy Institute.[85] The predominance of men in the camps is closely related to this point. According to Adrian Zenz, adults between thirty and fifty-four years of age—people who are the main source of family income and at the prime of their fertility—are overrepresented among those interned.[86] The concentration camps thus not only prevent Uyghurs from founding families but they also destroy family structures already in place. As mentioned, the same report also concluded that death rates have dramatically increased since 2017 and that birth rates have fallen drastically since 2015 in the densely populated Uyghur regions. As a result, the overall Uyghur population has sharply declined in the last few years.

The harmful conditions that the Chinese state has created for Uyghurs through the forced labor camps can be summarized as follows: first, sending mainly Uyghur women for many years of forced labor in inland China enforces a separation of the sexes and prohibits the marriage of these Uyghur women to Uyghur men in their community because they are not allowed to return to their community and partici-pate in reproduction. This technique to drastically reduce the population of Uyghurs is a serious violation of UN Genocide Convention Article 2(d). Second, removing family members, particularly breadwinners, and destroying the Uyghur family struc-ture is the deliberate infliction of conditions of life that could bring about the physi-cal destruction of a whole or in part of a people and is a serious violation of United Nations Genocide Convention law Article 2(c). To expand on this point, uprooting Uyghurs from their homeland and cultural, physical, and biological connections and sending them to inland China to do forced labor undermines their existence as a group or nation. Forcing the Uyghur population into low-paid or unpaid work destroys the economic conditions of the people of East Turkistan, who have already been segregated by the mainstream Chinese settlers. Uyghurs are dehumanized and commodified as they are sold as slaves. Uyghurs' freedom is restricted, and heavy punishment is imposed on those who attempt to escape from forced labor camps.

Some scholars have argued that the intention of colonial regimes is the exploita-tion of labor and natural resources, rather than the destruction of the labor source. They may have ignored the settler colonial dimensions of China's domination and missed the direct influence of labor exploitation on Uyghur population growth. It is true, in many cases, that forced labor and slavery may not violate Genocide Convention Article II(c) as the "intention" could be considered profit maximization rather than genocide. However, in the case of East Turkistan, if the intent is simply profit maximization, then none of the harmful conditions that I have listed earlier would have been created in advance. *Dolus indirectus* (indirect intention) was obvious here as China created the harmful conditions of the forced labor camp with full knowledge of the catastrophic consequences for the entire Uyghur population. In other words, creating harmful policies despite being aware of the catastrophic results proves that China's primary goal is to destroy the Uyghurs and other Turkic peoples. Simply put, it is not necessary to have a desire to kill them instead of using them as slave labor, since the end result would fulfill a desire to kill. We cannot become complacent. While China has not yet sent these people from concentration camps to extermination, this does not mean they will not in the future. Nazi policy became genocidal over time: Jews similarly faced restrictions on their movement before being forced into exploitative labor and, eventually, extermination.[87]

Second, people who are forcibly transferred for labor were not randomly or arbitrarily selected but selected based on their ethnicity, race, and religion. Zenz argued in his analysis of the "Xinjiang Papers" that China's forced labor targeted Uyghurs for political rather than economic reasons.[88] He cited a Chinese official's top-secret speech, which shows that nearly 3 million people were transferred from East Turkistan to industrial cities based on Xi Jinping's belief that this will prevent them from being influenced by "evil ideologies" and provide them with the opportunity to learn Chinese culture.[89]

The intent of these forced labor policies is to destroy the Uyghurs and other Turkic people in East Turkistan as a people by removing them from their homeland and reducing their population by separating the sexes. This clearly demonstrates China's genocidal mentality: general intent. It is also related to actus reus in ICC Article 30, and special intent (intent to destroy), achieved through reducing the Uyghur population.

Deportation to Secret Locations

An analysis published in the *New York Times* indicated that the population of East Turkestan accounted for less than 2% of China's population but 21% of arrests in 2017, while a greater share of defendants in the region were sentenced to prison terms of five years or longer. The same report also stated that the Chinese court sentenced a total of 230,000 people to prison or other punishments in 2017, significantly more than in any other period on record in decades for the region.[90] A large number of these prisoners were sent to secret locations that are unknown even to their families. These mass deportations also demonstrate genocidal intent: it is also a process of ethnic cleansing committed with the intent to destroy. Deporting Uyghur prisoners to secret prisons in inland China not only physically harmed them but, through disappearances, may also effect decline of the Uyghur population. Unlike ethnic cleansing cases without genocidal intent, these deported Uyghurs are not able to live and grow in their place of deportation. According to *Xinjiang Police File*, 30,000 prisoners were dispatched from the prisons of East Turkistan to the prison of Xinjiang Production and Construction Corps (XPCC) in 2018 and 2019. Alone in 2018, 222 were considered as serious offenders and sent to Qinghai, and 572 were sent to Sichuan and Gansu.[91]

A news report published by *Bitter Winter* stated that more than 500,000 Uyghur men were transferred from Ghulja in East Turkestan to secret prisons in inland China where no one can find them.[92] Drone footage posted on YouTube has also shown Chinese police herding hundreds of blindfolded and shackled men from a train station as they transfer them to an unknown location. Chinese characters clearly visible on inmates' uniforms say 喀什 "Kashgar," meaning these inmates are from the largest Uyghur city in East Turkistan.[93]

Thus, Chinese policies regarding concentration camps, forced labor camps, deportations, and excessive prison sentences are tearing families apart, expelling them *en masse* from their homes, and destroying the possibility of a healthy life, or even basic survival, for the people of East Turkistan. These policies will not only result in a significant population reduction but will eventually bring about the physical destruction in whole or in part of the Uyghur, as outlined in Articles II(d) and II(c) in the Genocide Convention. This is the intention of the Chinese state: the removal of the native population of East Turkistan opens the land for Han Chinese colonialism and extends Chinese nation-building. These policies also work to undermine any potential independence claim on the part of the people of East Turkistan by eliminating the territorial identity of the "nation" or "people" that belong to its territory. Although many scholars define a "people" on the basis of religion and ethnicity, language and culture, race, and common ancestry, to achieve self-determination under the law but a "people" must also share a common territory.[94] A "people" cannot be simply an ethnic group but must constitute a certain territorial and historical entity. Without land, without a shared territory, there is no "people" to have the right to self-determination because the referendum where the majority might determine the political status of the territory cannot make sense without territory.[95] China justifies its claim to the territory of East Turkistan both by emptying the land of Uyghurs and other Turkic Muslims and by making claims to that land as part of China.

CULTURAL GENOCIDE IS CLEAR EVIDENCE FOR INTENTION OF GENOCIDE

China is engaged in a multifaceted genocidal campaign against the Uyghurs and other peoples of the region, with the clear intent to annihilate them, including by destroying their sense of identity and memory. As noted earlier, this new campaign was launched in 2017, but it has much deeper roots, the Chinese government, which has controlled the region since the early 1950s, has long discriminated against the colonized people and favored the settlement of Han Chinese in what is now effectively a Chinese colony.

New laws, regulations, and policies have been introduced to reinforce this discrimination. For example, China's official policy of regulating all religious activities of Uyghurs and other Turkic Muslims was first implemented in 2000[96] and was then broadened and intensified with the Xinjiang Religious Affairs Regulation that took effect in March 2017.[97] According to the "Xinjiang Papers" leaked to the Uyghur Tribunal, Xi Jinping authorized this regulation, and it is directly linked to Beijing.[98] Based on these regulations, basic aspects of Islam such as clothing, teaching religion to children, and differentiating "halal" and "haram" are now all banned. Anyone who believes in Islam and practices this belief by praying or reading the Quran is punished, supposedly as part of a fight against the "Three Evil Forces." In reality, the criminalization of religion, as well as Uyghur language and culture, represents a form of collective punishment. A white paper published by the Chinese State Council Information Office also justified the ban on Uyghurs practicing Islam by stating that Islam is neither an indigenous nor the sole belief system of the Uyghur people.[99]

Similarly, a ban on Uyghur and other native languages has also been gradually but systematically implemented, and recently tightened, in an effort to eradicate Uyghur identity. In 2001, the Chinese State Council (central government) first adopted a "Resolution on the Reform of Fundamental Development," which began the recruitment of Uyghur middle school students to "Xinjiang classes" in Chinese cities, where they would study in Chinese only.[100] In East Turkistan itself, since early 2017, nearly all schools, including many elementary schools, have been transformed into boarding schools, to which students are confined except for weekend home visits. Recently, all the formerly bilingual schools in the region, including primary schools, were changed to Chinese language only, under the guidance of a new Chinese government document titled "The Standard Plan for Bilingual Education Curriculum in the Compulsory Education Phase of the Autonomous Region."[101] Uyghur place names and street names have been changed to Chinese. Uyghur history books are banned and Uyghur history distorted.[102] Anything that would help an Uyghur sense of belonging with each other is destroyed, suggesting the ultimate aim of exterminating the Uyghur nation.

It is well known that Raphael Lemkin, who coined the concept of genocide, also viewed the destruction of cultural and religious heritage, as well as languages, as an integral part of this defined crime. Indeed, this cultural genocide can also be seen in China's campaign to demolish mosques and other historical and archeological heritage sites. Beginning in 2016, in merely three months, 5,000 mosques were destroyed in East Turkestan; by 2020, a detailed report says "approximately 16,000 mosques in Xinjiang (65% of the total) have been destroyed or damaged as a result of government policies, mostly since 2017."[103] Uyghur-style houses, interior design, and cultural decorations have also been removed or destroyed to make their cultural identity to fit with the majority of Han Chinese traditions.[104] The Chinese government even committed the indignity of desecrating dead bodies and aggressively destroying Uyghur cemeteries, as well as sacred shrines and sites.[105] This targeting of Uyghurs' physical property should be included in actus reus per the Genocide Convention since China is systematically and deliberately attacking Uyghurs' conditions of life solely on the basis of their ethnicity and religion. The genocide in East Turkistan includes all these elements of religious and cultural heritage, and they should all be understood together, even as legal action necessarily is focused on those actions found to be crimes under the Genocide Convention and other bodies of international law. However, these aspects were excluded from the 1948 Genocide Convention, which was limited to the five criteria that still stand today as the legal definition. This exclusion occurred because European and other colonial powers did not want their own destruction of other cultures to be exposed or prosecuted.[106] In *Axis Rule*, Lemkin wrote that "genocide"

> does not necessarily mean the immediate destruction of a nation, except when accomplished by mass killings of all members of a nation. It is intended rather to signify coordinated plan of different actions aiming at the destruction of essential foundation of the life of national groups, with the aim of annihilating the groups themselves.[107]

The Genocide Convention has been considered as *a jus cogens* norm. As a consequence, it is not easy for legislators to change a norm, and no treaty or convention can displace it.[108] This is one of the obstacles to including cultural genocide in the Genocide Convention because states have to take collective action and intervene to solve the genocide as many legal scholars stated, and it is not easy to have a collective decision against states implementing genocide. However, as Lemkin would have recognized, even though these attacks on Uyghur language, culture, and religion are not directly enumerated in the text of the Genocide Convention, they do help reveal the Chinese government's overall genocidal intent.

SUMMARY

Genocidal acts were planned as state policy and repeatedly implemented despite their fatal impact on Uyghurs and other Turkic Muslims. Xi Jinping proudly confirmed the success of these policies by affirming that their policies against the Uyghurs and other Turks are totally correct.[109] Since Xi Jinping is the head of the Chinese state, his confirmation reveals China's "general" intent—that they knowingly and willingly implemented these policies that have fatal consequences. Significantly, China created these policies with a "special" intent to destroy Uyghurs and other Turkic Muslims since these policies are closely linked to their settler colonialism, which is eliminating these population and preparing living space for Han settlers. This special intent is clearly demonstrated in the aim and effects of population reduction.

NOTES

1. Convention on the Prevention and Punishment of the Crime of Genocide, December 9, 1948, 78 U.N.T.S. 277; S. Exec. Doc. O, 81-1 (1949).
2. First mentioned in chapter 3, note 5 and note 6.
3. *Id.*, 15
4. *Id.*

5. Guly Mahsut, Neq meydan: Beshinchi Iyul Ürümchi qirghinchiliqi eslimilirim: Dunya körüp baqmighan resim videolirim [Eyewitness: My recollections of the July 5 Massacre in Ürümchi: My photos and videos that the world has never seen before], YouTube video, 2:00:50, July 4, 2020, https://www.youtube.com/watch?v=axzAasB6wzI.

6. Zak, Doffman, "U.S. Accuses China of Detaining Up To 3M Xinjiang Muslims in 'Concentration Camps'," *Forbes*, May 4, 2019, accessed December 26, 2021, https://www.forbes.com/sites/zakdoffman/2019/05/04/xinjiang-u-s-accuses-china-of-putting-up-to-3m-muslims-in-concentration-camps/#1dfa2ade72b1.

7. Victims of Communism Memorial Foundation, *Xinjiang Police File* (Washington, DC: Victims of Communism Memorial Foundation, May 23, 2022), https://victimsofcommunism.org/xinjiang-police-files-summary-policy-recommendations/.

8. Victims of Communism Memorial Foundation, "China's Minister of Public Security Zhao Keji's June 2018 Speech on the Progress of Xinjiang Security Regime," in *Xinjiang Police File* (Washington, DC: Victims of Communism Memorial Foundation, May 23, 2022), 2, https://victimsofcommunism.org/xinjiang-police-files-summary-policy-recommendations/.

9. Ibid., 6.

10. Australian Strategic Policy Institute, *The Xinjiang Data Project* (Barton: Australian Strategic Policy Institute, 2020), https://xjdp.aspi.org.au; Megha Rajagopalan, Alison Killing, and Christo Buscheck, "China Secretly Built a Vast New Infrastructure to Imprison Muslims," *BuzzFeed,* January 29, 2020, accessed December 26, 2021, https://www.buzzfeednews.com/article/meghara/china-new-internment-camps-xinjiang-uighurs-muslims.

11. Yael Grauer, "The Revealed Massive Chinese Police Database," *The Intercept*, January 29, 2021, accessed December 26, 2021, https://theintercept.com/2021/01/29/china-uyghur-muslim-surveillance-police/.

12. Genocide Convention. 1949, supra note 1.

13. Bethany Allen-Ebrahimian, "Exposed: China's Operating Manuals for Mass Internment and Arrest by Algorithm," *International Consortium Investigative Journalist: China Cable,* November 24, 2019, accessed December 22, 2021, https://www.icij.org/investigations/china-cables/exposed-chinas-operating-manuals-for-mass-internment-and-arrest-by-algorithm/.

14. Lude Press 路德, "Lude fang wen mina nushi: jiang shu zai Xinjiang zao shou zhonggong guo bao pohai, shichu yi ge ji ge yue da de haizi, bei qiang po tuo yi jian cha de jingli" 路德访谈米娜女士：讲述在新疆遭受中共国宝迫害，失去一个几个月大的孩子，被强迫脱衣检查的经历 [Lude Press Interview With Mihrigul Tursun: Recounting the Experience of Being Persecuted by the CCP, Losing a Child a Few Months Old and Being Forced to Strip Naked for Inspections], YouTube video, 1:46, January 18, 2019, https://www.youtube.com/watch?v=P_By_N8U_YY&feature=youtu.be.

15. Shohret Hoshur, "At Least 150 Detainees Have Died in One Xinjiang Internment Camp: Police Officer," *Radio Free Asia*, October 29, 2019, accessed December 17, 2021, https://www.rfa.org/english/news/uyghur/deaths-10292019181322.html.

16. Shahit Biz, "Xinjiang Victim Database" *Shahit Biz,* January 2017, accessed December 1, 2021, https://shahit.biz/eng/#home. This list is derived from data on more than 37,961 victims reported by the Uyghur and Kazak diaspora.

17. "Tuìwǔ jūnrén jiē zhōnggòng zhènyā jiāng cáng gǎng rén de kǒngbù jīnglì" 退伍军人揭中共镇压疆藏港人的恐怖经历 [Veterans Expose the Chinese Communist Party's Horrific Oppression in Xinjiang and Tibet], 新唐人 *NTDTV* (webpage), last modified April 11, 2020, accessed March 15, 2022, https://www.ntdtv.com/gb/2020/04/10/a102820365.html.

18. Ibid.

19. Matthew P. Robertson, Raymond L. Hinde, and Jacob Lavee, "Analysis of Official Deceased Organ Donation Data Casts Doubt on the Credibility of China's Organ Transplant Reform," *BMC Medical Ethics* 20, no. 79 (2019). doi: 10.1186/s12910-019-0406-6.

20. Li Zaili, "Uyghurs Secretly Moved to Hide Mass Detentions," *Bitter Winter,* December 17, 2018, accessed March 25, 2022. https://bitterwinter.org/uyghurs-moved-to-hide-mass-detentions/.

21. Human Rights Watch, *China: Minority Region Collects DNA from Millions* (New York: Human Rights Watch, 2017), https://www.hrw.org/news/2017/12/13/china-minority-region-collects-dna-millions.

22. Ben Doherty, "Chinese Government May Have Falsified Organ Donation Numbers, Study Says," *The Guardian,* November 14, 2019, accessed December 22, 2021, https://www.theguardian.com/world/2019/nov/15/chinese-government-may-have-falsified-organ-donation-numbers-study-says; Nabila Ramdani, "Uyghur Camps Risk Being Turned Into 'Organ Banks'," *The Independent,* September 26, 2019, accessed March 22, 2022, https://www.gulftoday.ae/opinion/2019/09/26/uighur-camps-risk-being-turned-into-organ-banks.

23. Shohret Hoshur, "Young Uyghur Tour Director Dies Under Questioning by Xinjiang Authorities: Mother," *Radio Free Asia,* June 24, 2019, accessed March 22, 2022, https://www.rfa.org/english/news/uyghur/death-06242019143149.html; Voice memo of Aytursun's Eli's mother was published in Uyghur version of the news. Available at https://www.rfa.org/uyghur/xewerler/aytursun-eli-06192019225208.html.

24. Rita Uyghur (@0715Rita), "China's Live Organ Harvesting in Uyghur Region, This Sign Is in Urumchi Airport, It Says: Special Passengers, Human Organs Transport Corridor," Twitter Photo, February 28, 2019, https://twitter.com/0715Rita/status/1101085027809574912.

25. Keoni Everington, "Saudis Allegedly Buy 'Halal Organs' From 'Slaughtered' Xinjiang Muslims," *Taiwan News,* January 22, 2020, accessed May 22, 2020, https://www.taiwannews.com.tw/en/news/3862578.

26. Uyghur Human Rights Project, *Detained and Disappeared: Intellectuals Under Assault in the Uyghur Homeland* (Washington, DC: Uyghur Human Rights Project, 2019), https://uhrp.org/press-release/update---detained-and-disappeared-intellectuals-under-assault-uyghur-homeland.html.

27. Guo Rui, "Chinese State Media Denounces 'Two-Faced' Xinjiang Officials Accused of Colluding With Extremists," *South China Morning Post,* April 3, 2021, accessed February 7, 2022, https://www.scmp.com/news/china/politics/article/3128169/chinese-state-media-denoucestwo-faced-xinjiang-officials.

28. William Schabas, *Unimaginable Atrocities: Justice, Politics, and Rights at the War Crimes Tribunals* (Oxford: Oxford University Press, 2012), 146.

29. John Cooper, *Raphael Lemkin and the Struggle for the Genocide Convention* (Basingstoke, UK: Palgrave Macmillan, 2015), 154.

30. Abdullah Qazanchi, *Briefing the Disappearance of Uyghur Intellectual and Cultural Elites* (Washington, DC: Uyghur Human Rights Project, December 2021), accessed December 9, 2021, https://uhrp.org.

31. Shohret Hoshur, "Prominent Uyghur Intellectual Given Two-Year Suspended Death Sentence for 'Separatism'," *Radio Free Asia,* September 28, 2018, accessed December 9, 2021, https://www.rfa.org/english/news/uyghur/sentence-09282018145150.html.

32. Andreas Illmer, "Tashpolat Tiyip: Uyghur Leading Geographer Who Vanished in China," *BBC,* October 11, 2019, accessed December 9, 2021, https://www.bbc.com/news/world-asia-china-49956088.

33. Shohret Hoshur, "Uyghur Muslim Scholar Dies in Chinese Police Custody," *Radio Free Asia*, January 29, 2018, accessed December 9, 2021, https://www.rfa.org/english/news/uyghur/scholar-death-01292018180427.html.

34. Helen Davidson, "China Hands Death Sentences to Uyghur Former Officials," *The Guardian*, April 9, 2021, accessed December 9, 2021, https://www.theguardian.com/world/2021/apr/09/china-uyghur-death-sentences-xinjiang-education-directors.

35. Translation from original screen shot conversation. Translated by author.

36. Convention Against Torture and Other Cruel Inhuman or Degrading Treatment or Punishment, December 10, 1984, 1465 U.N.T.S. 85, 113; S. Treaty Doc. No. 100-20 (1988); 23 I.L.M. 1027 (1984) https://tbinternet.ohchr.org/_layouts/15/TreatyBodyExternal/Treaty.aspx?CountryID=36&Lang=EN.

37. Benjamin Hall, "Uyghur Internment Camp Survivor Reveals China's Horrifying Re-education Tactics," *Fox News,* February 6, 2021, accessed February 8, 2021. https://www.foxnews.com/world/uighur-internment-camp-survivor-reveals-chinas-horrifying-re-education-tactics.

38. Rukiye Turdush and Magnus Fiskesjo, "Dossier: Uyghur Women in China's Genocide," *Genocide Studies and Prevention: An International Journal* 15, no. 1 (2021): 22–43. doi: 10.5038/1911-9933.15.1.1834.

39. Gulbahar Jelilova, phone interview with author, March 24, 2021.

40. Istiqlal TV, "Exposed Silence (11) Unimaginable Oppression," September 5, 2018, YouTube video, 23:32, https://youtu.be/AGfPqG7f2F4.

41. Quote was from private video, obtained and saved by author. This video is not republished by author to protect the identity of the person in the video.

42. Zumret Dawut (Chinese concentration camp survivor, currently asked political asylum in United States), phone interview with author, March 24, 2021.

43. Zamira Rahim, "Muslim Prisoners in China's Xinjiang Concentration Camps Subjected to Gang Rape And Medical Experiments, Former Detainee Says," *The Independent*, October 22, 2019, accessed May 22, 2020, https://www.independent.co.uk/news/world/asia/china-xinjiang-uighur-muslim-detention-camps-xi-jinping-persecution-a9165896.html; for more reports see: Magnus Fiskesjö, *China's 'Re-education' / Concentration Camps in Xinjiang / East Turkestan and the Wider Campaign of Forced Assimilation Targeting Uyghurs, Kazakhs, etc, Bibliography of Select News Reports & Academic Works*(Washington, DC: Human Rights Project, July 2020), https://docs.uhrp.org/pdf/China%27s%20%27re-education%27%20concentration%20camps%20in%20Xinjiang%20-%20BIBLIO.pdf.

44. Rebecca Wright, Ivan Watson, Zahid Mahmood and Tom Booth, "'Some Are Just Psychopaths': Chinese Detective in Exile Reveals Extent of Torture Against Uyghurs," *CNN News,* October 5, 2021, accessed November 24, 2021, https://www.cnn.com/2021/10/04/china/xinjiang-detective-torture-intl-hnk-dst/index.html.

45. Ibid.

46. Rukiye Turdush (@parlabest), "Uyghur Kids Struggling to Understand Why Their Healthy Parents Mentally and Physically Harmed." Twitter, April 29, 2029, 2:09pm, https://twitter.com/parlabest/status/1167137218240159750.

47. Rukiye Turdush (@parlabest), "He Was a 32 years Old Healthy Man," Twitter, September 23, 2029, 11:44 am, https://twitter.com/parlabest/status/1308794408406593537.

48. Adile Kamran, in discussion with author, July 12, 2021. Pseudonyms are used to protect interviewee's identity.

49. Erkin Muhemmed, in discussion with author, July 14, 2021. Pseudonyms are used to protect interviewee's identity.

50. Gulbahar Haitiwaji and Rosenn Morgat, "'Our Souls Are Dead:' How I Survived a Chinese 'Re-education Camp' for Uyghurs," *The Guardian,* January 12, 2021, accessed in January 28, 2021, https://www.theguardian.com/world/2021/jan/12/uighur-xinjiang-re-education-camp-china-gulbahar-haitiwaji?CMP=share_btn_tw.

51. One of the author's Han Chinese contacts from Shanghai went to Ghulja city, Yengiyer county in East Turkistan to see the author's uncle Rishat Abdukadir who had just been released from Chinese concentration camp. She said, "Unfortunately, your uncle was arrested again. I learned most of the people who were released in this village were arrested again and put in prisons for long-term punishment. So impossible to find them. Better forget and never try to contact."

52. Alexandra Ma, "China is Reportedly Sending Men to Sleep in The Same Beds as Uyghur Women While Their Husbands Are in Prison Camps," *Business Insider,* November 4, 2019, accessed May 23, 2020, https://www.businessinsider.com/china-uighur-monitor-home-shared-bed-report-2019-11.

53. Drew Harwel and Eva Dou, "Huawei Tested AI Software That Could Recognize Uighur Minorities and Alert Police, Report Says," *Washington Post,* December 8, 2020, accessed November 24, 2021, https://www.washingtonpost.com/technology/2020/12/08/huawei-tested-ai-software-that-could-recognize-uighur-minorities-alert-police-report-says/.

54. Amy Qin, "In China's Crackdown On Muslims, Children Have Not Been Spared," *New York Times,* December 28, 2019, accessed February 6, 2022, https://www.nytimes.com/2019/12/28/world/asia/china-xinjiang-children-boarding-schools.html.

55. *The Economist* "How Xinjiang's Gulag Tears Families Apart," *The Economist,* October 17, 2020, accessed April 3, 2021, https://www.economist.com/china/2020/10/17/how-xinjiangs-gulag-tears-families-apart.

56. Original Video Posted by @majuismail1122 retweeted by Rukiye Turdush (@parlabest), "Uyghur Language Totally Banned," Twitter, March 6, 2021, 10:28 p.m., accessed December 3, 2021, https://twitter.com/parlabest/status/1368403090840432641?s=12.

57. Zunun and Amine, Interview with Parents of a Child Camp Survivor, October 9, 2021. Pseudonyms are used to protect interviewee's identity.

58. John Sudworth, "China Muslims: Xinjiang Schools Used to Separate Children From Families," *BBC News,* July 4, 2019, accessed May 23, 2020, https://www.bbc.com/news/world-asia-china-48825090.

59. Author's translation from original screen shot conversation. Emphasis added basis on the meaning of the language of conversation.

60. William Wan, "What Separation From Parents Does to Children: 'The Effect Is Catastrophic,'" *Washington Post,* June 18, 2018, accessed June 20, 2020, https://www.washingtonpost.com/national/health-science/what-separation-from-parents-does-to-children-the-effect-is-catastrophic/2018/06/18/c00c30ec-732c-11e8-805c-4b67019fcfe4_story.html.

61. Gulchehra Hoja and Shohret Hoshur, "Children of Detained Uyghurs Face 'Terrible' Conditions in Overcrowded Xinjiang Orphanages," *Radio Free Asia,* October 18, 2017, accessed May 23, 2020, https://www.rfa.org/english/news/uyghur/children-10182017144425.html.

62. Li Zaili 李在立, "Fùmǔ bèi guān jízhōngyíng wéizú értóng chéng 'gū'ér'" 母被關集中營　維族兒童成 孤兒 [Parents Are Held in Concentration Camps, Uyghur Children Become 'Orphans'], *Bitter Winter,* June 28, 2018, accessed May 23, 2020, https://zh.bitterwinter.org/china-muslim-parents-arrested-in-re-education-camps/.

63. Asiye Yasin (friends of Elfira Nury, currently asked political asylum in Europe), pseudonym is used to protect the identity for the victim and interviewee, phone interview with author, March 12, 2022.

64. Araphat Ablimit, in-person interview, Toronto Canada, April 12, 2022.

65. *Rome Statute of the International Criminal Court,* Adopted by the United Nations Diplomatic Conference of Plenipotentiaries on the Establishment of an International Criminal Court, July 17, 1998, UN Doc. A/CONF.183/9 [hereinafter *Rome Statute*], Art. 30, available online.

66. Xiaoli, in-person interview with author, November 2001, Beijing, China.

67. Miyesser, in-person interview with author, May 21, 2021, Toronto, Canada.

68. Government Information Public Platform of Kashi, "Guan yu yin fa 'ka shi di qu 2018 nian jian cha gong zuo yao dian ze ren fen jie fang a' de tong zhi" 关于印发《喀什地区2018年督查工作要点责任分解方案》的通知 [Notice on the Publication and Distribution of the 'Plan for Distributing Essential Inspection Work Tasks in the Kashgar Region, 2018], *Government Information Public Platform of Kashi,* March 6, 2018, https://web.archive.org/web/20180813115300; http://www.kashi.gov.cn/Government/PublicInfoShow.aspx?ID=2851.

69. Victims of Communism Memorial Foundation, "China's Minister of Public Security Zhao Keji's June 2018 Speech on the Progress of Xinjiang Security Regime," in *Xinjiang Police File,* 3.

70. Rukiye Turdush and Magnus Fiskesjo, "Uyghur Women in China's Genocide."

71. Zai Liang, "The Age of Migration in China," *Population and Development Review* 27, no.3 (2001): 499–524. http://csda.albany.edu/imc/Liang_PDR_2001.pdf.

72. People's Republic of China, "4-3 Total Population and Birth Rate, Death Rate and Natural Growth Rate by Region," *China's Statistical Yearbooks,* 1998, accessed May 24, 2021. http://www.stats.gov.cn/english/statisticaldata/yearlydata/YB1999e/d03e.htm.

73. People's Republic of China, "2-8 Total Population and Birth Rate, Death Rate and Natural Growth Rate by Region," *China's Statistical Year Books,* 2019, accessed May 24, 2021, http://www.stats.gov.cn/tjsj/ndsj/2019/indexeh.htm.

74. " Chinese Police Could Prevent Millions of Minority Births in Xinjiang: Report," France 24, August 6, 2021, accessed August 6, 2021,https://www.france24.com/en/live-news/20210608-chinese-policies-could-prevent-millions-of-minority-births-in-xinjiang-report.

75. Adrian Zenz, "The Xinjiang Papers: An Analysis of Key Findings and Implications for the Uyghur Tribunal in London," *Uyghur Tribunal,* December 9, 2021, accessed March 9, 2022, https://uyghurtribunal.com/wp-content/uploads/2021/12/The-Xinjiang-Papers-An-Analysis-for-the-Uyghur-Tribunal.pdf.

See also Adrian Zenz, "The Xinjiang Papers: An Introduction" *Uyghur Tribunal,* November 27, 2021, accessed March 9, 2022, https://uyghurtribunal.com/wp-content/uploads/2021/11/The-Xinjiang-Papers-An-Introduction-1.pdf.

76. Wang Luobu, " Guo ji fa da jiang tang di si shi yi qi: ru he zuo hao Xinjiang she hui wending yu chang zhi jiu'an di qi yan: 国际法大讲堂第四十一期——如何做活新疆社会稳定与长治久安的棋眼" [41th Session of International Law Lecture: How to Enlighten the Key of Social Stability in Xinjiang], *International Law Research Net,* 2015, accessed July 20, 2021, http://web.archive.org/web/20210305011946/http://sil.cupl.edu.cn/info/1040/1013.htm; Adrian Zenz, "'End the Dominance of the Uyghur Ethnic Group': An Analysis of Beijing's Population Optimization Strategy in Southern Xinjiang." *Central Asian Survey* 40, no. 3 (August 24, 2021): 291–312. doi: 10.1080/02634937.2021.1946483.

77. Rukiye Turdush and Magnus Fiskesjö, "Dossier: Uyghur Women in China's Genocide"; See also Qelbinur Tursun, video interview (what's app), January 17, 2019. Excerpts: "China implemented forced sterilization on Uyghur women to prevent births. I myself had

five children hidden from Chinese forces; 3 of them are illegal if they find out. To save my 6th baby, I escaped to Turkey. The Chinese government arrested my husband and sentenced him to 10 years after I escaped, just because we didn't kill our babies. Despite my parents' pleading the Chinese forces, they also took away my 5 children. No one knows their whereabouts. Just a few days ago, I recognized my daughter Ayisha in a Douyin video that a Chinese worker posted from Hoten's orphanage camp. She was three years old when I left, and 6 years old now. My home is in Kashgar city and she is in another city's orphanage camp right now. She was separated from her siblings and sent to another city. I don't know what happened to my other kids." This interview posted on Twitter by @ parlabest.

78. Hannekezi Aisa (sister of Nurbiye Aisa), Phone interview, April 20, 2022. note: Nurbiye Aisa contacted her and informed her that she had removed her name from the Chinese residential paper Hukou and that they would have no legal biological relationship and that she should never contact her again. Hannekezi claimed that her sister was frequently taken to the Chinese police station, where she was interrogated and mistreated even after she had been released. As a result, she said, "My sister terrified of contacting me and has even officially disowned my existence."

79. Adrian Zenz, "The Karakax List: Dissecting the Anatomy of Beijing's Internment Drive in Xinjiang," *Journal of Political Risk* 8, no. 2 (2020), https://www.jpolrisk.com/karakax/.

80. Rukiye Turdush and Magnus Fiskesjo, "Dossier: Uyghur Women in China's Genocide."

81. Dǒng yang 董洋, "Nóngcūn shèngyú láodònglì liúdòng duì xīnjiāng jīngjì de yǐngxiǎng: 农村剩余劳动力流动对新疆经济的影响" [Flow of Rural Surplus Labor Force Influence on Xinjiang's Economy], *Jingji Luntan* 经济论坛 , no. 3 (2007), http://cdmd.cnki .com.cn/Article/CDMD-10755-2007165567.htm.

82. Christopher Minster, "Spain's American Colonies and the Encomienda System," *Thought.Co* (web), May 30, 2019, accessed November 26, 2021, https://www.thoughtco.com /spains-american-colonies-encomienda-system-2136545.

83. Bai Jiayi 白嘉懿, "Shou ji Xīnjiāng nóngcūn fùyú láodònglì zhuǎnyí jiùyè chao 52.66 Wàn réncì" 首季新疆农村富余劳动力转移就业超 52.66万人次 [In the First Quarter of Xinjiang, Rural Surplus Labor Transferred Employment Exceeded 526,600 Person Times], *Chinanews.com*, April 4, 2019, accessed May 25, 2020, https://www.chinanews.com .cn/cj/2019/04-04/8800898.shtml.

84. "China Plans to Send Uygur Muslims From Xinjiang Re-education Camps to Work in Other Parts of Country," *South China Morning Post,* May 2, 2020, accessed May 25, 2020, https://www.scmp.com/news/china/politics/article/3082602/china-plans-send-ugyur -muslims-xinjiang-re-education-camps-work.

85. Vicky Xiuzhong Xu et al., *Uyghurs for Sale: "Re-Education," Forced Labour, and Surveillance Beyond Xinjiang* (Australian Strategic Policy Institute, March 1, 2020), accessed May 23, 2020, https://www.aspi.org.au/report/uyghurs-sale.

86. Adrian Zenz, "'Wash Brains, Cleanse Hearts': Evidence From Chinese Government Documents About the Nature and Extent of Xinjiang's Extrajudicial Internment Campaign," *Journal of Political Risk* 7, no. 11 (2019): figure 18, accessed May 20, 2020, http://www.jpol-risk.com/wash-brains-cleanse-hearts/.

87. William A. Schabas, *Genocide in International Law: The Crimes of Crimes* (New York: Cambridge University Press, 2000), 200.

88. Adrien Zen, "The Xinjiang Papers: An Introduction," *Uyghur Tribunal,* November 27, 2021, accessed January 1, 2022, https://uyghurtribunal.com/wp-content/uploads/2021 /11/The-Xinjiang-Papers-An-Introduction-01.pdf.

89. Ibid.

90. Chris Buckley, "China's Prisons Swell After Deluge of Arrests Engulfs Muslims,"*New York Times,* August 31, 2019, accessed May 25, 2020,

  https://www.nytimes.com/2019/08/31/world/asia/xinjiang-china-uighurs-prisons.html.

91. Victims of Communism Memorial Foundation, "China's Minister of Public Security Zhao Keji's June 2018 Speech on the Progress of Xinjiang Security Regime," in *Xinjiang Police File,* 9.

92. Li Zaili, "Uyghurs Secretly Moved to Hide Mass Detentions," *Bitter Winter,* Dec17, 2018, accessed May 25, 2021, https://bitterwinter.org/uyghurs-moved-to-hide-mass -detentions/.

93. War on Fear, "Xinjiang: A New Explanation," Online Video Clip, YouTube, 1:45, September 17, 2019, accessed May 30, 2021, https://www.youtube.com/watch?v =gGYoeJ5U7cQ.

94. Stefan Oeter, "The Role of Recognition and Non-Recognition With Regard to Secession," in *Self Determination and Secession in International Law,* ed. Christain Walter, Antje Von- Ungern Sternberg and Kavus Abushov, 1st ed. (Oxford: Oxford University Press, 2014), 54.

95. Ibid.

96. Human Rights Watch, *Devastating Blows: Religious Repression of Uyghurs in Xinjiang* (New York: Human Rights Watch, 2005), accessed May 19, 2020,

  https://www.hrw.org/report/2005/04/11/devastating-blows/religious-repression-uighurs -xinjiang.

97. China Law Translate, "Decision to Revise the 'Xinjiang Uighur Autonomous Region Regulation on De-Extremification,'" *China Law Translate,* October 10, 2018, accessed May 19, 2020, https://www.chinalawtranslate.com/en/decision-to-revise-the-xinjiang-uighur -autonomous-region-regulation-on-de-extremification/.

98. Uyghur Tribunal, "The Xinjiang Papers," *Uyghur Tribunal,* November 27, 2021, accessed December 19, 2021, https://uyghurtribunal.com/statements/.

99. China, The State Council Information Office, *Full Text: Employment and Labor Rights in Xinjiang* (Beijing: Foreign Languages Press Co. Ltd., 2020), http://www.xinhuanet.com/ english/2020-09/17/c_139373591.htm.

100. Baidu, "Guowuyuan guanyu jichu jiaoyu gaige yu fazhan de jueding" 国务院关于基础教育改革与发展的决定 [Decision of the State Council on the Reform and Development of Basic Education], *Baidu,* May 29, 2001, accessed May15, 2020, https:// baike.baidu.com/item/国务院关于基础教育改革与发展的决定.

101. Darren Byler, "Xinjiang Education Reform and Eradication of Uyghur Language Books," *SupChina,* October 2, 2019, accessed May 18, 2020, https://supchina.com/2019/10 /02/xinjiang-education-reform-and-the-eradication-of-uyghur-language-books/ ; Qiao Long and Yang Fen, "China Bans Use of Uyghur, Kazakh Textbooks, Materials in Xinjiang Schools." *Radio Free Asia,* October 13, 2017, accessed May 18, 2020, https://www.rfa.org/english/news /uyghur/ethnic-textbooks-10132017135316.html/.

102. Bai Yun Yi and Liu Xin, "White Paper Clarifies Historical Facts of Xinjiang," *Global Times,* July 19, 2019, accessed August 30, 2020, http://www.globaltimes.cn/content/1158660 .shtml.

103. Shohret Hoshur, "Chinese Authorities Continue to Destroy Mosques in Xinjiang," *Radio Free Asia, September* 7, 2018, accessed May 18, 2020, https://www.rfa.org/english/ news/uyghur/chinese-authorities-continue-to-destroy-mosques-in-xinjiang-09072018171910 .html; Nathan Ruser, James Leibold, Kelsey Munro and Tilla Hoja, *Cultural Erasure: Tracing*

the Destruction of Uyghur and Islamic Spaces in Xinjiang (Barton, Australia: Australian Strategic Policy Institute, 2020), https://www.aspi.org.au/report/cultural-erasure.

104. Rukiye Turdush (@parlabest), "Chinese Settlers Destroying Beautifully Decorated Uyghur Houses." Twitter, April 17, 2020, 12:37 pm, https://twitter.com/parlabest/status /1251188000832327682; Massimo Introvigne, "Uyghur Traditional House Destroyed by the CCP: Another Tool of Cultural Genocide," *Bitter Winter*, November 7, 2020, accessed September 7, 2020, https://bitterwinter.org/uyghur-traditional-houses-destroyed-by-the-ccp/.

105. Nicola Smith, "China Destroys Dozens of Cemeteries in Drive to 'Eradicate' Cultural History of Muslims," *The Telegraph,* October 9, 2019, accessed August 30, 2020,https://www .telegraph.co.uk/news/2019/10/09/china-destroys-dozens-uighur-cemeteries-drive-eradicate -cultural/; Rian Thum, "The Spatial Cleansing of Xinjiang: Mazar Desecration in Context," Made *in China,* August 24, 2020, accessed August 30, 2020, https://madeinchinajournal.com /2020/08/24/the-spatial-cleansing-of-xinjiang-mazar-desecration-in-context/.

106. John Cooper, *Raphael Lemkin and the Struggle for the Genocide Convention* (New York: Palgrave Macmillan, 2008), 158–59.

107. Raphael Lemkin, *Axis Rule in Occupied Europe: Laws of Occupation, Analysis of Government, Proposals for Redress* (Clark, NJ: The Law Book Exchange Ltd, 2005), 79.

108. Willam Shabah, *Unimagined Atrocities* (Oxford: Oxford University Press, 2012), 118.

109. Chris Buckley, "Brushing Off Criticism, China's Xi Calls Policies in Xinjiang 'Totally Correct,'" *The New York Times*, September 26, 2020, accessed September 26, 2020, https:// www.nytimes.com/2020/09/26/world/asia/xi-jinping- china-xinjiang.html.

6

Territory and Economy
in East Turkistan

The peoples of East Turkistan have never shared a historical homeland with the Chinese nation; Uyghurs and other Turkic Muslims are indigenous to the land of East Turkistan. Some statistics help illustrate this fact. As of the early 1940s, there are very few ethnic Han Chinese populations but Buddhist people such as Manchus, Sibos, and Salons constituted 5.7% of the population of East Turkistan and Muslims are 92.22%.[1] In the early 1950s, according to the census of the People's Republic of China (PRC), there were 4.87 million people in the region, of which 75% were Uyghur.[2] In 2010, almost sixty years later, the Han Chinese proportion of the population increased to 40.48%, while that of the Uyghurs decreased to 45.84%.[3] That change is due entirely to in-migration. Following the Chinese Communist Party (CCP)'s introduction of the "Open Up the West" (*Xibu da kaifa*) program in 1999, there was an increased focus on massive infrastructure investment in the region, while natural resources were extracted more aggressively for the benefit of the Chinese state.[4] As a result, the Chinese government attracted a vast number of Han Chinese settlers into East Turkistan.

The benefits of economic development accrue overwhelmingly to these newly arrived Han immigrants. Article 118 of the Constitution of the PRC clearly states:

> Autonomous organs of ethnic autonomous areas shall, under the guidance of state plans, autonomously plan for and manage local economic development. When the state is exploiting resources or establishing enterprises in an ethnic autonomous area, it should be attentive to the interests of that area.[5]

However, the PRC has failed to implement its own laws to benefit the people of the so-called "Xinjiang Uyghur Autonomous Region." Rather, members of the Uyghur and other Turkic Muslim populations are coercively enslaved through forced labor to the benefit of the Chinese state. Additionally, the natural resources of East Turkistan are exploited to benefit the Chinese state and its Han people, rather than the Uyghurs and other local Muslims. Meanwhile, even territorial functions of which every citizen could have such as property ownership in any state were gradually denied to the people in the region despite China considered them a part of the Chinese nation after they had been colonized.

THE XINJIANG PRODUCTION
AND CONSTRUCTION CORPS

This section outlines the history of Han Chinese settlement in the region with specific attention to the organization that most facilitates the region's exploitation, the Xinjiang Production and Construction Corps (XPCC). As of 2016, the XPCC had a population of about 2.8 million, equating to around 12% of the total population for the region and 86% are Han Chinese.[6]

Before the 1990s, the colonization of East Turkistan was a component of the Chinese government's policy of controlling the region militarily. In 1949, Chinese general Wang Zhen invaded East Turkistan with 70,000 troops from the Chinese army. Soon, between 1954 and 1966, 170,500 more Han Chinese soldiers entered, this time not as formal members of the military but as armed workers of the "XPCC" (XPCC, *Xinjiang Shengchan Jianshe Bingtuan*).[7] The Corps, commonly called the *Bingtuan*, was officially tasked with helping develop and reconstruct the colonized East Turkistan. In reality, it represented a major strategic deployment of Chinese armed forces into East Turkistan, as well as an influx of state-sponsored civilian settlers, although not volunteer settlers. The existence of the XPCC gave the lie to the so-called Xinjiang Uyghur Autonomous Region that was proclaimed in 1955. In reality, each district of this region was heavily populated with Uyghurs and other Turks, who were in turn surrounded by the XPCC.

In 1975, during the Cultural Revolution (1966–1976), the XPCC was dissolved, but it was quickly restored in the early 1980s after the clash happened between the Uyghurs in Aksu and South Xinjiang Military District to stabilize the relationship between Han Chinese and Uyghurs.[8] In 1981, Chinese president Deng Xiaoping highlighted the important role of XPCC in China's ideological, governmental, and military control of East Turkistan, saying that "its task is to combine the Party, the government, and the army. . . . The Xinjiang Production and Construction Corps is the core of stabilizing Xinjiang and must be restored."[9] The XPCC has played that role ever since.

Nevertheless, the XPCC remains poorly understood by outsiders. In 2008, Bao Yajun, a former fellow at the Development Research Center of China's State Council, was sent by the Central Organization Department to study the XPCC's management structure. Bao's later report describes a massive paramilitary apparatus. According to him, the XPCC has fourteen divisions spread in almost every city of East Turkistan, including Kashgar, Khotan, Aksu, Urumchi, Karamay, Ghulja, and

Turpan, and 176 regimental farms, with each regiment having a population of over 10,000. XPCC members do not wear military uniforms, but they receive military payments, and they have never been demobilized.[10]

The XPCC comprises a military, political, and economic system that integrates soldiers into agriculture and uses labor to support the military. Indeed, its political position makes it a powerful military "kingdom" in East Turkistan possessing vast territory and economic dominance. It governs its own administrative, education, science, technology, and infrastructure, and it has its public security apparatus, courts, procuratorate, judiciary, and jails. XPCC's special role that played important role in oppressing East Turkistani people as a "four-in-one" system of joint defense that links the People's Liberation Army (PLA), the armed police, the XPCC, and the ordinary people praised in China's white paper.[11] In 2018, to round up Uyghurs and put them in prisons, Chinese National Development and Reform Commission supported seven new prison development projects in the XPCC with a total investment of 2.25 billion yuan and twenty-seven projects for extending (existing) prisons in East Turkistan with a total investment of 2.27 billion yuan.[12] The XPCC also handles its own economic affairs, including agricultural production, solar power, iron, steel, and coal mining, all under the direct control of Beijing.[13] In the early years, they established many large state-owned enterprises, including textile and sugar factories, and they continuously deprived local people of their farms and water.

The XPCC has squeezed out local farmers and occupied hundreds of thousands of acres of agricultural land. It has expanded its territorial occupation by urbanizing Uyghur towns and villages and confiscating Uyghur farmland and houses. The XPCC now governs eight of its own cities, including Shihezi, Alar, Tumshuk, Beitun, Tiemenguan, Shuanghe, Kokdala, and Kunyu. According to official documents, the XPCC is planning to establish twenty more XPCC cities by 2030.[14] It attracts Chinese settlers from other parts of China to migrate into these cities by providing free houses and job opportunities, as the original population of East Turkistan has been reduced through genocidal policies. The Chinese government's preferential economic policies since the beginning of "Open Up the West" have become highly attractive to XPCC settlers. XPCC workers enjoy a variety of social security benefits and receive regular pensions.

Bao Yajun infers, based on his interviews with XPCC members, that during the winter, when conditions are unsuitable for agriculture, XPCC divisions and regiments organize militia training. The XPCC has about 100,000 trained militia.[15] The main aim thereof is to help the police and the standing army to control, oppress, and assault the Uyghur and other Turkic populations in East Turkistan under the pretext of "eliminating terrorists." Chinese state media asserts that the Corps is ready for any joint operations with the military or police and that they have participated in putting down resistance by Uyghurs and other Turkic Muslims.[16]

The state has given free rein to the XPCC's arbitrary arrests and murders of Uyghurs and other Turkic Muslims. The XPCC collaborated with armed police in the bloody crackdown on Uyghur farmers in Baren in April 1990.[17] On February 5, 1997, Uyghur youth in Ghulja demonstrated against China's injustices, particularly the ban on Uyghur cultural and educational events such as *meshrep*.[18] Once again, the Chinese government dispatched the XPCC's Fourth Division, headquartered in Ghulja, to crack down on the demonstrators. Amnesty International estimates that authorities detained 3,000–5,000 people in XPCC prison facilities run by the 4th Division. Most of these detainees were executed, tortured, forcibly disappeared, or sentenced to long-term imprisonment.[19] During the "July Fifth" riots in Urumchi in 2009, XPCC militia rapidly deployed in Urumchi and played a significant role.[20] According to several eyewitnesses, XPCC militia joined armed police in the crackdown. They also participated in the cleanup of murdered civilians' corpses and performed nighttime patrols. [21] Later, in 2012, the XPCC established an internal National Security Bureau to exercise its power of administrative enforcement and conduct so-called "criminal investigation."[22] This has targeted the people of East Turkistan in the name of protecting the territorial, political, and economic stability of China.

Xinjiang party secretary Chen Quanguo gave a speech at the Tenth Plenary Session of the Ninth Party Committee of the Autonomous Region in October 2020 in which he emphasized the XPCC's role in China's military, political, territorial, and economic colonialism. Again he invoked the goal of "development":

> We must fully support the XPCC on a continuous deepening of reforms, strengthen stability maintenance capabilities, firmly stand to develop southern Xinjiang, promote the integration of military and civilian development, and continuously enhance the XPCC's organizational advantages and mobilization capabilities to better play its unique role.[23]

The XPCC is certainly "unique." Today, there is no "production corps" in any other Chinese province or region, not even Tibet or Inner Mongolia. This uniqueness demonstrates that, while China claims that East Turkistan is "a part of China," it is not in fact treated as such but as an occupied territory distinct from the rest of China.

THE CHINESE SETTLERS

While XPCC members were originally sent to East Turkistan to gain both military and economic control, other Chinese settlers have no military training. Many of them do not understand the geopolitical importance of this colonial region. In the early years of colonization, most of these Chinese farmers were scared to come to East Turkistan, as they saw it as a "foreign land." The author herself remembers how, before the 1990s, there were very few Han Chinese in her hometown of Ghulja. Han Chinese civilian settlers' gradual migration to East Turkistan contrasts with the large-scale settlement undertaken by the XPCC.

As noted at the beginning of this chapter, in the early 1950s, there were 4.87 million people in East Turkistan, of which 75% were Uyghur.[24] In 2010, almost sixty years later, the Han Chinese proportion of the population increased to 40.48%, while that of the Uyghurs decreased to 45.84%.[25] By 2018, the total population had already risen to nearly 25 million, representing a fivefold increase over the 1950s, including more than 9 million Han Chinese.[26] According to Chinese state media, compared to the Chinese national census in 2010, there is an increase of 2,174,000, or 24.86 %, of Han Chinese, including 1,948,000 new Han settlers between 2015 and 2018.[27] The XPCC alone contributed 18.3% of the Han population growth during the past decade.[28]

China created an interconnected institution to exploit non-Han Chinese people, as they were racialized and seen as non-human. Exploitation and settler colonialism was achieved first by confiscating Uyghur and other Turkic people's land and water resources. This was initially for XPCC and then gradually for Chinese settlers as well. Han settlement, XPCC, and the so-called "Open Up the West" project are not intended to develop rural lands to help locals economically but rather to dominate their property to create industrial farms, oilfields, and real estate. These projects benefitted millions of Han Chinese settlers, who moved into Uyghurs' land, causing Uyghur and other Turkic people to lose their property and houses.[29] Not long ago, 70–90% of Uyghurs were farmers, but, as a result of the XPCC and settlement, Uyghurs were forced to abandon their land or be marginalized to desert areas.

Since colonization, the Chinese government has decided the legal value of the land of Uyghurs and other Turkic Muslims, much of which it confiscated as "collective land" belonging to the state. In the 1950s, the land became "commercial," as the local government confiscated farmers' land for commercial transactions, in order to do business with Han Chinese investors or use it for government projects.[30] Uyghur farmers are not allowed to possess the original versions of land-related documents, such as deeds. These documents are registered and held by the Chinese government. The reason the Chinese government gives for this reveals anti-Uyghur prejudice, for example, "Uyghurs are backward, disorganized and illiterate, they do not know how to keep these papers."[31] For this reason, legal documents regarding farmers' property claims are very weak, and authorities can seize the land with or without providing due compensation. There are countless such cases of conflicts between Uyghur farmers and the government over land confiscations used to invest in infrastructure or real estate projects.

An undercover Uyghur journalist was told during an interview in 2006 that Uyghur women were forced to work in a factory in Tianjin, China. One interviewee told him,

> Government officials threatened our parents with confiscating our houses, or else we would have to pay a 3,000-5,000-yuan fine. If not, they would destroy our houses with a bulldozer and take our land if we refused to come here to work.[32]

Since 2017, following the incarceration of millions of Uyghurs, many Uyghurs who have been imprisoned have had their homes confiscated by the Chinese government and sold to Han Chinese settlers. The Uyghur Human Rights Project detailed twelve recent cases of imprisoned Uyghurs whose property was auctioned off by the Chinese government.[33] Property owners who were compensated received as little as 10% of the value of their homes. According to an interview with one

Uyghur recently able to escape abroad, in many cases, villagers received no payment at all.[34] Meanwhile, farmers are burdened by heavy taxes and forced to buy agricultural goods that the Chinese government cannot sell elsewhere. Consequently, this imposes heavy debts on farmers and forces them to sell their agricultural assets and lands to the government and to settlers for a nominal price.

The Chinese government has incentivized the mass movement of Han Chinese into East Turkistan, including both XPCC and civilian settlers, to grow and produce cotton and tomato products. Based on statistics from 2020, 85% of Chinese cotton products and 35% of tomatoes exported to the world are from Uyghur lands occupied by Han Chinese settlers.[35] The influx of Chinese settlers has led to their dominance of agricultural industries traditionally controlled by native Uyghurs, such as raisin production in Turpan. Local Uyghurs have historically used a traditional air-drying method to produce raisins and avoided selling their grape fields to outsiders, as they consider that to be a significant source of connection to their roots, as well as their economic lifelines. However, the Chinese government imposed heavy taxes, putting the local population in crisis levels of debt, in order to coerce Uyghurs to give up their farmland. Confiscated farmlands were given to Chinese settlers as both a welcome present and a reward for their acceptance of settling in East Turkistan.[36] In some cases, farmland was not simply given to settlers, it was sold to settlers cheaply. East Turkistan has historically boasted a variety of agricultural products, such as the massive, thin-skinned walnuts of Khotan; the nutritious, sweet red dates of Qumul; the vast pomegranate fields of Yarkand; the figs of Kashgar; and the flat peaches and mulberries of Kucha. Tragically, all of these local fruit industries have been taken away one by one and given to Chinese settlers.[37]

In recent years, the Chinese government has accelerated infrastructure construction with the goal of "trying a belt around the inside of Xinjiang to speed Xinjiang's import-export" (*Jiang nei huan qi lai, jin chu Jiang kuai qi lai*).[38] The government has long planned to reconstruct East Turkistan as a core area of the New Silk Road Economic Belt and act as a transportation hub for countries west of China.[39] Major railways now connect the region to China and facilitate the transport of Han settlers into East Turkistan, as well as the flow of natural resources out to China. Special air cargo flights are opening up "air corridors" directly to consumer markets. For example, Korla Airport has opened cargo flights for consumer products such as pears, apricots, tomatoes, peaches, "chestnut pumpkins," and "plumps," allowing melons and fruits to directly fly to inland Chinese cities.[40]

The expropriation of land is tied closely to a system of forced labor, in which Uyghur farmers work without compensation for one to three months each year for many years.[41] The XPCC's mining, food, and agricultural industries are heavily involved with forced labor. Currently, the XPCC has eleven traded subsidiaries, listed in table 6.1, many of which have been sanctioned for that reason:[42]

Uyghurs are forced to work for little or no payment in cotton production, in which the land is deprived of Uyghurs and controlled either privately or by state-run Han Chinese companies. A thirty-six-year-old Uyghur farmer in Ghulja who

Table 6.1   Xinjiang Production and Construction Corps Traded Subsidiaries

XPCC Subsidiary	Primary Industry
Xinjiang Baihuacun C., Ltd.	Information technology
Xinjiang Tianye C., Ltd.	Plastics
Xinjiang Suntime International Economic- Trading C., Ltd.	International trade
Xinjiang Talimu Agriculture Development Co., Ltd.	Cotton
Xinjiang Sayram Modern Agriculture Co., L.	Cotton
Xinjiang Yilite Industry Co., Ltd	Alcohol
Xinjiang Chalkis Co., Ltd.	Tomatoes and related industries
Xinjiang Tianhong Paper making Co., Ltd.	Paper manufacturing
Xinjiang Tianfu Thermoelectric Co., Ltd	Electricity
Xinjiang Guannong Fruit & Antler Co., Ltd.	Fruits and animal husbandry
Xinjiang Qingsong Cement Co., Ltd.	Cement

Source: Adapted from Rongxing Guo, China's Spatial (Dis)integration: Political Economy of the Interethnic, (Kidlington UK: Elsevier Ltd, 2015), 18.

previously owned 50 mu chili pepper fields and currently working for the Han Chinese owner said:

> It depends on Han Chinese owners. Some of them pay nothing at the end of the season. And you can't go anywhere to ask for your rights because you are Uyghur. Some of them pay little if they want to when they need us again.[43]

This is the common explanation from many Uyghurs who lived in the villages in East Turkistan. Uyghurs who have survived despite heavy taxation and forced labor have not been allowed to produce goods independently to compete with Chinese settlers.

> They destroyed our house and took over our land. It is to benefit Han Chinese [and at the] same time to disconnect our ethnic spiritual ties to the mother land, it is same as taking our life. Currently two of my brothers are in concentration camps and their beautiful houses and apple yards were confiscated.[44]

Such views are also common to the Uyghurs and Kazaks who are indigenous to East Turkistan. As made apparent by the previous paragraph, it is evident that China's territorial occupation in East Turkistan is both economic and political, as it is aimed to destroy the Uyghur and other Turkic people's economic and social conditions, as well as uproot their physical, cultural, and spiritual attachment to the land of their colonized country.

EXPLOITATION OF NATURAL RESOURCES AND ECONOMIC SEGREGATION

The people of East Turkistan should have the right to freely dispose of their natural wealth and resources, according to the UN's International Covenant on Civil and

Political Rights, which entered into force in March 1976. The Covenant clearly states in Article 1, paragraphs 1 and 2, as follows:

1. All peoples have the right of self-determination. By virtue of that right they freely determine their political status and freely pursue their economic, social and cultural development.
2. All peoples may, for their own ends, freely dispose of their natural wealth and resources without prejudice to any obligations arising out of international economic co-operation, based upon the principle of mutual benefit, and international law. In no case may a people be deprived of its own means of subsistence.[45]

Even though China signed the Convention in October 1998, it has yet to ratify it. One of the reasons that China has repeatedly refused to ratify the convention is to avoid being bound by the covenant in accordance with the provisions of Article 49. That would oblige China to recognize the rights of the people of East Turkistan to possess their natural wealth and resources freely. As a result of the unequal distribution of wealth across areas inhabited by the people of East Turkistan and Han Chinese settlers, Uyghurs and other Turkic Muslims in the region have become visibly segregated. Furthermore, they suffer greatly from a lack of educational and employment opportunities, as well as access to health care, credit, and financial services.

Alessandra Cappelletti in her article "Socio-Economic Disparities and Development Gap in Xinjiang" provides vivid examples of political and economic inequalities between Han Chinese and Turkic Muslims in the region.[46] Cappelletti illuminates the sufferings and socioeconomic disadvantages of Uyghurs by examining the substantial economic and developmental inequality between the Uyghur-majority city of Kashgar and the Han Chinese-majority city of Shihezi. According to her case study, the per capita GDP in Shihezi is six times higher than that of Kashgar. Furthermore, in 2011, the unemployment rate of Kashgar was 4%, while that of Shihezi was 2.02%. The average life expectancy of Uyghurs is about ten years shorter than that of Han Chinese in the region.[47] Further research demonstrates that "[i]n life expectancy, infant mortality, maternal mortality and morbidity Uyghur people are much worse off than Han."

Around 90–92% of Uyghurs live in rural areas, where income is much lower, especially in the southern part of East Turkistan. In 1993, rural Uyghur farmers' total income averaged 732 yuan, compared to Han farmers' 2,680 yuan.[48] Chinese government statistics in 2008 revealed that the average annual per capita of "Xinjiang's" GDP was 19,000 yuan, but we must disaggregate that figure: the average per capita income in rural areas was 3,800 yuan ($560), but farmers in southern "Xinjiang" received 2,226 yuan.[49] In many Uyghur villages in the south, the average annual income was lower than 1,500 yuan ($221). Moreover, according to official Xinjiang statistics, the income gap between Han-dominated urban and Uyghur-dominated rural areas widened from 2.1 times in 1980 to 3.24 times in 2007.[50] According to Anthony Howell's survey of Urumchi in 2008, the city was mainly populated by Han Chinese, with only 12% being Uyghur, while the average monthly earnings of Han Chinese were 28% higher than those of Uyghurs.[51] This was despite the fact that Uyghur residents in Urumchi are fluent in Han Chinese and mainly consist of educated and skilled people. The Chinese government does not release its own statistics showing average income by ethnicity. However, since 2017, Uyghurs and other Turks have been forced into slavery and extreme poverty as a result of China's genocidal policies, including slavery and forced labor, as well as the incarceration of many heads of households, who are usually the primary wage earners. Xinhua news agency reported that Xinjiang's GDP was 1.36 trillion yuan in 2019 and annual growth rate was 7.2% since 2014.[52] Uyghurs and other Turkic people's income are sharply lower than Han Chinese income and economy is dominantly Chinese central state owned, high GDP means has no links with people of East Turkistan but strongly link to Han Chinese or China's economy.

Following China's "Open Up the West" campaign, the Chinese government invested billions to exploit natural resources and build railroads, bridges, and airlines to help facilitate the migration of Han Chinese settlers. For example, in early 2003, the Chinese government invested more than 70 billion yuan (US$8.36 billion) in "highways, power plants, dams and telecommunications facilities," of which investment in road transportation alone hit a historic high of 10 billion yuan (1.2 billion USD).[53] However, this development only benefitted the Chinese government and Chinese settlers. Consequently, for the Uyghurs and other Turkic Muslims, this development intensified the exploitation of the rich natural resources of East Turkistan, which were then directly controlled by Beijing and Chinese state-owned enterprises.

In July 2002, China began to construct the West-East Gas Pipeline that begins at the Tarim Basin oil and natural gas fields and carries those resources to Chinese major cities such as Shanghai, Guangzhou, and Fuzhou.[54] The annual natural gas production of East Turkistan is estimated at 1,800 million cubic meters and oil resources at 2.08 billion tons, accounting for 30% of China's continental oil.[55] Five billion cubic meters of natural gas flow from East Turkistan to Chinese provinces every year.[56] The coal resources of East Turkistan account for 40% of China's estimated gross national resources. The Geological and Mineral Bureau of Xinjiang found fifteen new mineral fields in 2015, including iron, coal, nickel, gold, lead, and zinc ores.[57] As for agriculture, the total planting area of cotton in East Turkistan was more than 2.54 million hectares in 2019, accounting for more than 76% of China's total cotton production.[58]

Unjust exploitation of these natural resources by Chinese state firms has no benefit for people of East Turkistan.[59] Uyghurs and other Turkic Muslims are disenfranchised from the economic benefits, wealth, and resources that other Chinese citizens enjoy. Access to such vast amounts of natural resources is of paramount geostrategic importance to China, and these resources determine China's economic wealth and national security. China has, among other reasons, chosen to transform East Turkistan into an inseparable part of its nation out of an increasing demand for resources and the fear of losing this rich, illegally occupied territory. The state has thus created a police state in East Turkistan in order to exploit it. Additionally, this has also motivated the Chinese government's intent to eliminate the real territorial owners of this region, the Uyghurs and other Turkic peoples, and replace them with Han settlers.

SUMMARY

It is undeniable that XPCC and Han Chinese settlers are a massive force of China's military and demographic colonization in East Turkistan. Uyghurs and other Turkic Muslims in their colonized country East Turkistan were subjected to elimination through gradual territorial dispossession, including genocide. To camouflage its genocide as an internal affair, China called it is as a policy for nation-building. However, if these people belong to China's nation as China propagandized, they would have a Chinese national identity in terms of rights and obligations, and China would allow them to perform political, economic, and territorial functions.

As we mentioned in the introduction of part II, Anthony Smith analyzed in his book *National Identity* that external functions such as legal-political, territorial, and economic are important to defining the identity of a nation. Particularly, the territorial and economic function can provide people with the ability to live, work, and develop their territorial space and play an essential role in their other obligations and rights as a citizen. After the colonization of East Turkistan, China destroyed the historical national identity of the people of East Turkistan. Furthermore, instead of treating them equally as a Chinese nation that can have legal-political, territorial, and economic rights and obligations, China deprived their fundamental human rights and redistributed their resources and properties to the Han settlers. Reengineering these people's identity and forcibly creating an artificial Chinese nation can be functional only in assimilation into Han culture, as we can see that many Uyghurs and other Turkic Muslims were already sinicized. But it is not functional in terms of performing China's national identity as China did not provide rights and obligations to them that nations of the state could have.

To analyze the right to independence of East Turkistan in the circumstances outside of the colonial sphere, this chapter did not focus on historical national ownership of the state territory of East Turkistan but argued China's aggressive violation against the natural rights of property ownership of the colonized people in the region. As discussed in this chapter, XPCC and the Chinese government forcibly took over Uyghurs' houses and farmlands, forced them to move out for rental places, or most of them were rounded up in concentration camps and forced labor camps. Their privately owned properties were given or sold to Han settlers as a welcome gift for immigrating to East Turkistan. Apparently, not providing any territorial functions to the people also justifies China's illegitimacy of ruling these people as China's own nation. The international community who do not support and is implicitly against the independence of East Turkistan should ask: Will they not judge their own morality by allowing China to destroy more than 20 million Uyghur and other Turkic people with the excuse of respecting China's so-called nation-building as an internal affair of China? Why China needs settlement colonialism and implement genocidal policies in the region if these people belong to China's nation and should be considered as China's internal affairs? Uyghurs and other Turkic Muslims in the free world should also ask: Will China grant them to perform their political, territorial, and economic function equal to Han Chinese if they give up their historical national identity? Will they still survive and flourish at least as ethnic people with religious and ethnic identity? History already answered those questions, as we can see in the following chapters.

NOTES

1. Central Intelligence Agency Electronic Reading Room, "The Chinese Population of Sinkiang," May 1, 2013, CIA-RDP82-00047R000200210003-2. https://www.cia.gov/readingroom/document/cia-rdp82-00047r000200210003-2.

2. Stanley Toops, "Demographics and Development of Xinjiang After 1949" (Working Paper, no.1, Analysis and Publications, East- West Center, Washington, DC, 2004), https://www.eastwestcenter.org/system/tdf/private/EWCWwp001.pdf?file=1&type=node &id=32004.

3. Stanley Toops, "Spatial Results of the 2010 Census in Xinjiang," Asia Dialog (blog), March 7, 2016, accessed October 10, 2021, https://theasiadialogue.com/2016/03/07/spatial -results-of-the-2010-census-in-xinjiang/.

4. Michael E. Clarke, *Xinjiang and China's Rise in Central Asia 1949–2009* (London: Routledge, 2011), 151.

5. Constitutions of People's Republic of China (Adopted by the Standing Committee of the National People's Cong., December 4, 1982), P.R.C. Laws of 1982, art. 118, accessed October 15, 2021, http://english.www.gov.cn/archive/lawsregulations/201911/20/content _WS5ed8856ec6d0b3f0e9499913.html.

6. Bao Yajun, "The Xinjiang Production and Construction Corps: An Insider's Perspective," *China: An International Journal* 18, no. 2 (May 2020): 161–74. muse.jhu.edu/article/75 6368.

7. Bao, "The Xinjiang Production and Construction Corps," 164.

8. Donald H. McMillen, "Xinjiang and the Production and Construction Corps: A Han Organisation in a Non-Han Region," *The Australian Journal of Chinese Affairs* 6 (July 1981): 65–96. doi: 10.2307/2159052.

9. Zhan Fan and Li Jingquan, "Xinjiang bingtuan tunken shubian hefa xing ji qianzai hefa xing weiji tanxi" [On the Legitimacy of the Xinjiang Production and Construction Corps' Garrisoning of the Border and Military Farming] in *Zhongnan daxue xuebao (shehui kexue ban)* 18, No. 2 (2012): 102; Fang Yingkai方英楷, *"Xinjiang Bingtuan tunken shubian shi"* 新疆兵团屯垦戍边史[History of the Xinjiang Production and Construction Corps in Farming and Defending the Frontier], ed. LiFusheng 李福生(Wulumuqi: Xinjiang keji weisheng chubanshe 新疆科技卫生出版社, 1997), 886–14.

10. Bao, "The Xinjiang Production and Construction Corps," 162.

11. China, The State Council Information Office, Full Text of *White Paper on History and Development of Xinjiang* (Beijing: Foreign Languages Press Co. Ltd., 2003), sec. IX, http://en .people.cn/200305/26/eng20030526_117240.shtml.

12. This investment was not included investment for detention centers and so-called re-education centers. See Victims of Communism Memorial Foundation, "China's Minister of Public Security Zhao Keji's June 2018 Speech on the Progress of Xinjiang Security Regime," in *Xinjiang Police File* (Washington, DC: Victims of Communism Memorial Foundation, May 23, 2022), 9, https://victimsofcommunism.org/xinjiang-police-files-summary-policy-recommendations/.

13. Ibid.

14. Bao, "The Xinjiang Production and Construction Corps," 166.

15. Ibid., 172.

16. *China Daily*, "Full Text: The History and Development of the Xinjiang Production and Construction Corps," *China Daily*, Last Updated October 5, 2014, accessed December 20, 2021, https://www.chinadaily.com.cn/china/2014-10/05/content_18698088.htm.

17. Uyghur Human Rights Project, *The Bingtuan, China's Paramilitary Colonizing Force in East Turkestan* (Washington, DC: Uyghur Human Rights Project, 2018), 19, accessed December 12, 2021, https://uhrp.org/press-release/uhrp-releases-new-report-'-bingtuan-china's-paramilitary-colonizing-force-east.

18. Author's note: The *Meshrep* was banned by the Chinese government in 1995 because of the increased role of *meshrep* groups in community activism, anti-drug abuse and anti-alcohol advocacy, establishing local youth sports leagues, and social mobilization. See Jay Dautcher, *Down a Narrow Road: Identity and Masculinity in a Uyghur Community in Xinjiang China* (Cambridge: Harvard University Asia Center, 2009), 328.

19. Ibid.; Uyghur Human Rights Project, *The Bingtuan, China's Paramilitary Colonizing Force in East Turkestan*, 19.

20. *China Daily*, "Full Text: The History and Development of the Xinjiang Production and Construction Corps."

21. Interview with Rishat Ibrahim, Aliye Qurban, and Ismail (Uyghur Refugees in Canada and Europe) in discussion with the author, October 2021. Pseudonyms are used to protect interviewee's identity.; Zhang, Fan, and Li Jingquan. 张凡, 李景全 "Xinjiang bingtuan tunken shùbiān héfǎ xìng jí qiánzài héfǎ xìng wéijī tànxī" 新疆兵团屯垦戍边合法性及潜在合法性危机探析[Analysis on the Legality and Potential Legality Crisis of Xinjiang Corps], *South China University Gazette* 18, no. 2 (2012),http://www.zndxsk.com.cn/upfile/soft/20120329/17-p101-skbs4.pdf, Chinese language PDFversion is available at: http://www.zndxsk.com.cn/upfile/soft/20120329/17-p101-skbs4.pdf.

22. Zhonguo Xinwen wang 中国新闻网, "Xinjiang sheng chan jianli she bingtuan guo jia an chuan ju chengli," 新疆生产建设兵团国家安全局成立 [Xinjiang Production and Construction Corps National Security Bureau Was Established], *Zhonguo Xinwen wang* 中国新闻网, March 28, 2012, accessed December 12, 2021, http://www.chinanews.com/gn/2012/03-28/3779628.shtml.

23. Xinjiang Ribao 新疆日报, "Zìzhìqū dǎngwěi jiǔ jiè shí cì quánhuì zhàokai"自治区党委九届十次全会召开[The Tenth Plenary Session of the Ninth Party Committee Meeting of the Autonomous Region Was Held], *Xinjiang Ribao* 新疆日报, October 11, 2020, accessed Dec 13, 2021, http://news.ts.cn/system/2020/10/11/036459586.shtml.

24. Toops, "Demographics and Development of Xinjiang After 1949."

25. Toops, "Spatial Results of the 2010 Census in Xinjiang."

26. Lixiao xia, "An Analysis Report on Population Change in Xinjiang," *Global Times*, January 7, 2021, accessed December 15, 2021. https://www.globaltimes.cn/page/202101/1212073.shtml.

27. *Global Times*, "Populations of Han, Ethnic Minorities in Xinjiang Rise Markedly Over Past Decade: Communiqué" *Global Times,* June 14, 2021, accessed December 15, 2021. https://www.globaltimes.cn/page/202106/1226080.shtml; Adrian Zenz, *Sterilizations, IUDs, and Mandatory Birth Control: The CCP's Campaign to Suppress Uyghur Birth Rates in Xinjiang* (Washington, DC: Jamestown Foundation, 2021), accessed December 11, 2021 https://jamestown.org/product/sterilizations-iuds-and-mandatory-birth-control-the-ccps-campaign-to-suppre ss-uyghur-birthrates-in-xinjiang/.

28. Zenz, "Sterilizations"; "Populations of Han, Ethnic Minorities in Xinjiang Rise Markedly Over Past Decade: Communiqué," *GlobalTimes.*

29. Darren Byler, "Why Xinjiang Is an Internal Settler Colony," *SupChina*, September 1, 2021, accessed December 12, 2021, https://supchina.com/2021/09/01/why-xinjiang-is-an-internal-settler-colony/ (This essay is adapted from Darren Byler's forthcoming book, *Terror Capitalism: Uyghur Dispossession and Masculinity in a Chinese City*, published by Duke University Press).

30. Alessandra Cappelletti, "Socio-economic Disparities and Economic Gap in Xinjiang," in *Inside Xinjiang: Space, Place and Power in China's Far North West*, ed. Anna Hayes and Michael Clarke (Abingdon: Routledge, 2018), 171.

31. Cappelletti, "Socio-economic Disparities," 172.

32. Quote was from a private video, provided by East Turkistan Information Center. This video is not published publicly to protect the identities of the forced labor workers in the video. This quote also cited in Rukiye Turdush and Magnus Fiskesjö, "Dossier: Uyghur Women in China's Genocide," *Genocide Studies and Prevention: An International Journal* 15, no. 1 (May 2021): 22–43. doi: 10.5038/1911-9933.15.1.1834.

33. Uyghur Human Rights Project, *Under Gavel: Evidence of Uyghur-owned Property Seized and Sold Online* (Washington, DC: Uyghur Human Rights Project, 2021), accessed December 12, 2021, https://uhrp.org/report/under-the-gavel-evidence-of-uyghur-owned-property-seized-and-sold-online/.

34. Zumret Dawut (camp survivor), phone interview with author, December 12, 2021.

35. Byler, "Why Xinjiang Is an Internal Settler Colony."

36. *Radio Free Asia*, "Han Migrant Influx Threatens Uyghur Farms," *Radio Free Asia,* March 11, 2013, accessed December 14, 2021, https://www.rfa.org/english/news/uyghur/farmers-03112013164151.html/.

37. Video evidence shows Han Chinese families owned Fruitland of East Turkistan. These videos downloaded and saved by the author. Originally posted in Duoyin, the Chinese Social media platform.

38. Jingji Ribao–Zhonguo Jingji wang 经济日报–中国经济网, "Jiāotōng gǎishàn dàidòng tèsè chǎnyè jiāsù fāzhǎn! Xīnjiāng zài tuījìn xībù dà kāifā zhōng qiánghuà jīchǔ shèshī guīhuà jiànshè" 交通改善带动特色产业加速发展！新疆在推进西部大开发中强化基础设施规划建设 [Improved Transportation to Accelerate Special Characteristic Industries Development! In the Process of Development of Western Region, Strengthen Infrastructure Planning and Construction], *Jingji Ribao- Zhonguo Jingji wang* 经济日报-中国经济网, January 4, 2021, accessed December 20, 2021, http://www.ce.cn/xwzx/gnsz/gdxw/202101/04/t20210104_36184892.shtml.

39. China, The State Council Information Office, *Guiding Opinions of the Central Committee of the Communist Party of China and the State Council on Promoting the Development of the Western Region in the New Era to Form a New Pattern* (Beijing: Chinalawinfo. Co., Ltd. 2020).

40. "Jiaotong Gaishan." *Zhongguo Jingji Ribao.*

41. Local Uyghurs have come to refer to this system as *Hashar*.

42. Rongxing Guo, *China's Spatial (Dis)integration: Political Economy of the Interethnic* (Kidlington UK: Elsevier Ltd, 2015), 18.

43. Halmurat Eziz (Uyghur farmer in Ghulja), social media chat conversation, July 23, 2018. He was forced to abandon his farm land to a Chinese settler for very little price, after XPCC dominated water sources and made him unable to grow peppers. I learned in May 2020 through my contacts that Eziz and his wife were both arrested for Chinese concentration camps in 2019, his wife died in the camp and their children were sent to children's concentration camps.

44. Sureyya Abdurahman (currently she asked political asylum in Turkey), Phone Interview, July 26, 2018.

45. International Covenant on Civil and Political Rights, Dec.16, 1966,
   999 U.N.T.S. 171; S. Exec. Doc. E, 95-2 (1978); S. Treaty Doc. 95-20; 6 I.L.M. 368 (1967). See also Optional Protocol to the International Covenant on Civil and Political Rights, December 16, 1966, https://www.ohchr.org/en/professionalinterest/pages/ccpr.aspx.

46. Cappelletti, "Socio-Economic Disparities," 153–57.

47. Brenda L. Schuster, "Disparities in the Xinjiang Uyghur Autonomous Region of China," *China Quarterly* 198, (June 2009): 1–6. doi: 10.1017/S0305741009000393.

48. Barry Sautman, "Preferential Policies for Ethnic Minorities in China: The Case of Xinjiang," *Nation- alism and Ethnic Politics* 4, no. 1 (1998): 86–118, quoted in Anthony Howell, and C. Cindy Fan. "Migration and Inequality in Xinjiang: A Survey of Han and Uyghur Migrants in Urumqi," in *Eurasian Geography and Economics* 52, no. 1 (April 2011): 124.

49. Ilham Tohti, "Yī lì hā mù: Hépíng, gōngkāi, píngděng, zūnzhòng, shànyì, cái shì jiějué wèntí de gēnběn" 伊力哈木:和平、公开、平等、尊重、善意，才是解决问题的根本 [Ilham: Peace, Openness, Equality, Respect, Goodwill, Is the Root of the Problem], *Still Darkness*(blog) July 7, 2009, accessed and saved by the author in October 18, 2014.

50. Kathrin Hille and Richard McGregor, "Trouble At the Margin," *Financial Times*, July 10, 2009, accessed January 6, 2022, https://www.ft.com/content/fe6d1666-6d92-11de-8b19-00144feabdc0.

51. Anthony Howell, "Chinese Minority Income Disparity in Urumqi: An Analysis of Han-Uyghur Labour Market Outcomes in the Formal and Informal Economies," *China an International Journal*, 11, no. 3 (December 2013): 17.

52. Hua xia, "Xinjiang's GDP Grows 7.2 pct Annually From 2014 to 2019," *Xinhua Net*, February 5, 2021, accessed February 9, 2022, http://www.xinhuanet.com/english/2021-02/05/c_139724143.htm.

53. Nicolas Becquelin, "Staged Development in Xinjiang," *China Quarterly* 178 (July 2004): 358–78, 370.

54. Guo, *China's Spatial (Dis)integration*, 11.

55. Edward Wong, "China Invests in Region Rich in Oil, Coal and Also Strife," *New York Times,* December 20, 2014. Accessed October 14, 2020, https://www.nytimes.com/2014/12/21/world/asia/china-invests-in-xinjiang-region-rich-in-oil-coal-and-also-strife.html; Ji Zen Tu, "Energy and Natural Resources of Xinjiang," in *Xinjiang: China's Northwest Frontier*, ed. Warikoo Kulbhushan (London: Routledge Press, 2019), 22–29.

56. Guo, *China's Spatial (Dis)integration*, 21.

57. Ibid.

58. Mao Weihua and Zheng Caixiong, "Xinjiang Still China's Largest Cotton Producer in 2019," *China Daily,* January 8, 2020, accessed May 14, 2020, https://www.chinadaily.com.cn /a/202001/08/WS5e156c70a310cf3e3558336b.html.

59. Becquelin, "Staged Development in Xinjiang."

7

History of Resistance Movements against Chinese Communist Colonialism

Various UN resolutions and legal instruments confusingly use the terms "all peoples" and "territories and countries" with regard to people's right to self-determination. This can lead to a lack of clarity when defining movements by people within states. To be clear, those resolutions regarding external self-determination refer to colonized countries that have not yet attained independence, such as the Uyghurs and other Turkic Muslims, as the term "all peoples" refers to the people of a colonized country or colonized territories, such as East Turkistan. This fact can be explained in several ways in the issues of East Turkistan.

Importantly, the issue of East Turkistan's self-determination should not be confused with that of an ethnic minority's effort to separate from the territory of a state to which they have migrated, nor with a self-styled liberation movement by an ethnic minority within a civic nation-state. First, the peoples of East Turkistan are not "separatists" as China has claimed—they are colonized peoples, as the foregoing chapters have established. Second, the peoples of East Turkistan are not Chinese ethnic minorities, since they are not in China—to the contrary, it is the people of China, the Han, who are in East Turkistan. The people of East Turkistan—including Uyghurs, Kazaks, Mongols, and Hui—are distinct from those of the Han Chinese state. Third, it is not possible to solve China's gross violations of the rights of Turkic Muslims in East Turkistan through the restoration of respect for some, but not all of their basic human rights. It is not a domestic situation that China can solve through internal reforms. The scope of the issue encompasses all the peoples of the colonial country of East Turkistan whose struggles have continued since China's invasion. It is also about genocide and crimes against humanity that are impossible to solve without independence for East Turkistan's people.

The history of major resistance movements in East Turkistan presented in this chapter reflects the strongly independent identity of the region's people. This historical account will help to answer the following questions: Are the people of East Turkistan ethnic minority secessionists who want to withdraw from their state because of their ethnicity? Or are they colonized nations who want to regain their independent state? Have they ever placed a greater emphasis on fighting for basic human rights and asking genuine autonomy? If so, what was the outcome?

INDEPENDENCE MOVEMENTS

During the People's Republic of China (PRC)'s invasion in 1949 under General Wang Zhen, the people of East Turkistan resisted. Then they resisted the mass killings that Wang undertook, and they did not cease in the decades after. The following major resistance movements occurred between 1949 and the 1980s.

In the 1950s, the Chinese government launched political campaigns against counterrevolutionaries, which involved the Land Reform program that killed half a million people, including intellectuals and landowners, in East Turkistan. Pro-independence activists established the *Salam* (peace) government as a shadow government, which rose against Chinese occupation and land reform.[1] Chinese territorial occupation and oppression were the leading cause of the uprising that started in Khotan. The Chinese government sent heavily armed police units and soldiers to crack down on the rebels. Resisters attacked a labor camp in Buzha and freed its prisoners, but one of the Chinese guards managed to escape and inform the Chinese headquarters. According to several eyewitnesses, most of the insurgents were either arrested or killed, and during that time, the Chinese government terrorized Khotan. The following proclamation of the independence fighters was released by the Chinese police later on, and it indicates that religion and ethnicity played a significant role in organizing the resistance movement but did not ignite the movement:

> The enemy of religion, the CCP, has occupied the Muslim homeland, has plundered Muslim land, minerals and other property and has imposed its laws on the laws of Islam. It allows our people to labour but does not allow us to be the masters of the fruits of our labour. According to Islamic law, if the infidel invades Muslim lands, resisting the infidel is the duty of all Muslims. The time for rebellion is here.[2]

In the 1950s and 1960s, Uyghurs and other Turkic people organized independence movements in various cities and towns in the north and south of East Turkistan. In 1958, Uyghur and Kazak intellectuals, both inside and outside of the Chinese Communist Party (CCP) and of the so-called Xinjiang Uyghur Autonomous Region's government, were firmly against China's policy of false autonomy. Subsequently, they demanded the separation of the autonomous region from the PRC and demanded the departure of the Chinese from the region.[3] According to meeting records between deputy chairman of the People's Committee of the Xinjiang Uyghur Autonomous Region Xin Lanting and Consul-General of the USSR in Ürümchi G. Dobashin, the head of the Department of Culture Ziya Sämädi, pronouncements by the head of the Department of Internal Affairs Ibrahim Turdi, deputy head of the Department of Public Security Aliev, chairman of the autonomous region Trade and Industry Association, and mayor of Ürümchi Abdurehim Saidov are strongly against the fake autonomy of Xinjiang and insists China and its people to leave from East Turkistan.[4] These intellectuals and many ordinary young people who spoke up against China's illegal occupation and unjust policies were secretly killed, arrested, or harshly oppressed. Islamic organizations and bazaars were closed down to prevent people from gathering and organizing against China. The CCP's heavily oppressive campaign against the people of East Turkistan started under the name of eliminating "local nationalism." As a result, countless Uyghur and other Turkic Muslims were arrested, tortured, imprisoned, or killed under China's increasingly severe crackdown.

In 1966, Mao Zedong started China's Cultural Revolution. The people of East Turkistan became the most vulnerable victims of the Cultural Revolution as they were considered aliens in the Chinese colony. Their culture, power, dignity, and resistance were intentionally destroyed on many fronts. Even the simple act of demanding basic human rights, such as when young women Uyghurs refused to cut their hair short in Chinese style, was considered a crime against the CCP. Many Uyghurs who witnessed Chinese communist policies in East Turkistan during these years described brutal punishment of Uyghurs who were labeled as ideological enemies of China, ethnic nationalists, and Soviet revisionists due to their adherence to their ethnic roots and religious and ideological beliefs. An ethnic Uyghur named Muhemmet Ehmet, who lives in Turkey at the present time, narrated to the author a traumatic experience from his boyhood that took place during the Cultural Revolution. He said the following:

It was the early winter of 1972. I witnessed, with my own eyes, the murder of Jemshit Kari Hajim by Chinese civilian soldiers known as *Minbing* in Chinese language at the time. He was religious scholar, and they dragged him out from his home and threw him into a deep dirty water pond in my neighbourhood in Hoten city. Every time he lifted his head out of the water to try to escape, they threw stones at him. People from my neighbourhood was forced to gather and watch him be tortured and die. I was only 12 years old at the time, and I still have night mares about the scene to this day.[5]

Turdush Kasim, who now lives in Canada, detailed China's horror in Ghulja during the Cultural Revolution as follows:

I witnessed that almost every adult male that I know including my two older brothers, was arrested, put to death and myself and my friends given 10-20 years in prison in Gulja in 1970s. We were called "ethnic nationalist" or "Soviet revisionists." Even though, most of these arrested people were released from prison after Mao Zedong died and Deng Xiaoping come to power, the generation that lived through the Chinese cultural revolution did not trust Deng Xiaoping either. We hated China, but feared, cautious and obedient.[6]

Following the end of the Cultural Revolution and the death of Mao Zedong, the Chinese people began a period of recovery. They were able to recover from the

Cultural Revolution's pain and ruin. Nonetheless, China has not only shown any intention of leaving East Turkistan but has also made no significant improvement in its policy in the region. As we noted in the previous chapter, Xinjiang Production and Construction Corps (XPCC) was re-established, and Chinese general Wangzhen insisted on harsh tactics to govern East Turkistan. He asked his followers to burn his body if he dies and spread his ashes in the Tengri mountains of East Turkistan, meaning that they would never leave the region even if they perished.

General Wangzhen and other Chinese government officials fiercely criticized Chinese official Hu Yaobang for suggesting genuine autonomy and a more relaxed policy approach to governance in East Turkistan. In the early 1980s, Hu Yaobang briefly became CCP secretary-general. He proposed a "six points" reform program to enact genuine autonomy. His proposed policy was softer than the other "six points" plan for Tibet, as he suggested that the "Xinjiang" issue was not as complicated, since it has no exiled religious leader or active independence movement in exile. However, General Wang Zhen adamantly opposed him. Soon after Hu proposed the reform program, Han chauvinists removed him from his position.[7] The author of one interesting report from this era was Yuan Ming, the former deputy director of Theoretical Research Office of Central Party School. He visited and interviewed many Uyghur local cadres and farms, after which he confirmed that people in "Xinjiang" wanted genuine autonomy and were against Chinese oppression:

> Even the most radical minority cadres in Xinjiang we came across were not antagonistic to all Han people and Han cadres. Nor did they advocate total independence from China. All they wanted was genuine autonomy and the freedom to be the true master of the territory of Xinjiang. They were opposed to Han chauvinists like Wang Zhen and Deng Liqun who bullied and oppressed them. They welcomed Han friends who helped them, like Hu Yaobang and Xi Zhongxun. All the Uygur, Kazak, Uzbek, and Tajik cadres we met were open, candid, not at all inhibited.[8]

He also mentioned the words of Han Chinese cadres in East Turkistan who supported Wang Zhen's oppressive policies:

> What the hell does Hu Yaobang know? Full autonomy! You give them autonomy and they would only turn around and create an East Turkistan. Hu Yaobang also wants to withdraw Han cadres to the interior. That would be like surrendering Xinjiang to the Soviet Union and Turkey. Only a traitor would do such a thing. To stabilize Xinjiang, we must send hard-liners like Wang Zhen and Deng Liqun here.[9]

After Hu Yaobang was removed as CCP secretary-general, the people of East Turkistan quickly realized that it would be nearly impossible to gain genuine autonomy. Consequently, two different reactions emerged among Uyghur and other Turkic populations. The ideology of "independence or die" was felt among those who realized very well that living under Chinese control is equivalent to destruction. Others simply wanted to gain basic human rights and thought that this would be possible with help from international pressure. They believed that the international community could provide at least some relief, and they had reason to believe as much: UN Resolution 1514 provides that

> all armed action or repressive measures of all kinds directed against dependent peoples shall cease in order to enable them to exercise peacefully and freely their right to complete independence, and the integrity of their national territory shall be respected.[10]

Nevertheless, this resolution was not enforced in China.

Instead, all resistance and freedom movements were brutally repressed. A prime example of recent resistance was the Baren Uprising, in which Uyghurs and other Turkic Muslims directly demanded the end of Chinese colonization. In April 1990, in Baren village, located in the Kizilsu Kyrgyz Autonomous Prefecture, Uyghur farmers protested against the Chinese state's multifaceted oppression. They refused to participate in forced labor, refused to pay taxes, rejected the Chinese government, and stood up against Chinese birth prevention measurements and nuclear testing. Protestors attacked the local police station, bombed the village government building, hung the East Turkistan flag on that building, and demanded that Han Chinese settlers leave East Turkistan. The protest's leader, Zeynidin Yusuf, read a manifesto against China's colonization when protestors surrounded the police station. According to one of the organizers, Abdulahat Memet, who managed to escape from Baren to Central Asia, the Baren manifesto was as follows:

> Killing innocent lives is a crime everywhere. Why is China's killings of innocent babies before they have been delivered to this world not counted as a crime and punished? East Turkistan is the land of Uyghurs and other Turkic Muslims. Why [do] they have to pay land tax and many other taxes to Chinese invaders? We refuse to pay tax to the Chinese government! We demand that the Chinese government stop hashar! (slave labor!). On the pretext of population control, the Chinese government is killing our babies. If the Chinese government wants to control population growth, they should stop migrating Han Chinese settlers into East Turkistan! [W]e demand that Han Chinese settlers leave East Turkistan! We demand that the Chinese government and its Party and its military forces leave East Turkistan! We declare war against the Chinese government's birth control policy and slave labor! We demand that the Chinese government stop nuclear testing in our land![11]

Subsequently, China reacted to the Baren Uprising with a bloody crackdown. The Chinese government sent thousands of armed police officers and troops to suppress the protestors, resulting in thousands being killed and arrested. Additionally, the whole village was sealed off for three years.

The Baren Uprising was probably the clearest and most goal-oriented independence movement organized by Uyghur farmers who lived under extremely harsh conditions in a particularly poor village. Later resistance movements, uprisings, or expressions of discontent since the 1990s, such as the 1997 Ghulja Uprising and

2009 Urumchi protests, only demanded justice, equality, and self-governance. These will be discussed in the next section.

Nevertheless, there have also been signs of large-scale resistance since 1990. The Yarkand resistance in July 2014 also clearly demonstrated a protest against Chinese colonization. A few months after Xi Jinping's order to accelerate the XPCC's settlement of the South,[12] around 100 Uyghur villagers armed with knives attacked the government office and police station in Yarkand County. According to a Chinese official report, this incident resulted in the killings of 37 police officers and Chinese officials, and Chinese forces killed 59 of the attackers and arrested 215 people.[13] However, anonymous Uyghur witnesses attest that more than 4,000 Uyghurs were killed during the protest and afterward in Yarkand by the Chinese security forces and Chinese drones. Chinese official Wang Yongzhi was soon afterward appointed to run Yarkand County, with the result that he built a new detention facility in the county, signaling the beginning of mass detentions. By 2017, it was estimated that 20,000 Uyghurs were detained in this facility alone.[14]

Several other scattered, unorganized Uyghur resistance activities have occurred since the harsh crackdown on the Urumchi protests. Most of these violent acts targeted Chinese police stations, government buildings, and Chinese officials—not Chinese civilians. China labeled all these attacks as "terrorism." However, Turkic Muslims have seen these unorganized attacks as resistance fighters' activities against China's colonialism or an individual reaction of oppressed and angry people. These scattered, violent reactions led people in all Uyghur villages or towns to pay a heavy price collectively, for example, by being arrested, regardless of whether they have a connection with violent resistance.

DEMANDING AUTONOMY

The people of East Turkistan after 1990 largely changed their strategy, retreating from independence to demand instead the autonomy that China guarantees in its Constitution (this does not mean a total step down. There are still independence resistances like Yarkand resistance and some scattered underground independence activities. But the main strategy did not include those activities). Demanding fundamental human rights, equal treatment with Han Chinese citizens, and respect for autonomy means lending legitimacy to China's legal obligation to protect Turkic people as Chinese citizens. At the same time, East Turkistan's continued inclusion within China's territory also legitimizes the people's demands for basic rights and protections from China. However, China has continually refused to uphold its national and international obligations. Furthermore, the state even considers Turkic people's very existence and indigeneity in the colonized land as a Chinese national security threat. Instead of choosing from a myriad of other potential responses, including negotiations, the Chinese government has chosen to repress Turkic people's demands violently.

Uyghurs Protest in Ghulja

Local Uyghur youth leaders in Ghulja organized a cultural event called a *Meshrep* to preserve Uyghur culture and prevent the widespread drug and alcohol use, which the Chinese government had encouraged. *Meshrep* leaders publicly criticized China's unfair regulations and ill-treatment of Uyghurs during these gatherings. Furthermore, they demanded that the Chinese government respect its Constitution's commitment to allow autonomous regions to govern their own local and financial affairs. On February 5 and 6, 1997, Uyghur youths in Ghulja protested in front of the city hall and demanded their arrested *Meshrep* leaders' release. In response, the Chinese government sent police units. At first, the XPCC took advantage of the cold weather and used high-pressure hoses and tear gas to try to disperse the demonstrators in February's freezing cold weather. Numerous eyewitnesses, whom the author interviewed during a visit to Ghulja shortly after the protests, attest that the XPCC then started to fire at the crowds of protestors.[15]

The protest was peaceful and only demanded the retention of cultural, as well as religious freedom, some political and economic rights. Unlike other armed resistance activities, those in Ghulja did not openly demand or fight for independence. Nevertheless, the reaction of the Chinese government and their behavior against the protestors were no different. The Chinese security forces, composed of the Public Security Bureau and the People's Armed Police, brutally crushed the protest by shooting and killing a number of unarmed demonstrators. Casualty figures vary depending on sources. In the few months following the protest, Uyghur youths' arrests and house searches were constant and resulted in thousands of Uyghurs being arrested and many others forcibly disappeared. The author also learned during her visit to Ghulja that most of her male high school classmates and friends in Ghulja were either arrested, executed, or disappeared in the wake of the protests. It is significant because it was and continues to be emblematic of the Chinese government's brutal treatment and criminalization of Uyghurs and other Turkic people, as well as the inhumane policies that were used to govern the supposedly "autonomous" region.

Protest in Urumchi

Uyghur university students protested in Urumchi on July 5, 2009, to demand justice for the Uyghur youths who had been brutally killed in a Chinese toy factory in Shaoguan, Guangdong on June 25. According to a Reuters news report, Han Chinese workers attacked Uyghur workers who had been newly recruited from East Turkistan, leading to three deaths and 118 injuries.[16] The fight was triggered by an internet poster who falsely alleged that Uyghur male workers had raped a young Han Chinese woman after she mistakenly walked into an Uyghur male dormitory. This false report, which was later disproven, caused serious ethnic conflict in the Shaoguan manufactory.

Following the June 25 incident, violent and bloody videos from Shaoguan were circulated showing how thousands of Chinese attacked Uyghurs, stabbing them to death. While official reports claimed only two Uyghur youths had been killed, unofficial sources reported a much greater loss of life, owing to the disappearance of hundreds of Uyghur workers from the Shaoguan factory. Uyghur students who organized the protest in People's Square in Urumchi had asked permission to hold a protest, but the authorities refused. Nevertheless, organizers decided to continue, and around 300–400 people gathered. This group called for a proper investigation into the events in Shaoguan. Notably, they raised the red Chinese flag and asked the Chinese government to treat Uyghurs equally with Han Chinese citizens in accordance with the law. However, these peaceful demonstrators faced a bloody crackdown as the Chinese government sent security forces and opened fire instead of responding to their legitimate demands. An eyewitness, Rishat Elkun, who currently lives in Europe, used to live close to where the demonstration took place on July 5. Elkun, recalling that night, told the author: "The gunshots did not stop all night, we know those Uyghur youths have nothing in their hands, but Chinese security forces are fully armed."[17] Other eyewitness reports and videos distributed on social media show that the protest turned violent after Chinese armed forces blocked the protestors and opened fire. Uyghurs in the streets attacked Han Chinese people to take revenge after deep resentment built up over years of oppression and Han Chinese settlers' discrimination.

On July 6, 2009, an additional 20,000 security personnel, including police, armed paramilitary police, and the military, were deployed to Urumchi.[18] Despite the already heavy security presence, those forces also distributed metal sticks to Han Chinese civilians in every neighborhood and encouraged them to attack Uyghurs in the name of self-defense. Han Chinese mobs attacked and killed anyone in the streets who looked like an Uyghur.[19] Chinese figures reported the death toll at 197, with 134 of them being Han Chinese, and more than 1,600 injured.[20] However, the former president of the World Uyghur Congress (WUC) Rebiya Kadeer claimed that 400 Uyghurs had been killed in Urumchi alone and probably more in Kashgar.

As a result of the Urumchi protests, internet access and telephone communication were disconnected, while Facebook, Twitter, and video-sharing sites such as YouTube were blocked throughout China. Wang Lequan, the CCP secretary who directed the Urumchi massacre, proudly told the Han Chinese mobs in the street that the CCP's dictatorial force alone could be enough to oppress Uyghurs: "Comrades, to start with, such action fundamentally not necessary, our dictatorial force is fully able to knock out evildoers, so there is no need to take such action."[21] His provocative words labeled Uyghur protestors as the evildoers, despite the fact that Han Chinese mobs were also attacking Uyghurs, which indicates that the Chinese government failed and was unjust in their response to the Uyghurs' legal rights.

Ilham Tohti's Ideology

The Chinese government effectively manipulated the Global War on Terrorism for the purpose of justifying its oppression of Uyghurs and other Turkic Muslims. Anyone who demanded greater rights or internal self-determination was labeled a terrorist, separatist, or religious radical and received severe punishments. Uyghur scholar Ilham Tohti is a unique figure because he was not simply one of the millions of ordinary people against China's colonization. Rather, he was a peacemaker who was genuinely dedicated to erasing ethnic tensions between Han Chinese and Uyghurs by advocating equal treatment, mutual understanding, fundamental human rights, and harmonizing society for peaceful China. He did not participate in any Uyghur resistance movements or peaceful demonstrations such as those in Ghulja or Urumchi. However, as an academic, he demanded equal treatment for Uyghurs under the Chinese Constitution.

Ilham Tohti's nonviolent strategy to create mutual understanding between Han Chinese and Uyghurs relied on social media and academic networks. He established the website "Uyghur Online" at the end of 2005 in an attempt to open up dialogue in order to ease the ethnic tensions. "Uyghur Online" provided a platform for the Chinese people, as well as the world, to understand Uyghurs. The website strictly forbade pro-independence speech. Ilham then began to make an effort to gain Han intellectuals' attention on the "Xinjiang" problem and Uyghurs' suffering.[22]

Meanwhile, he raised awareness about social discrimination and economic issues that Uyghurs had been experiencing since 2006.[23] He criticized the Chinese government's so-called "economic development policy" that took advantage of and exploited Uyghurs. He stated that, even if China improved its economic policies to benefit Uyghurs, it would still not satisfy their cultural and political autonomy, unless the Chinese government improved its heavy-handed political control in the region.[24] He regarded the Chinese government as the legitimate government for China, including East Turkistan. Ilham Tohti stated this in an article:

The Han Chinese nation is the ruling nation in China, so it should take responsibility for this country and our destiny. It is you who want us to integrate with you. It is you who came in to lead us, and the leader must be responsible and tolerant. If 1.3 billion Han people cannot tolerate 10 million Uyghurs, how could you talk about the unity of the country?[25]

Ilham Tohti was against racism and Chinese nationalism and tried instead to promote an equal and harmonious relationship between Han Chinese and other nations in East Turkistan. As he pointedly put it, "There is a certain degree of speech freedom and internet freedom for Han Chinese and not for the Uyghurs. The Chinese government is very vocal to criticize racism in Western countries while ignoring its internal racist and fascist mentalities."[26]

Professor Tohti, an economist, also conducted research with his students to submit to the Chinese government as a demonstration of the demands of East Turkistan's majority. His research methods included direct interviews of 312 participants and 4,500 online survey questionnaires. The interviewees, mostly Uyghur, were selected as a random sample in three prefectures, six cities, and two counties in East Turkistan. Research was conducted from October to December 2009, January to March 2010, and May to September 2010. They also distributed 600 survey questionnaires to Uyghurs who were living in other Chinese cities, in which they interviewed ninety-eight people in those cities, including fifty-three Uyghurs and forty-five Hans.[27] According to his research, 12.3% of Uyghurs believe that independence can solve Uyghur-Han issues, while 81.3% believe that a high degree of autonomy can do so. The credibility of the survey should be questioned since it was conducted in East Turkistan under the Chinese occupation, where there is no freedom of speech. However, at the very least, the survey results reflected a consensus around the idea of obtaining true autonomy and fundamental rights, while also recognizing that there is currently no hope for the possibility of independence.[28] Nevertheless, such demands were rejected.

Moreover, Ilham Tohti's efforts to educate Han Chinese people and gain their support tragically failed and eventually resulted in his arrest. He was charged with separatism and sentenced to life in prison in January 2014.[29] The failure of his peaceful ideology and efforts proves that the Chinese state's intention is not to create peace and treat Uyghurs and other Turkic Muslims equally with Chinese citizens but rather to eliminate them.

POLITICAL ACTIVITIES OF EXILED UYGHURS

Ilham Tohti's imprisonment portended the genocide that began following Xi Jinping's articulation of the "China Dream" of a stronger nation with a stronger military.[30] The actions and reactions of the Uyghur exile diaspora have paralleled the progressively worsening political and economic situation of the people living in East Turkistan.

Exiled Uyghurs and other Turkic Muslims who escaped in the early 1950s to Central Asia and Turkey never lost the hope of regaining freedom and independence for their beloved country. In 1949, The president of the East Turkistan Republic Elihan Tore was abducted by the Soviet forces and placed under house arrest in Uzbekistan, after which other top leaders were killed in a plane crash while on their way to a diplomatic meeting in Beijing. Only a few leading elites were able to escape to neighboring Central Asian countries or Turkey. However, it was impossible for them to establish the East Turkistan government while in exile. Nor were they able to promote independence for East Turkistan from neighboring Central Asian countries, as these regions were under Soviet administration until the 1990s. Even though the independence of many Central Asian countries in the 1990s provided some hope for the people of East Turkistan, it was nearly impossible for the movement to thrive in these newly independent countries, as they were both weak and authoritarian. Most significantly, these countries were and remain under the strong influence of Russia and quickly became close allies of China with the creation of the Shanghai Five security organization in April 1996. Consequently, Uyghurs' political activism in these countries is continuously repressed.

Political activities developed in Turkey between the 1960s and 1990s and expanded to Europe and North America in the 1990s. Muhammad Emin Bughra, one of the founders of the East Turkistan Islamic Republic in 1933, was exiled to Turkey during Communist China's invasion in 1949.[31] Isa Yusuf Alptekin, the self-styled former secretary-general of the East Turkistan government, previously served the Chinese Nationalist (Kuo mintang) government to secure East Turkistan from Soviet Communist influence. He had asked the Chinese Nationalists for full autonomy for East Turkistan and was subsequently also exiled to Turkey.[32] These leaders' activities were committed to gaining recognition and support for the East Turkistan cause. They established the National Center for the Liberation of East Turkistan, wrote articles, published magazines and newspapers, and sent letters to international leaders. In a May 1954 letter from Muhammed Emin Bughra to his friend Yolbarshan explained how the ambassador of the Republic of China (Chinese Nationalist or Kuomintang) in Turkey had tried to put pressure on him. The account and his response are as follows:

> [T]wo months ago, at the Chinese Embassy in Ankara, he had wanted to speak with me in person, and we have done so. He told me "you are advocating for the secession of Xinjiang from the Republic of China from abroad. Your actions and words are centered on this task. You should desist from such actions and words. The Chinese government will not grant you independence [freedom]. You should first go to Taiwan to take a look at our strength before you do your thing. If you keep emphasizing this task of yours, the results will not be in your favor." My reply at the time was: "Our independence movement is not something that has just begun today, we started doing this twenty-two years ago. This is not some empty rhetoric; sometimes it involves real battles, and sometimes it is sought through discourse. We will not stop until our homeland is free. The best sort of solution is for the Chinese government to take a benign stance in supporting Xinjiang's independence. We think that our liberation is in the interests of both sides."[33]

Some leading elites from East Turkistan had some degree of diplomatic relations with China, as represented by the Nationalist government. However, they were firmly against any Chinese government's control of East Turkistan. Muhammed Emin Bughra's red line was very clear. Similarly, many other Uyghur leaders, such as Elihan Tore, received support from the Soviet Union and Communist groups and yet did not accept being part of Communist China or of the Soviet Union.

Exiled Uyghur leaders in Turkey sent a letter to the Advisor of the State Department of the Government of the United States in 1950 to inform him how the independent East Turkistan Republic in the North fell under the control of the Soviet government and Communist China, and he asked for help concerning in relation to Uyghur refugees in India.[34] Even though they did not fully explain the complicated situation in the letter, this letter can also prove their frustration with the Soviet government's involvement in putting down the independent East Turkistan. These exiled leaders also had established relationships with anti-communist Chinese officials in Taiwan to gain their support.

Isa Yusuf Alptekin likewise received support from anti-communist powers in Turkey. Unlike before, he promoted freedom both for East Turkistan under Chinese colonization and for Western Turkistan under the control of the Soviet Union. Alptekin participated in the Bandung Conference (aka the Afro-Asian Conference) in New Delhi in 1960 and the Baghdad Conference of the Islamic Countries in 1961.[35] He also presented a special memorandum in 1962 at the Karachi Islamic

World Conference and the Muslim League in Mecca in 1963, as well as the General Islamic Congress in 1964, in which he asked Muslim countries and peace-loving countries to put into practice resolutions concerning Turkistan (East and West Turkistan) that had been passed.[36] He also wrote a letter to President Nixon on July 23, 1969, requesting that the United States recognize East Turkistan as a captive nation and express disappointment about the captive nation resolution proposed by Senator Douglas and his eighteen friends in "Captive Nations Week" on June 22, 1959, in which East Turkistan was not mentioned.[37] During his presidency of the National Liberation Centre of East Turkistan, US Congressman John M. Murphy introduced Alptekin and his appeal on the House floor on March 3, 1970. Alptekin asked for help from the Free World in his petition; he stated the following wishes of the people of East Turkistan:

> That the nations of the free world use their good office to persuade the Government of Nationalist China to declare that Eastern Turkestan is independent;
> That the nations of the free world especially the Moslem states try to bring the problem of Eastern Turkestan before the United Nations Organization as an item for debate;
> That the influx of Chinese colonists from China to Eastern Turkestan be protested; and that genocide and persecution be condemned;
> That academic institutes be founded to undertake research work concerning Eastern Turkestan;
> That a freedom movement for the people of Eastern Turkestan be sponsored;
> That the children of the Eastern Turkestani exiles be granted scholarships to study in various countries of the world.[38]

However, the Nixon government, following Kissinger's foreign policy, was interested in improving its relationship with China and thus refused to support the East Turkistan cause.[39]

In December 1998, the East Turkistan National Centre (ETNC) was established in Turkey as a potential basis for the future establishment of an East Turkistan Government-in-Exile (ETGE).[40] The headquarters of ETNC moved to Germany soon after. In October 1999, during the Second East Turkistan National Assembly, the center was renamed the East Turkistan National Congress, which was to function as a global umbrella organization and already included eighteen diaspora organizations. In April 2004, the East Turkistan National Congress merged with the World Uyghur Youth Congress, and they changed the name of the organization to the WUC. Additionally, they changed their strategy from promoting the independence of East Turkistan to promoting democracy, human rights, and religious freedom for the Uyghur people, as well as using peaceful, nonviolent, and democratic means to determine East Turkistan's future.[41] In order to avoid using the word "independence," the WUC put the term "self-determination" in their Constitution, without specifying external or internal self-determination. There are several possible reasons for this gesture:

Firstly, the WUC requires financial and moral support from non-governmental and intergovernmental organizations to raise awareness. Many such donor organizations are only minimally opposed to trade relations with China. Meanwhile, they may see the Uyghur issue as a Chinese internal matter and do not want to get involved directly, but they are interested in providing moral and financial support if the WUC's political objectives are focused on human rights within the framework of international self-determination law. This provides the leadership of WUC with a safe path to financial and professional resources.

Second, most of the prominent leaders of the WUC believe that it is not the right time to ask for independence and that it is challenging to gather support for independence against an assertive and dominant country such as China. Significantly, some of the WUC leaders think the political strategy of the Uyghur cause must be led in a way that parallels the aspirations of people in East Turkistan who demand genuine autonomy and fundamental human rights, particularly in support of Ilham Tohti's ideas. The leaders may believe that, if they do so, China would not have to be afraid of Uyghurs' independence and may agree to negotiations. However, it should be noted here that the people in East Turkistan cannot express their true national aspirations while they are not free, so it is not accurate to say that support for Ilham Tohti's ideas comprises a genuine national aspiration. Furthermore, China's intention to destroy the people of East Turkistan is not motivated only by the fear of their independence. Regardless, these perceptions have already been invalidated by the fact that China's genocide in East Turkistan also targets people who neither dare to ask for independence nor dare to demand human rights.

Third, it is also a reality that WUC has no specific published strategy and plan for organizing institutions, establishing political parties, or electing officials who could represent the political views of the East Turkistani population that could highlight their potential statehood agenda. Dr. Erkin Ekrem, one of the founders of the WUC and its current vice president, drafted a three-stage roadmap for Uyghurs' political struggle in the diaspora in 2003. However, it is unclear whether WUC will rigorously implement this strategy. The first stage of his strategy is to promote East Turkistan's national identity in the diaspora, alongside Uyghur ethnic identity. I myself wrote the book *Ethnicity, Nation, Identity, and Liberal Nationalism* (*Étnik, ulus, kimlik we uluschiliq*) to support Dr. Erkin Ekrem's strategy, promote a civic nation-state identity of East Turkistani people, and prevent Uyghur ethnonationalism, in order to achieve territorial independence. The East Turkistan Youth Congress, established in 2019, tirelessly promoted East Turkistan national identity (*Ulus kimliki*), while the WUC is focusing on ethnic Uyghur identity issues. The second stage of Dr. Erkin Ekrem's strategy is focused on pursuing a viable political program in the international arena to legitimize the rights of East Turkistan's people through governments and states political, economic, trade, internal security, education, cultural, and religious affairs, including their recognition as a captive nation and securing the passage of Uyghur human rights policy acts in various countries. The goal is to secure protection from international powers. The third strategy is to establish the East Turkistan National Congress jointly with all domestic and diaspora political organizations of Uyghurs and other Turkic Muslims of East Turkistan, and that this National Congress will determine the form of the future independent state of East Turkistan. While the current language used by the WUC is not very consistent with the elements of Dr. Erkin Ekrem's strategy, nevertheless, the WUC is also working hard to secure the rights of Uyghurs and other Turkic Muslims as an ethnic group in order to secure international protection.

Lastly, the WUC may wish to take a soft approach to China and prioritize specific issues instead of independence of East Turkistan and ask for human rights. The WUC, considering East Turkistan's weak position, therefore decided to cooperate with overseas anti-CCP Chinese people, while avoiding the territorial issue. However, tragically, all of these efforts have failed. Despite the moderate approach of Uyghurs both in East Turkistan and in the diaspora, China has not changed its actions nor intention to destroy the people of East Turkistan. International powers led by United States have strongly criticized China verbally, yet avoid putting heavy sanctions on China, despite extensive evidence of genocide. Furthermore, many other developing countries, particularly Muslim countries continue to even blatantly deny the genocide and instead support China because of their great dependency on the Chinese economy.

The ETGE was established following the dissolution of the East Turkistan National Congress in September 2004 in Washington, DC, to promote the independence of East Turkistan. However, the ETGE took on a symbolic role and failed to become active in lobbying. Again, the reason that ETGE was left inactive and powerless was the reluctance of governments, non government orgnaizations (NGO), Intergovernmental organizations (IGO) and international non-governmental organizations (INGO) to support the independence of East Turkistan. No one, not even influential countries such as the United States, wanted to take on that burden, which could harm their relationship with China, in part because the UN principle of territorial integrity under international law misleadingly and officially recognizes East Turkistan as part of China. Nevertheless, as shown in figure 7.1, in 2001, the US government had a letter exchange with the East Turkistan National Freedom Center (which later merged into the ETGE) but only concerned China's violation of human rights issues in East Turkistan.[42]

The ETGE represents the genuine aspirations of the people of East Turkistan, and it was established by prominent Uyghur, Kazakh, and other East Turkistani leaders, representing over a dozen organizations from across the East Turkistan diaspora. Nevertheless, people in the diaspora did not lend the ETGE their support but believed that the WUC's strategy would be effective in fighting for the rights of Uyghurs since they have the financial resources to do the job. Most significantly, internal power challenges and political quarrels among the ETGE leadership jeopardized its credibility in the eyes of the diaspora.

For both East Turkistani people and China, the strategy of stepping back from the existential national aspirations of people inside and outside East Turkistan made no difference. On the contrary, starting in 2017, China disclosed its genocidal intent by committing atrocities. Members of the East Turkistani diaspora lost connection with their family members at home. Most of these people had not participated in any anti-colonization activities until the events of 2017. Now the people of East Turkistan finally realized that it would be impossible to survive without

United States Department of State

Washington, D.C. 20520

July 20, 2001

Mr. Anwar Yusuf Turani
President
Eastern Turkestan National Freedom Center
P.O. Box 76488
Washington, D.C. 20013

Dear Mr. Turani:

 Thank you for your letter of May 10 to President Bush
concerning the situation of Uighur Muslims in China,
including issues relating to violations of human rights.
The President has asked me to reply to your letter. We
regret the delay in responding to your inquiry.

Please be assured that the United States Government is
committed to protecting the fundamental human rights -- the
rights to freedom of association, assembly, religion,
belief, conscience, and expression -- of Uighurs and others
living in China. These issues have been, and will continue
to be, a central part of our agenda with the Chinese
Government.

 I hope this information is helpful in addressing your
concerns.

Sincerely,

David S. Sedney
Acting Director
Office of Chinese and
Mongolian Affairs

Figure 7.1 Original Letter Sent by David S. Shedney, Acting Director, Office of Chinese and Mongolian Affairs of US Department of State, to President of East Turkistan National Freedom Center, Anwar Yusuf Turani.

independence. Recently, young Uyghurs in the diaspora formed the East Turkistan Youth Congress, joined by seventeen different Uyghur and East Turkistani organizations. They rejected the WUC's mission, collected 10,000 signatures, and declared that the WUC could not be the sole legitimate organization representing the genuine national aspirations of all people in East Turkistan and the diaspora.[43] This organization became popular among young Uyghurs, despite the fact that the WUC is gaining remarkable support in the international community.

SUMMARY

Uyghurs and Turkic Muslims desperately need to stop the Chinese state's current genocide. On the basis of their historical experiences in dealing with China, Uyghurs understand that, as long as China is autocratically ruled, it will probably always want to destroy democracy, freedom, and equality. However, except for a few Western nations led by the United States, which sees China as a direct danger to its hegemony, all other governments are hesitant to stand firm against China, which would eventually create a vacuum and drive China's autocratic, illiberal power to attempt to conquer the world. The realities displayed since 2017 made the people of East Turkistan quickly and deeply realize that, as long as Uyghurs live under Chinese colonization, severe oppression will continue. East Turkistan's failed struggle for freedom has in many ways led to two final choices that they are faced with today: either the people of East Turkistan suffer under state-sanctioned genocide or China's colonial rule in East Turkistan must come to an end.

NOTES

1. Michael Dillon, *Xinjiang: China's Muslim Far North West* (London and New York: Rutledge Curzon, 2004), 53.
2. Quoted in Dillon, *Xinjiang*, 55.
3. "Memorandum of a Discussion held by USSR Consul-General in Ürümchi, G. S. Dobashin, with First Secretary of the Party Committee of the Xinjiang Uyghur Autonomous Region, Comrade Wang Enmao, and Chair of the People's Committee, Comrade S. Äzizov," January 17, 1958, RGANI, fond 5, opis 49, delo 130, listy 54-56, trans. David Brophy, "Local Nationalisim" in Xinjiang 1957-1958, History and Public Policy Program Digital Archive, Wilson Center, Washington DC, https://digitalarchive.wilsoncenter.org/document/175894.
4. "Memorandum on a Discussion Held By the Consul-General of the USSR in Ürümchi, G.S. Dobashin, with Deputy Chairman of the People's Committee of the Xinjiang Uyghur Autonomous Region, Comrade Xin Lanting," January 12, 1958, "Local Nationalism" in Xinjiang 1957–1958, History and Public Policy Program Digital Archive, Wilson Center, Washington, DC, online at https://digitalarchive.wilsoncenter.org/document/175895.
5. Muhemmet Ehmet (eye witness), Phone interview, April 15, 2022.
6. Turdush Kasim (eye witness), Phone interview, April 16, 2022.

7. Dillon, *Xinjiang*, 36.

8. Yuan Ming, "Missed Historic Opportunity Recalled," June 11, 1992, 79–80, JPRC-CAR-92-039, JPRS Report, Foreign Broadcast Information Service, reproduced by US Department of Commerce National Technical Information Service, accessed October 21, 2021, https://apps.dtic.mil/sti/pdfs/ADA335616.pdf.

9. Ibid.

10. G.A. Res. 1514 (XV), Declaration on the Granting of Independence to Colonial Countries and Peoples, ¶4 (December 14, 1960), https://www.sfu.ca/~palys/UN-Resolution%201514.pdf.

11. Abdulehet Mehmet, telephone interview, September 6, 2021. Author's translation. Abdulehet Mehmet was able to hide and get away because, before the Chinese military arrived, he went to a nearby village to coordinate with Baren supporters. This manifesto is recorded on the basis of his memoir, and it was confirmed with other several witnesses who learned about it through Chinese radio broadcast at the time.

12. Austin Ramzy and Chris Buckley, "'Absolute No Mercy:' Leaked Files Expose How China Organized Mass Detentions of Muslims," *The New York Times,* November 16, 2019, accessed June 21, 2021, https://www.nytimes.com/interactive/2019/11/16/world/asia/china-xinjiang-documents.html.

13. Rong xing Guo, *China's Spatial (Dis)integration: Political Economy of the Interethnic Unrest in Xinjiang* (Kidlington, UK: Elsevier Ltd, 2015), 14.

14. Austin Ramzy and Chris Buckley, "'Absolute No Mercy:' Leaked Files," *The New York Times.*

15. Qemer, Sajide, Tursun, Mehmet, Nurgul, Group interview, conducted by author in Ghulja, April 1998 (redact last names for the protection of interviewees identity).

16. Antoine Blua, "China Says Ethnic Violence In Check Amid Heavy Troop Presence," *Radio Free Europe and Radio Liberty*, July 8, 2009, accessed January 5, 2022, https://www.rferl.org/a/Chinas_Ethnic_Violence_In_Check_Amid_Heavy_Troop_Presence/1772210.html.

17. Rishat Elkun, Phone interview, September 13, 2021.

18. Human Rights Watch Report, *We Are Afraid to Even Look for Them* (New York: Human Rights Watch, October 2019), accessed December 29, 2021, https://www.hrw.org/sites/default/files/reports/xinjiang1009webwcover.pdf.

19. Al Jazeera, "Troops Deployed in Uighur City" *Al Jazeera,* July 7, 2009, accessed December 23, 2021, https://www.google.com/search?client=safari&rls=en&q=%E2%80%9CTroops+deployed+in+Uighur+city%E2%80%9D+Al+Jazeera&ie=UTF-8&oe=UTF-8.

20. *Xinhua Net*, "Innocent Civilians Make up 156 in Urumqi Riot Death Toll," *Xinhua Net,* August 5, 2009, accessed August 5, 2009, http://www.xinhuanet.com/english/urumqiriot/latestnews.htm.

21. Michael Wines, "A Strongman Is China's Rock in Ethnic Strife," *New York Times*, July 20, 2009, accessed January 27, 2022, https://www.nytimes.com/2009/07/11/world/asia/11xinjiang.html.

22. Ilham Tohti, "My Ideals and Career Path I have Chosen," *Ilham Tohti Institute* (website), March 2020, accessed October 10, 2020, http://www.ilhamtohtiinstitute.org/?p=108.

23. Ibid.

24. Ilham Tohti, 伊力哈木, "Yilihamu. Toheti: Beijing de zhengce rang Xinjiang hui jiao tu geng bu man" 伊力哈木•土赫提:北京的政策让新疆回教徒更不满 [Ilham Tohti: Policy of Beijing Dissatisfied Muslims in Xinjiang More Than Ever], *Da Jiyuan,* June 14, 2010, accessed March3, 2022, https://www.epochtimes.com/b5/10/6/14/n2937204.htm.

25. Ilham Tohti, 伊力哈木, "Yilihamu: women shi yi ge zi ji zuo bu liao zhu de minzu," 伊力哈木: 我们是一个对自己作不了主的民族 [Ilham: We Are the People Who Cannot Rule Themselves] *weiwuer zai xian. [uighurbiz.net]*, December 13, 2012, accessed December 16, 2012.

26. Ibid.

27. Ilham Tohti 伊力哈木, "Diàochá:12.3% de wéiwú'ěr rén yào dúlì jiànguó, ér 81.3%Yào gāodù zìzhì" 调查：12.3%维吾尔人希望建立独立国家, 81.3%希望高度自治 [Survey: 12.3% of Uighurs Want to Establish an Independent Country, While 81.3% Want a High Degree of Autonomy], November 12, 2010, www.uighurbiz.net website was delated by the Chinese government. Article was saved by author as PDF. Article also can be find at https://uyghurbiz.org/调查：12-3的维吾尔人要独立建国，而81-3要高度自治/.

28. Ibid.

29. *Front Line Defenders* "Ilham Tohti Sentenced to Life Imprisonment," *Front Line Defenders*, January 15, 2018, accessed October 6, 2020, https://www.frontlinedefenders.org/en/case/ilham-tohti-sentenced-life-imprisonment.

30. BBC News, "What Does Xi Jinping's China Dream Mean?" *BBC News*, June 6, 2013, accessed November 19, 2021, https://www.bbc.com/news/world-asia-china-22726375.

31. Muhammmed Emin Bughra, *History of Est Turkistan*, last edition (Ankara: Ankara publishing, 1987), 422.

32. "Hon. John M. Murphy of New York, in the House of Representatives, 'Isa Yusuf Alptekin--Defender of Freedom'," Congressional Record (Bound Edition), Volume 116, Part 5 (March 3, 1970 to March 11, 1970), Extensions of Remarks, March 3, 1970, 5795–5796. History and Public Policy Program Digital Archive, Wilson Center, Washington, DC, https://digitalarchive.wilsoncenter.org/document/208600.

33. "Letter from Mohammad Emin Bugra, Former Deputy Chairman of Xinjiang Province, to Yolbars Khan, Chairman of the Office for the Xinjiang Provincial Government," May 10, 1954, History and Public Policy Program Digital Archive, 11-04-01-09-02-005. "Xinjiang nanmin yiju Tuerqi," West Asia Division, Ministry of Foreign Affairs, Archives of the Institute of Modern History, Academia Sinica, obtained by Justin Jacobs and translated by Caixia Lu, https://digitalarchive.wilsoncenter.org/document/123643.

34. "Letter, Muhammad Amin Bughra, Isa Yusuf Alptekin, and Colonel Adam Sabri to Owen Lattimore," April 6, 1950, Folder 14 "Sinkiang Refugees 1950–1951," Box 5, Subseries 3 (Correspondence), Series 4 (Owen Lattimore), Subgroup 2 (Administrative Records, 1924-1955), Record Group 08.010. Records of Walter Hines Page School of International Relations 1923/1955, Ferdinand Hamburger Archives, Sheridan Libraries. Johns Hopkins University," Obtained by Charles Kraus, History and Public Policy Program Digital Archive, Wilson Center, Washington, DC, http://digitalarchive.wilsoncenter.org/document/134644. [correct spelling of Muhammad Amin Bughra's name in Uyghur language: Muhammed Emin Bughra].

35. Jacob M. Landau, *Radical Politics in Modern Turkey*, Vol. 6 (New York: Routledge, 2016), 203.

36. Ibid.

37. "Isa Yusuf Alptekin, 'Memorandum Sent to Richard Nixon, President of the United States of America,'" July 12, 1969, History and Public Policy Program Digital Archive, Wilson Center, Washington, DC, https://digitalarchive.wilsoncenter.org/document/208601; Sea also "Isa Yusuf Alptekin, Doğu Türkistan İnsanlıktan Yardım İstiyor" [East Turkistan Expects Help from Humankind] (Otağ Matbaası, 1974): 112–13.

38. "Hon. John M. Murphy of New York, in the House of Representatives, 'Isa Yusuf Alptekin—Defender of Freedom'," Congressional Record (Bound Edition), Volume 116, Part 5 (March 3, 1970 to March 11, 1970), Extensions of Remarks, March 3, 1970, 5795–5796. History and Public Policy Program Digital Archive, Wilson Center, Washington, DC, https://digitalarchive.wilsoncenter.org/document/208600.

39. Yitzhak Shichor, "Dialogue of the Deaf: The Role of Uyghur Diaspora Organization Versus Beijing," in *The Uyghur Community: Diaspora, Identity and Geoplolitics,* ed. Guljanat Kurmangaliyeva Ercilasun and Konuralp Ercilasun (New York: Palgrave Macmillan 2018), 126.

40. Yitzhak Shichor, "Virtual Transnationalism: Uyghur Communities in Europe and the Quest for Eastern Turkestan Independence," in *Muslim Networks and Transnational Communities in and Across Europe,* ed. S. Allievi and J.S. Nielsen (Leiden, Boston: Brill, 2003), 294.

41. World Uyghur Congress, "Mission Statement," *World Uyghur Congress* (website), https://www.uyghurcongress.org/en/introducing-the-world-uyghur-congress/.

42. Original letter sent by the David S. Shedney, Acting Director Office of Chinese and Mongolian Affairs of United States Department of State to president of East Turkistan National Freedom Center Anwar Yusuf Turani.

43. Xelq Imza Herkiti, "World Uyghur Congress Does Not Represent The Collective Interest of Uyghurs," *Xelq Imza Herkiti(website),* January 2022, accessed January 7, 2022, https://xelqimzaherikiti.net.

8

China's Broken Promise of Internal Self-Determination

ARTIFICIAL AUTONOMY

The absolute right to self-determination of all people in colonial territories, as described in various UN resolutions discussed in the previous chapter, has always been understood to refer to all classic colonial peoples. The colonial status of East Turkistan demonstrates that it also falls under that paradigm. Even if it were not the case that East Turkistan were a colonial territory, independence would still be warranted, on the basis of China's failure to provide legally guaranteed autonomy, its harsh oppression, and its ongoing genocide against the region's peoples. If the people concerned are experiencing genocide and face elimination, it is impossible to maintain their existence under the political and legal system of the currently existing state. The international community therefore must resort to securing the independence of East Turkistan to prevent genocide and ensure peace.

The people of East Turkistan have never freely chosen to be associated with China. As explained in chapter 1, the so-called "peaceful liberation" was a forced annexation. The Chinese government never intended to establish real autonomy in East Turkistan. Even though Article 4 of the PRC Constitution states, "Regional autonomy is practised in areas where people of minority nationalities live in compact communities; in these areas organs of self-government are established for the exercise of the right of autonomy,"[1] this has never been implemented. Article 2 of the Regional Ethnic Autonomous Law states that "all ethnic autonomous areas are integral parts of the People's Republic of China."[2] This means autonomous regions, including East Turkistan (as the "Xinjiang Uyghur Autonomous Region"), do not have nominal rights to sovereignty in the Chinese constitution. Article 3 of this law requires, "Ethnic autonomous areas establish autonomous agencies that function as local agencies of state power at their respective levels. Autonomous agencies in ethnic autonomous areas shall apply the principle of democratic centralism."[3] This indicates the principle that the local government has to be run under the unified leadership of the Chinese central government. Even so, the people of East Turkistan are not allowed to elect their representatives and participate in the government of the territory.

From the beginning, CCP general Wang Zhen, who governed Xinjiang after 1949, had maximum power to control the region under China's central government administration. In February 1951, fifty-one intellectuals in East Turkistan, including Uyghurs, Kazaks, and Russians, held a secret meeting where they discussed demanding the withdrawal of the People's Liberation Army (PLA) from East Turkistan, self-governance, and sending a representative of the Uyghurstan Republic to the United Nations with the PRC delegation. Wang discovered this meeting, and the intellectuals were harshly criticized. According to his translator's memoir, Wang threatened them with death and said: "Demanding federating with China with some kind of republic is separatism! The 'fifty-one meeting' is treason! Their heads will roll!"[4] Subsequently, according to a CIA report, the Communist government trained a mass cohort of Uyghur and other ethnic minority cadres far more intensely than in other ethnic regions, in order to ensure their loyalty before announcing the establishment of "Xinjiang Uyghur Autonomous Region" in 1955.[5] According to the same report's estimates, 2,600,000 books and periodicals were published in the region by the CCP to promote patriotism for China and internationalism.[6] Furthermore, between 1951 and 1952, every woman and man was required to secure a certificate of loyalty to the CCP and one of the personal loyalty certificates to Mao Zedong.[7] Although Seypidin Ezizi, an ethnic Uyghur, was appointed as the chairman of the People's Council of the new "autonomous region," real power was in the hands of Party Secretary Wang Enmao and PLA General Wang Zhen, both ethnic Han Chinese. Turkic Muslims held no leadership positions with decision-making or executive power, and those leaders were appointed or elected only for propaganda purposes. This system successfully hid settler colonialism and artificial autonomy by creating an image of Han and non-Han officials coexisting.

The situation has not changed since. According to a report by the Australian Strategic Policy Institute (ASPI), more than 170 CCP offices, including government, military, paramilitary, and hybrid administrative entities, have participated in oppressing Uyghurs and other Turkic Muslims.[8] Further research also confirms that not a single crucial leadership post in "Xinjiang," including of course the party secretary, is held by an Uyghur or other local non-Han. Unlike every one of China's provincial-level government's vice governors, only "Xinjiang's" vice governors are CCP members and are absolutely in line with China's party-state lines.[9]

The same power division is mirrored at every regional-, prefecture-, city-, county-, and township-level government administrative office, educational institution, public health institution, civil affairs office, propaganda office, and so on. The central government has appointed each successive executive for the government of "Xinjiang," while the Supreme People's Court and Supreme People's Procuratorate hold supreme power over the region's courts and legal system.[10] The presiding judge, deputy presiding judge, integrity inspector, and secretary of the Sixth Circuit of the Supreme People's Court, which includes East Turkistan, are Han. So is the party secretary of the People's Procuratorate of Xinjiang.[11] The Uyghur Human Rights Project has documented that Han Chinese occupy 64% of senior posts and Uyghurs barely 20% in eighty-one regional positions.[12] Recently, Chinese state media published an article announcing that all ethnic groups practice democracy and enjoy voting rights, electing county- and township-level people's congress members, and that these members voted and elected sixty-one representatives to the regional-level people's congress and thirty-eight of them non-Han.[13] However, the entire population of East Turkistan is under digital surveillance and extreme scrutiny to ensure loyalty, which obviously gives the lie to any claims of genuine democracy.

OPPRESSIVE RULE

The people of East Turkistan have no right to equal citizenship with Han since their political, territorial, and economic functions were never granted. China's Regional Ethnic Autonomy Law, Article 32, states:

> Autonomous agencies in ethnic autonomous areas have the power to autonomously administer the finances of their areas. All revenues accruing to the ethnic autonomous areas under the financial system of the state shall be managed and used by autonomous agencies in these areas on their own.[14]

However, the so-called Xinjiang Uyghur Autonomous Region has no freedom to manage and use revenues or manage independently local economic development, education, science, and public health, or exercise their rights to develop and protect their cultural heritage. The central government operates the region's two dominant industries, oil and gas. China National Petroleum Corporation has the majority share of the region's oil industry. Chinese state-owned enterprises (SOEs), such as energy giants PetroChina and Sinopec, exploit oil and natural gas resources in East Turkistan, and these pay income tax to Beijing instead of "Xinjiang."[15]

The autonomy promised to the people of East Turkistan has been denied, while they have been denied basic economic benefits from their prosperous land, moving through gradual deprivation to total destruction. The Eighth National People's Congress promulgated the Labor Law of the PRC on July 5, 1994, Article 12 of which states: "Laborers, regardless of their ethnic group, race, sex, or religious belief, shall not be discriminated against in employment."[16] However, economic segregation and refusal to hire Uyghurs in urban areas are common, even if they fluently speak Chinese and are well-educated. As of 2010, only 0.45% of Uyghurs were employed in government institutions, party organizations, enterprises, and business units in "Xinjiang," compared to 3.37% of Chinese.[17] These figures are disproportionate to the region's overall population, in which Uyghurs accounted for 45.84% and Han 40.47% that year. Further statistics show that Uyghurs and other Turkic people were mainly employed in the agricultural sector, while Han Chinese were employed in secondary (construction and manufacturing) and tertiary industries (service, schools, hotels, and restaurants).[18] Those statistics, it must be emphasized, do not indicate that Uyghurs have land ownership rights—as discussed in chapter 7, XPCC and Chinese settlers have gradually driven Uyghur and other Turkic farmers off of their land, and they increasingly work for those settlers. Populations statistics abruptly changed in 2017, when the Chinese government rounded up Uyghurs for forced labor manufacturing jobs with little or no payment. A Chinese government white paper estimates that 2.76 million "surplus rural workers" had been "transferred" or "relocated" annually, though the white paper does not specify how many times people were transferred for forced labor.[19] Mass incarceration and state-sponsored relocation affected 90% of Uyghur agricultural and residential towns, villages, and counties. Some villages have been completely evacuated.[20] This could dramatically affect Turkic people's basic living conditions, long-term survival, and growth, leading to the total destruction of the nation of East Turkistan.

SELF-GOVERNMENT IN LOCAL AFFAIRS: RELIGION, EDUCATION, AND CULTURE

The regional government has almost no freedom to manage education, science, and public health, each of which the Chinese central government strictly controls, despite the fact that Article 1 of the Regional Ethnic Autonomy law guarantees regional autonomy.[21] The Autonomous Region government instead has to ask permission from the Standing Committee of the National People's Congress, as stated in Article 116 of the PRC's 1982 Constitution:

> The people's congresses of ethnic autonomous areas shall have the power to formulate autonomous regulations and local-specific regulations in accordance with the political, economic and cultural characteristics of the ethnic groups in their areas. The autonomous regulations and local-specific regulations of autonomous regions shall go into effect after submission to the National People's Congress Standing Committee and receipt of approval. The autonomous regulations and local-specific regulations of autonomous prefectures and autonomous counties shall go into effect after submission to the standing committees of the people's congresses of their provinces or autonomous regions and receipt of approval, and shall be reported to the National People's Congress Standing Committee to be placed on record.[22]

The Standing Committee of the National People's Congress, which thus has the final approval on any and all regional policies, does not permit the formulation or implementation of any policy to benefit ethnic people in the region but instead favors Han settlers.

Such control is particularly dissonant with the Autonomous Region government's guaranteed right to govern culture independently. The regional government has the right to determine the educational plan, the establishment of schools, school system, the forms by which schools are run, curricula, the language of teaching, and the method of enrollment, in accordance with principles concerning education and legal provisions of the state basis on the Regional Autonomy and Ethnic Minority law of China.[23] Article 121 of the 1982 PRC Constitution also states that autonomous governments are to use local non-Han languages:

> In performing their functions, the organs of self-government of the national autonomous areas, in accordance with the autonomy regulations of the respective areas, employ the spoken and written language or languages in common use in the locality. [24]

However, since 1997, the Xinjiang authority has implemented an Orwellian "bilingual education" policy, according to which Uyghur and other non-Han students are sent to inland China as part of "Xinjiang classes" to learn only the Chinese language.[25] Today, the Uyghur language is gradually being eliminated, as Uyghur schools have been shut down, and Uyghur children have been sent to mandatory Chinese-language boarding schools where they are not allowed to speak the Uyghur language.[26] Since early 2017, nearly all schools in East Turkistan have been transformed into monolingual Chinese-language boarding schools, under the guidance of a new Chinese government document titled "The Standard Plan for Bilingual Education Curriculum in the Compulsory Education Phase of the Autonomous Region."[27] In 2018, an ethnic Han Chinese was appointed president of "Xinjiang" University.[28] This is another example of the central government's total control of education in the region.

In violation of Section 3, Article 4, of China's Regional Ethnic Autonomy Law, "Respecting and Guaranteeing the Freedom of Religious Belief of Ethnic Minorities," religious institutions are also tightly controlled by the central government, which is gradually achieving the eradication of Islam. This effort was enshrined in law in 2018 with the "Decision to Revise the 'Xinjiang Uighur Autonomous Region Regulation on De-Extremification,'" which could criminalize Muslims for engaging with basic Islamic beliefs and practices.[29] This law, specific to the Autonomous Region, was directly approved by Xi Jinping. Article 43 of the regulation emphasizes the Sinicization of religion:

> Religious schools and institutions should adhere to the direction of sinocizing religion, and earnestly perform the duties of cultivating and training religious professionals, to prevent permeation by extremification.

Article 4 not only specifies that these efforts shall persist, it also implies an inherent opposition between Islam and Chinese culture:

> De-extremification shall persist in the basic directives of the party's work on religion, persist in an orientation of making religion more Chinese and under law, and actively guide religions to become compatible with a socialist society.

The suggestion here is that "socialist society" is equivalent to Han culture, and that Han culture is in turn nonreligious. This is false, as religion has no commonplace in China, and religion and Chinese culture are in any case conceptually distinct. This law conflates them.

Before these religious restrictions came into effect, the central government gradually took control of religious institutions through the Islamic Association of China, which is responsible for training and appointing imams. Those imams are tightly controlled and directed by the party. Party-trained clerics use their propaganda power to control Muslims in the region, and they are often effective. They distort Islam to the benefit of Chinese imperialism and the party. At the end of 2017, China's State Administration of Religious Affairs (SARA) and State Ethnic Affairs Commission (SEAC) were both absorbed by China's United Front Work Department (*tongyi zhanxian gongzuo bu* 统一战线工作部), which means that the religion and ethnicity East Turkistan's people are directly controlled by party and its Han leaders.[30] The United Front Work Department is the most potent party organization, designated to penetrate every section of people's lives and liaise with all forces outside the CCP. It is strictly controlled by the CCP and implements its orders. It has four bureaus related to the East Turkistan crisis, including the Xinjiang Work Bureau, Ethnic Work Bureau, and two different Religious Work Bureaus whose concrete functional differences remain obscure.[31] These latter two bureaus were added in 2018 to prioritize and specifically target and control Uyghur and other Turkic Muslims. Since 2015, "Sinicization of religion" has become the CCP's main anti-Islam slogan in East Turkistan, and this apparatus implements it.

In October 2017, under Xi Jinping's "Thoughts on Socialism with Chinese Characteristics for a New Era," Chinese authorities intensified the "Sinicization of Islam."[32] This reflected an immediate implementation of the "Regulations on Religious Affairs" published in East Turkistan in September 2017.[33] Xi Jinping gave several speeches about how to develop religion in the Chinese context, in which he stated: "Religions in China have increasingly been Chinese in orientation, and religious groups have kept enhancing their recognition of the motherland, the Chinese nation, the Chinese culture, the CPC and socialism with Chinese characteristics." He also stressed training puppet religious personnel: "Fostering a group of religious figures who are politically reliable, have noble characters and religious accomplishments, and can play their role at critical times."[34] Chen Quanguo, the former party secretary of "Xinjiang," gave a speech at the standing committee of the regional party committee, in which he also emphasized the "Sinification of Islam."[35] It is self-evident that this policy refers to assimilating Turkic Muslims' religious beliefs to Xi Jinping thought, as the party restricts Islam and forces Muslims to memorize his writings.

Even though autonomous regions have the constitutional right to protect and preserve cultural heritage and develop culture according to international laws, China has destroyed Uyghur cultural heritage sites. Chinese authorities demolished the Old City of Kashgar, rebuilding or eradicating this ancient Uyghur city.[36] Satellite imagery has also found that more than 100 Muslim cemeteries in the region have been demolished in an effort to destroy Uyghurs' cultural connection to the land.[37]

Uyghur-style houses have also been destroyed, and Uyghurs are no longer allowed to decorate their house in Uyghur cultural style.

SUMMARY

Xi Jinping explained his approach and the role of the CCP at the Nineteenth Party Congress in 2017: "Government, the military, society and schools, north, south, east and west—the Party leads them all."[38] His speech reflects how the Chinese Party-state has secured and seeks to maintain total control everywhere, including in its colonies. China's central government possesses the decision-making power at every institutional level of the "Xinjiang Uyghur Autonomous Region" government, from legal institutions to educational institutions and religious institutions, and from policymaking to exploiting natural resources. Research by the ASPI even found that the Central Committee of the CCP, led by Xi in Beijing, directly administers East Turkistan's neighborhood subdistrict committees (*shequ* 社区), which are responsible for local party control and have engaged and played a big role in the genocidal operation against Turkic people in East Turkistan since 2014.[39] Under such conditions, it is obvious that "autonomy" is a myth, even by the narrow definitions provided by Chinese law. It is furthermore clear that China has restricted and redefined regional autonomy in order to neuter it of any power to protect or promote non-Han people in East Turkistan.

NOTES

1. XIANFA art. 4 (2004) (China).
2. Zhonghua Renmin Gonghe Guo Minzu Quyu Zizhi Fa (中华人民共和国民族区域自治法)
[Regional Ethnic Autonomy Law of the People's Republic of China] (promulgated by the Standing Comm. Nat'l People's Cong., May 31, 1984, effective October 1, 1984, amended at February 28, 2001) 1984 STANDING COMM NAT'I PEOPLES CONG. GAZ. art. 2 (China).
3. *Id.* art.3.
4. Chen ping, 陈 平,"Xīnjiāng shēngchǎn jiànshè bīngtuán de ruògān lìshǐ wèntí sīkǎo" 新疆生产建设兵团的若干历史问题思考[Analysis of Several Historical Issues of Xinjiang Production and Construction Corps], *Department of Sociology of Peking University*, PDF version available at: http://www.shehui.pku.edu.cn/upload/editor/file/20180829/20180829184531_5822.pdf.
5. Central Intelligence Agency Electronic Reading Room, "Autonomous Governments in Minority Inhabited Areas of Communist China," September 21, 1991, CIA/RR-G-7, p45, Geographic Intelligence Report, accessed October 14, 2020, https://www.cia.gov/library/readingroom/docs/CIA-RDP79T01018A000100070001-3.pdf.
6. Ibid., 46.
7. Central Intelligence Agency Electronic Reading Room, "Chinese Communist Regime in Sinkiang Province," October 29, 2009, CIA-RDP80-00810A001400020009-5, General

CIA Record, accessed October 14, 2020, https://www.cia.gov/library/readingroom/docs/CIA
-RDP80-00810A001400020009-5.pdf.

8. Ibid.

9. Cheng Li, "Ethnic Minority Elites in China's Party-State Leadership: An Empirical
Assessment," *Brookings,* June 20, 2008, accessed November 10, 2021, https://www.brookings
.edu/articles/ethnic-minority-elites-in-chinas-party-state-leadership-an-empirical-assessment/.

10. Gardner Bovingdon, *The Uyghurs: Strangers in Their Own Land* (New York: Columbia
University Press, 2010), 49; See also: 中华人民共和国检察官法 (Zhōnghuá rénmín gòng-
héguó jiǎnchá guān fǎ) [Procurators Law of the People's Republic of China] (promulgated
by the Standing Comm. Nat'l People's Cong., February 28, 1995, amended and adopted at
September 1, 2017, rev'd. April 23, 2019) 1995 STANDING COMM NAT'I PEOPLES
CONG. GAZ. Chap. IV. art. 18 (China).

11. Uyghur Human Rights Project, *Simulated Autonomy: Uyghur Underrepresentation in
Political Office,* September 2017, https://www.academia.edu/35113506/Simulated_Auton-
omy_Uyghur_Underrepresentation_in_Political_Office.

12. Ibid.

13. Liu Xin and Fan Lingzhi, "Xinjiang Regional Government Introduces Democracy
Practices, Lashes Out at US democratic Hegemony," *Global Times,* December 6, 2021,
accessed December 7, 2021, https://www.globaltimes.cn/page/202112/1240812.shtml.

14. Regional Ethnic Autonomy Law of the People's Republic of China, supra note 2, art
32.

15. Shan, Wei, and Cuifen Weng. "China's New policy in Xinjiang and Its Challenges." *East Asian Policy* 2, no. 3 (2010): 60.

16. Zhong Hua Renmin Gongheguo Laodong Fa (中华人民共和国劳动法) [Labour
Law of the People's Republic of China,] (promulgated by the Standing Comm. Nat'l People's
Cong., July 5, 1994, effective Jan.1, 1995) 1994 STANDING COMM NAT'I PEOPLES
CONG. GAZ. Chap. IV. art. 12 (China).

17. Li Jianxin and Chang Qingling, 李建新, 常庆玲 "Xīnjiāng gè zhǔyào mínzú rénkǒu
xiànzhuàng jí biànhuà tèzhēng" 新疆各主要民族人口 现状及变化特征 [The Current
Situation and Changing Characteristics of Major Ethnic Group Population in Xinjiang]
Xīběi mínzú yánjiū 西北民族研究 [N. W. Journal of Ethnology], 3, (2015): 28–29,
accessed December 30, 2021, http://www.shehui.pku.edu.cn/upload/editor/file/20171212
/20171212180106_2459.pdf.

18. Ibid.

19. The State Council Information Office of the People's Republic of China, *Full Text:
Employment and Labour Rights in Xinjiang* (Beijing: Foreign Language Press Co Ltd, September 17, 2020), accessed December 11, 2021, http://english.www.gov.cn/archive/whitepaper
/202009/17/content_WS5f62cef6c6d0f7257693c192.html.

20. Photographer and Traveller "Speaking Turkish With Turkish Uyghurs- Xinjiang
Uyghur Autonomous Region in China-2" YouTube video, 00:10:12, uploaded December 22,
2018, accessed January 17, 2022, https://www.youtube.com/watch?v=03vSjiyLgK0.

21. Regional Ethnic Autonomy Law, supra note 2, art. 1.

22. XIANFA, supra note 1, art. 116.

23. Regional Ethnic Autonomy Law, supra note 2, art. 10.

24. XIANFA, supra note 1, art. 121.

25. United States, Congressional – Executive Commission on China, *2012 Annual
Report,* accessed March8, 2022 https://www.cecc.gov/publications/annual-reports/2012
-annual-report#IV.%20Xinjiang.

26. See chapter 2 for more detail.

27. Qiao Long and Yang Fen, "China Bans Use of Uyghur, Kazakh Textbooks, Materials in Xinjiang Schools," *Radio Free Asia,* October 13, 2017, accessed October 18, 2020, https://www.rfa.org/english/news/uyghur/ethnic-textbooks-10132017135316.html/.

28. Yojana Sharma," Alarm Over Choice of New Leader for Xinjiang University," *University World News,* October15, 2020, accessed October 16, 2020, https://www.universityworld-news.com/post.php?story=20201015084137568.

29. China Law Translate, "Decision to Revise the 'Xinjiang Uighur Autonomous Region Regulation on De-Extremification,'" *China Law Translate* (webpage), October 10, 2018, accessed May 19, 2020, https://www.chinalawtranslate.com/en/decision-to-revise-the-xinji-ang-uighur-autonomous-region-regulation-on-de-extremification/.

30. World Watch Monitor, "China's Communist Party Increases Control Over Religious Affairs," *World Watch Monitor,* March 27, 2018, accessed May 7, 2021, https://www.world-watchmonitor.org/coe/chinas-communist-party-increases-control-over-religious-affairs/.

31. Alex Joske, "Reorganizing the United Front Work Department: New Structures for a New Era of Diaspora and Religious Affairs Work," *China Brief,*19, no. 9 (May 2019), accessed February 3, 2022, https://jamestown.org/program/reorganizing-the-united-front-work-department-new-structures-for-a-new-era-of-diaspora-and-religious-affairs-work/.

32. Benoît Vermander, "Sinicizing Religions, Sinicizing Religious Studies," *Religions* 10, no. 2 (2019): 137. doi: 10.3390/rel10020137.

33. Zongjiao Shiwu Tiaolie (宗教事务条例) [Regulations on Religious Affairs] (promul-gated by the Standing Comm. Nat'l People's Cong., June 14, 2017, effective February 1, 2018) 2017 STANDING COMM NAT'I PEOPLES CONG. GAZ.

34. Xinhua Net, "Xi Stresses Developing Religions in Chinese Context," *Xinhua Net,* December 4, 2021, accessed January 18, 2022, http://www.news.cn/english/2021-12/04/c_1310352026.htm.

35. Xinjiang Ribao 新疆日报 " Zizhiqu dangwei hui zhuchi huiyi Chenchuanguo jiang hua" 自治区党委常委会主持会议 陈全国讲话[The Standing Committee of the Autonomous Region Party Committee Chaired the Meeting: Chen Quanguo's Speech], *Xinjiang Ribao* 新疆日报October 11, 2020, accessed October 20, 2020, http://news.ts.cn/system/2020/10/11/036459586.shtml.

36. United States, Congressional – Executive Commission on China, *2012 Annual Report.*

37. Ibid.

38. Nectar Gan," Xi Jinping Thought- the Communist Party's Tighter Grip on China in 16th Characters," *South China Morning Post,* October 25, 2017, accessed October 20, 2020, https://www.scmp.com/news/china/policies-politics/article/2116836/xi-jinping-thought-communist-partys-tighter-grip-china.

39. Vicky Xiuzhong Xu, James Leibold, and Daria Impiombato, *Exposing the Chinese Government's Oppression of Xinjiang's Uyghurs* (Canberra: Australian Strategic Policy Institute, October 2021), accessed January 17, 2022, https://www.aspistrategist.org.au/exposing-the-chinese-governments-oppression-of-xinjiangs-uyghurs/.

Conclusion

The Meaning of the Right to Sovereignty

LEGAL DIMENSIONS

Article 5 of the International Convention on the Elimination of All Forms of Racial Discrimination delineates several key aspects of internal self-determination. These include the right to equal treatment before the law, the right to the security of person, and, significantly,

> Political rights, in particular the rights to participate in elections to vote and to stand for election on the basis of universal and equal suffrage, to take part in the Government as well as in the conduct of public affairs at any level and to have equal access to public service.[1]

Clearly, the establishment of a democratic state structure and equality is a prerequisite for achieving internal self-determination. However, China is an undemocratic colonial power. Under that state, the people of East Turkistan have suspended their struggle for "must have" lawful rights—that is, independence—in order to fulfill their "urgent needs," which include equal rights, as well as basic human rights, despite the fact that they have no such prerequisite circumstances for their demand. Not unexpectedly, China has aggressively opposed their demands and retaliated with genocide.

The failure to secure basic human rights internally seems to leave the people of East Turkistan with no options. In today's world, international law has only recognized the need for external self-determination in extreme cases of the denial of internal self-determination, such as that of Kosovo. When we turn to the democratic states of the West, we find that the Canadian Supreme Court is one of few that have considered the question of external self-determination—which is to say,

143

independence—on a domestic basis. In the case of Quebec, the Canadian Supreme Court stated:

> A number of commentators have further asserted that the right to self-determination may ground a right to unilateral secession in a third circumstance. Although this third circumstance has been described in several ways, the underlying proposition is that, when a people is blocked from the meaningful exercise of its right to self-determination internally, it is entitled, as a last resort, to exercise it by secession. The *Vienna Declaration* requirement that governments represent "the whole people belonging to the territory without distinction of any kind" adds credence to the assertion that such a complete blockage may potentially give rise to a right of secession.[2]

That is to say that when internal self-determination is denied, and people are deprived of the possibility of pursuing access to political, economic, social, and cultural rights, this may indeed form a legal basis for the "last resort" of secession. For now, Quebec's guaranteed internal self-determination leads the Canadian Supreme Court to rule against Quebec's external self-determination or independence. However, the Supreme Court's ruling leaves open the possibility of independence in the case that the people of Quebec lose their internal rights.

It follows that, in the case of East Turkistan, where internal self-determination was never granted under the authority of the Chinese state, the false autonomy of the so-called "Xinjiang Uyghur Autonomous Region" forms a basis for internal self-determination. As we argued in the preceding pages, China's invasion of East Turkistan in 1949 violated the state integrity law stated in UN Charter Article 2(4). This same law has also become the main impediment to East Turkistan's peaceful independence today, as China claims that East Turkistan is an inseparable part of China and that its independence would consequently mean a violation of China's state integrity. Nonetheless, China's assertion of state integrity contradicts the UN General Assembly's Friendly Relations Declaration of 1970, which addresses the subject of conflicts between state integrity and self-determination on the basis of the principle of self-determination and equal rights of people. It emphasizes that a state will be recognized or considered a legitimate representative of its people only so long as it does not impede the political participation of people within the territory on the basis of their "race, creed, or color":

> [n]othing in the forgoing paragraphs shall be construed as authorizing or encouraging any action which would dismember or impair, totally or in part, the territorial integrity or political unity of sovereign and independent States conducting themselves in compliance with the principle of equal rights and self-determination of peoples as described above and thus possessed of a government representing the whole people belonging to the territory without distinction as to race, creed or colour.[3]

As we have detailed throughout this book, China neither represents the people of East Turkistan nor intends to do so, without such distinction. On the contrary, China has remanded the people of East Turkistan to second-class citizenship and now intends to eliminate them as a racial, religious, and ethnic group. It is

strange that China has received so little censure, and the independence movements of oppressed peoples within its territory so little support, when the international community is nominally united in its support for decolonization and
self-determination.

Consequently, the question of whether the right to be independent of East
Turkistan beyond the context of decolonization here should be answered basis on
"remedial secession" theory. This theory was introduced by Lee Buchheit,[4] and it
received broad support in academia, including by Ryngaert and Griffioen, who
elaborated the conditions granting the right to unilateral secession as follows:

1. [If] the "people" has a distinct identity, and represents a clear majority within
    a given territory;
2. massive violations of basic human rights and systematic discrimination at the
    hands of a repressive regime have taken place;
3. violations cannot be prevented and remedied because the "people" is excluded
    from political participation, and is not given internal self-determination;
4. negotiation between the "repressive" regime and "people" lead nowhere.[5]

As we have discussed, the people of East Turkistan should be regarded as a people
belonging to a state of East Turkistan, whose right to internal self-determination
has been denied since China colonized the region. Currently, the people of East
Turkistan are suffering ongoing genocide, and, as we have shown, the government
at every level, from Xi Jinping downward, has declared that this policy is correct.[6]
That means that there is no adequate remedy to prevent this genocide, and that, at
this point, there is no hope for attaining genuine autonomy. Nor, for that matter,
is autonomy appropriate to the situation of East Turkistan, as it cannot bring lasting peace. First, the people of East Turkistan have learned through experience that
the autonomy guaranteed them has never been implemented, and surely never will
be, as demands for autonomy were brutally rejected. As long as China exists as an
autocratic state, there will be no democratic mechanism to guarantee their rights.
Furthermore, it is impossible to establish mutual trust and guarantee the absence of
violent conflict between the people of East Turkistan and the Chinese government,
including ethnic Han Chinese settlers.

Thus, external self-determination—independence—is the true last resort for the
restoration of the human rights of the people of East Turkistan. Furthermore, the
historical colonization of the territory substantially supports East Turkistan's claim
to external self-determination according to the principles of international law. Many
conventional laws and resolutions related to self-determination are linked to the
Convention on the Prevention and Punishment of the Crime of Genocide in terms
of peace and security of humanity because the crime of genocide is a significant
violation of human security and peace. For example, Article 1, Paragraph 2 of the
UN Charter proclaims the principle of equal rights and self-determination: "To
develop friendly relations among nations based on respect for the principle of equal
rights and self-determination of peoples, and to take other appropriate measures

to strengthen universal peace."[7] Article 55 also specifically proclaims the principle of equal rights and self-determination of peoples.[8] Moreover, Articles 2 and 56; Article 73, Chapter XI, regarding the Declaration Regarding Non-Self Governing Territories; and Article 76, Chapter XII, regarding the International Trusteeship System all indirectly created obligations for UN Member States with regard to the implementation of the provisions of Articles 1 and 55.[9] Many recent international instruments have also confirmed the principle of self-determination as articulated in Articles 1, 55, 73, and 76, which was also confirmed by Security Council Resolution 246 (1968) of March 1968.[10]

The principle of self-determination is not only a conventional law as stated in the Charter, but also in many General Assembly declarations and resolutions, including Resolution 1547 (XV) in December 1960, Resolution 2621 (XXV) of October 12, 1970, and the Declaration on the Occasion of the Twenty-fifth Anniversary of the United Nations (General Assembly Resolution 2627 (XXV)). Resolution 2621 (XXV) reaffirmed that "colonial peoples have the inherent right to struggle by all necessary means at their disposal against colonial Powers which suppress their aspiration for freedom and independence."[11] Program of action 7 in the same resolution also stated:

> All states shall undertake measures aimed at enhancing public awareness of the need for assistance in the achievement of complete decolonization and, in particular, creating satisfactory conditions for activities by national and international non-government organizations in support of the people under colonial domination.[12]

In the Declaration on the Deepening and Consolidation of International Détente, the Member States of the United Nations declared their reaffirmation of the Declaration on the Granting of Independence to Colonial Countries and People on December 14, 1960.[13] The Security Council, in Resolutions 183 (1963) and 218 (1965), has also reaffirmed the validity of the principle of the right to self-determination as stated in General Assembly Resolution 1514 (XV).[14]

Many other soft laws incorporate the principle of self-determination. These include the International Covenant on Civil and Political Rights[15] and the International Covenant on Economic, Social, and Cultural Rights, both of which entered into force in 1976;[16] the African Charter of Human and Peoples' Rights of April 1981;[17] and the Vienna Declaration and Programme of Action of June 1993. The Vienna Declaration, adopted by the World Conference on Human Rights in Vienna on June 25, 1993, recognizes the right of people to take any legitimate action in accordance with the Charter of the United Nations to realize their inalienable right of self-determination.[18] The declaration considers the denial of the right of self-determination to be a violation of human rights and underlines the importance of the effective realization of this right.

The justification for China's unlawful occupation of East Turkistan outlined in part I of this book should be enough to establish East Turkistan's intrinsic right to independence. However, China violates these fundamental rights, and other great powers and UN Member States have permitted that infringement. The former Soviet Union was instrumental in this breach and aided China's geopolitical maneuvering.

Today, in an era of international peace, East Turkistan's geopolitical significance may be different. The dissolution of the Soviet Union, China's hegemonic ambitions via the New Silk Road, and Russia's aggressive military invasion of its neighbors, in addition to China's never-implemented autonomy in the region and now genocide, have at least made the world aware of the dangers of ignoring imperialistic regimes. East Turkistan's genocide is not a human rights issue that China can address alone. As is customary, it is a geopolitical issue that is inextricably linked to global peace. In order to ensure the efficacy of General Assembly Resolution 738 (VIII) of November 28, 1953, which describes "the importance of the observance of and respect for the right of self-determination in the promotion of world peace and of friendly relations between peoples and nations,"[19] it is important for the people of East Turkistan to attain an independent and free state through the principle of the right to self-determination.

In 1960, the Declaration on the Granting of Independence for Colonial Countries and Peoples declared the unconditional necessity of guaranteeing independence from colonialism. Paragraph 4 of the declaration states that "all repression measures of all kind directed against dependent peoples should cease in order to enable them to exercise peacefully and freely their right to complete independence, and the integrity of their national territory shall be respected."[20] On the basis of this declaration and many others, and of conventional laws and resolutions in international law related to the principles of equal rights and self-determination, the external self-determination of the people of East Turkistan should be seen as legitimate, given both the history of colonization in the region as well as the present concern of genocide.

However, whether international law provides "remedial secession" to the people under oppression in contexts beyond decolonization has given rise to significant debate. As the International Court of Justice's (ICJ) Advisory Opinion on Kosovo states:

> Whether, outside the context of non-self-governing territories and peoples subject to alien subjugation, domination and exploitation, the international law of self-determination confers upon part of the population of an existing State a right to separate from that State is, however, a subject on which radically different views were expressed by those taking part in the proceedings and expressing a position on the question. Similar differences existed regarding whether international law provides for a right of "remedial secession" and, if so, in what circumstances.[21]

The ICJ's report answers the above question in Paragraph 83: "To answer that question, the Court need only determine whether the declaration of independence violated either general international law or the *lex specialis* created by Security Council resolution 1244 (1999)."[22] In Paragraph 95, the ICJ report also mentions how Security Council Resolution 1244 (1999), Paragraph 8 envisions a long-term solution:

> [a] political process towards the establishment of an interim political framework agreement providing for a substantial self-government for Kosovo, taking full account of the Rambouillet accords and the principles of sovereignty and territorial integrity of the

Federal Republic of Yugoslavia (FRY) and the other countries of the region, and the demilitarization of the KLA.[23]

So, it is unquestionable that international law supported Kosovo's self-determination only under the condition that the Federal Republic of Yugoslavia (FRY) was already dismantled. As a result, Security Council Resolution 1244 (1999) did not challenge the territorial integrity of the FRY. However, whether international law provides for a right of "remedial secession" to East Turkistan should also be decided according to its unique situation. There is no conflict between the integrity of the Chinese state and the right to self-determination of East Turkistan which aims to preserve collective identity and secure survival and freedom for its more than 12 million people. Even if China raises an objection to East Turkistan's "remedial secession" on the basis of Chinese state integrity, its claim should be rejected based on the context of illegal occupation and the degree of oppression.

INTERNAL AND EXTERNAL FACTORS
INDICATE ATTAINMENT OF INDEPENDENCE

The preceding section presented the legal dimensions of East Turkistan's independence based on the principles of equal rights and self-determination. This section will look at other aspects of independence through the lens of self-determination law. As stated earlier, Article 73 of the UN Charter, Resolution 1541, Principle VI requires countries to allow non-self-governing states to gain independence or freely associate with other states or integration on the basis of equality.[24] According to Principle I, Principle VI relates to non-self-governing territories known to be colonial. Although East Turkistan was not listed as a non-self-governing territory in General Assembly Resolution 66 (I), this does not alter its colonial status as an illegally occupied state. Furthermore, this list was determined by UN Member States, not by residents of occupied territories themselves. General Assembly Resolution 742 (VIII) lists factors that indicate the attainment of independence or self-government through another system. These factors are both internal and external including full international responsibility for the territory, UN membership eligibility, internal and territorial self-government, complete autonomy in terms of economic, cultural, and social affairs, as well as the sovereign right to its own national self-defense.[25] East Turkistan does not fully meet any of these conditions yet. However, it does have the potential capacity and legitimate right to meet all of them. The following analysis will provide the internal context and external dimensions of East Turkistan's case to conclude why its people should regain their independent state based on the "factors indicative of attainment of independence" in Resolution 742(VIII), in accordance with the will of a colonized people.

Internal Context

This section summarizes the internal context of East Turkistan and its people in support of its pursuit of independence. According to Resolution 742 (VIII), a people's right to self-determination depends on their possession of a clear collective national identity and historical or current attachment to or ownership of the territory. They also should have an agenda for democratic statehood and a national will for independence in the internal context, as well as external factors that support their attaining independence rather than attaining autonomy.

East Turkistan is a region that is territorially, ethnically, religiously, and linguistically distinct from China. It was home to historically independent states prior to the Manchu invasion. There were two established, independent republics after the fall of the Manchu Qing Empire in 1912 and before Communist China's invasion in 1949. As the following section will demonstrate, tradition of statehood and its core values survive in political movements outside of China.

The national will of the people of East Turkistan is to regain their statehood and achieve full independence. This national desire has not arisen simply because they differ religiously, linguistically, or ethnically from the Chinese people. It existed prior to their sovereignty being violated and their territory being colonized. Even though people in East Turkistan have occasionally abandoned the legitimate demand for independence in favor of internal self-determination, nevertheless, doing so did not and could not represent their genuine national aspirations, as they had no freedom to express their political, territorial will and were compelled by geopolitical disadvantages, a lack of power, and suffering under harsh oppression without external assistance. Currently, because of China's genocide in the region, the national will to regain self-rule in response to the genocide is very strong. A strong demand for independence can be seen in the diasporas of all Uyghur and other Turkic Muslims, and this may represent the true voice of the people both inside and outside of East Turkistan's territory.

Not only does East Turkistan possess a history of democratic, independent statehood, but its people have also suffered for so long under an autocratic colonial regime that they yearn for freedom and democracy. Respect and tolerance for different races, colors, and religions are cultural values shared by Uyghurs and other Muslims in East Turkistan. They are also cultivating a national culture of spreading peace in order to strengthen their resilience in the face of Chinese state violence and oppression. The peaceful resistance of Uyghurs in the diaspora to China's current genocide is a prime example of this.

Members of East Turkistani diaspora organizations continue the long-established tradition of democratic statehood in the homeland. First of all, they derive some of their values from the four principles of the East Turkistan Islamic Republic founded in 1933: Islam, Freedom, Justice, and Brotherhood. Article 1 of the Constitution of the Republic stated that it was established in accordance with the commandments of the Holy Qur'an and principles of Islamic law. However, this does not mean that an independent East Turkistan will be governed solely by Islamic law—rather, democracy has seen not contrary to Islamic principles as Article 4 of the Constitution stresses free discussion, populism (will of the people), and democratic free and fair elections are core East Turkistani political values and democratic form to defend needs of ordinary citizens. Populism was included here to ensure a clear focus on people's needs, equal participation, and equal standing in front of the rule of law as they seek emancipation from oppression.

Furthermore, both republics in 1933 and 1944 recognized Islam as a main religion of the country. The East Turkistan Government in Exile and other main political organizations in diaspora today likewise respect Islam as a religion of the majority of East Turkistan. Nevertheless, their statehood agenda promotes religious freedom and a secular state that includes separation of state and religion. Furthermore, achieving the "Free and Sovereign State of East Turkistan" was one of the very significant and core principles of the East Turkistan Islamic Republic, as well as today's national aspiration of the people of East Turkistan. Justice (*adalat*) was also emphasized in the East Turkistan Islamic Republic's emblem along with two important sections (*suras*) from the Qur'an that related to justice. The English translation of these *suras* from the Qur'an and the national emblem as shown in figure 9.1 are follows:

> Indeed, Allah commands you to return trusts to their rightful owners; and when you judge between people, judge with fairness. What a noble commandment from Allah to you! Surely Allah is All-Hearing, All-Seeing.[26] (Qur'an 4:58, *an-Nisa*) Allah enjoins to do justice and adopt good behavior and to give relatives (their due rights), and forbids shameful acts, evil deeds and oppressive attitude. He exhorts you, so that you may be mindful.[27] (Qur'an 16: 90, *an-Nahl*)

The principle of justice was reflected in the national character of the East Turkistan government in 1933. That state was founded to promote justice and equality and was opposed to all forms of oppression. Justice was established through the rule of law to ensure that all of East Turkistan's institutions, entities, and people were held accountable to the law. The principle of "brotherhood" referred to relations with all humanity, including peace-loving people, rather than only Muslims. One article published in the

Figure 9.1 National Emblem of Islamic Republic of East Turkistan. *Source*: Reprinted from Bughra, Muhemmed Emin. *History of East Turkistan*, Last edition. Ankara: Ankara Publishing, 1987.

East Turkistan Republic's state newspaper *Free East Turkistan*, "Either Unity or War" (*Ya Ittipaq Ya Harab*), in 1933 clarified the meaning of "brotherhood" as follows:

> People can be united and can form brotherhood because of their language, religion, territory or because of common problems. Mongols in East Turkistan are not Muslims, but there is enough reason that they can be our brothers.[28]

The statehood vision and agenda of East Turkistan organizations in the diaspora on behalf of all East Turkistan have been developed further on the basis of these four principles from the East Turkistan Republics of 1933 and 1944. The statehood agenda aims to usher in a new era of liberation for East Turkistan, establishing equality, peace, and justice for all ethnic groups in the country. The Uyghur Research Institute, based in Ankara, Turkey, is led by Dr Erkin Ekrem and his assistant Nijat Turghun, who amended these principles and submitted them to Uyghur organizations for discussion. The principles of "brotherhood" amended to "peace," and the "welfare state" has been added. Uyghur intellectuals and leaders briefly revised these amended principles of statehood agenda at the Uyghur Research Institute's Belgium conference in April 2018 and the Utrecht conference in November 2019. The author added, "knowledge and science" for further discussion. The author's draft interpretation and further development of the amended statehood agenda principles are follows:

1. *Freedom:* People of East Turkistan will establish a free and sovereign state, against any kind of oppression and colonization.
2. *Politically Secular State:* Islam is the religion of the majority population of East Turkistan. However, the State of East Turkistan will be formulated according to political secularism and protect everybody's freedom of conscience, religion, and belief, by maintaining neutrality between them.
3. *Justice:* Independent East Turkistan will establish equality and rule of law to ensure citizens are all equal under the law itself and develop principles of political, social, and legal rights, including the right to vote, the right to freedom of expression, the right to participate in political activities, the right of freedom to move around in East Turkistan, the right to live or leave, the right to work and education within East Turkistan, and the right to have freedom, equality, and security.
4. *Peace:* Independent East Turkistan will establish friendly relationships with all peace-loving nations in respect of the UN Declaration on Principles of International Law Friendly Relations and Co-operation among States in Accordance with Charter of the United Nations.
5. *Welfare State:* Independent East Turkistan will ensure peace and prosperity, including the vision of a welfare state that protects the security and economic and social well-being of all people in East Turkistan. It will establish public provision of basic education, health services, and housing, as well as anti-poverty programs.

6. *Knowledge and Science:* The East Turkistan state will attach great importance to knowledge and development of science. It will provide equal opportunity to access all kinds of education for the people of East Turkistan.[29]

A question related to the principle of justice will need to be addressed if there is a referendum; this concerns the voting rights of the Chinese settlers who migrated to East Turkistan. Even though this question was not included in the draft statehood agenda, according to the author's research, most Uyghurs and other Turkic Muslims in the diaspora agree that Han Chinese settlers should not be allowed to vote in a referendum. The main reason for this opinion is apparent and logical. First and foremost, the case of East Turkistan, should be considered both in the context decolonization and beyond it, particularly given the fact of an active genocide. So, it is necessary to define the Uyghurs and other Turkic Muslims in the region as colonized and oppressed "people" who are not a minority ethnic group within the Chinese nation-state. The term "people" in international law refers to the territory of the colonized state as well as to an oppressed nation; it is not to be confused with any other definition of "people." Thus, Han Chinese settlers in East Turkistan should not be defined as "people" of East Turkistan and should not have the right to vote if there is a democratic, peaceful process of independence because they do not fall into the category of colonial peoples or oppressed peoples.

In the diaspora, exile organizations and newly formed political organizations work hard to preserve Uyghur culture, religion, and language. They also work hard to raise awareness about China's egregious violations, protect East Turkistan's legitimate territorial and political rights, fight for East Turkistan's collective rights, and cultivate a democratic, peace-loving statehood vision. They have also pledged to work with peace-loving states, institutions, governments, and non-governmental organizations. Ultimately, the goal is for East Turkistan to gain independence based on moral and legal principles of international law. Article 9 of the Constitution of the East Turkistan Government in Exile (ETGE), for example, states:

> The essential tasks of the Government-in-Exile . . . are to gain the support of those nations amongst the Free World who adhere to principles of democracy, rule of law, peace and respect for human rights, as well as all international organizations under the leadership of United Nations, and all international human rights organizations that cooperate therewith, in order to oppose China's state terrorism against the people of East Turkistan, and in order to achieve the independence of our country, East Turkistan.[30]

East Turkistan Youth Congress's (ETYC) political program Article 2 similarly states its goals as follows:

> Endeavors for the peaceful establishment of the democratic and secular East Turkistan Republic in accordance with international law, in which the cultural identity, political rights and religious freedom of the people of East Turkistan (currently colonized and occupied by the Chinese regime and territory is identified as Xinjiang Uyghur

Autonomous Region, which translated from Chinese as New Colony/Frontier, Uyghur Autonomous Region) are protected. Our goal is to protect our countrymen/women in the diaspora from the Chinese regime's threat and empower them by working with like-minded people who strive for the same goal as we do.[31]

The ETGE and ETYC both strictly promote the national aspiration for independence and collective rights of the people of East Turkistan and are working diligently to promote and practice the principles of democracy and democratic elections in the diaspora.

The unpublished Constitution of World Uyghur Congress (WUC), the most powerful Uyghur organization in the diaspora, states that its principle is to initiate and proceed with activities to protect the national interests of East Turkistan.[32] Even though the WUC's stated goal in its constitution is to gain self-determination, it is not clearly specified whether the national interest of East Turkistan is internal self-determination or independence. Like other organizations in the Uyghur Diaspora, in Principle 5(3) of their constitution, the WUC expresses, "WUC agrees to act according to the principles of separation of religion and state and of majority democracy, and is opposed to totalitarian systems of any kind."[33] Even though the organizational name "World Uyghur Congress" only refers to the Uyghur ethnicity in East Turkistan, they nevertheless promote equal rights for all the people of East Turkistan. Article 5(2) of their constitution states one of their principles: "WUC agrees to respect the rights of all peoples living in East Turkistan alongside the Uyghurs, regardless of their race, creed or language, and to be committed to their equality and promote the development of the individual cultures."[34]

Another organization, the International Union of the East Turkistan Organizations (IUETO), which includes a major Uyghur organization, called Maarif, but separated from WUC, ETGE, and ETYC, also firmly advocates for the independence of East Turkistan in its constitution.[35] Article 9 of the IUETO Constitution states, "Our organization will endeavor all legitimate means and possible solutions that are not conflicting to our national principles and national interests in order to attain complete independence of our homeland East Turkistan and establish an independent state."[36] They have also followed the principle of "brotherhood" from the East Turkistan Republic in 1933 to promote peace in their constitution as follows:

> Our organization appeals all states and organizations in the world to free East Turkestan from the Chinese occupation and we will cooperate with them on the basis of our national interest. In the process of attaining this, we will never give up on national principles and will prefer the moderate pathway to achieve our political aspiration.

Consequently, we can see that East Turkistani diaspora organizations not only continue to uphold longstanding democratic principles and institutions from the region but may also express the national will for independence. This also makes the position of Uyghur and other Turkic Muslims in the diaspora more likely to be compatible with any powers that might face direct or indirect threat and harm from

China. In that sense, the East Turkistani people are ideally positioned in their ability to play a crucial role and develop coalitions, making them a significant source of freedom defenders in the face of China's expansion.

Armed conflict remains a remote possibility. According to Article 1(4) of the Additional Protocol (I) to the Geneva Conventions of August 12, 1949, "Armed conflicts in which peoples are fighting against colonial domination, alien occupation or racist regimes are to be considered international conflict."[37] However, this is exclusively humanitarian and does not affect the legal status of the party as Geneva Conventions, as Article 3(4), specifies.[38] Paragraph 165 of Article 4 of the Commentary of 1987, Legal Status of the Parties to the Conflict, also emphasizes this:

> As stated in the Commentary to the Conventions, (6) paragraph 4 of common Article 3 is essential; without it, neither Article 3 nor any other in its place would ever have been adopted, because it was necessary to indicate in the clearest possible way that the article is exclusively of a humanitarian nature, and cannot confer any special protection or immunity on a Party, or increase its authority or power in any way.[39]

In other words, even if there is a chance for the people of East Turkistan to use armed forces, the United Nations cannot consider their struggle as self-defense and provide special protection but only humanitarian assistance. East Turkistan's exile forces perfectly understand the meaning of this convention. However, if survival from genocide is not possible through peaceful means, and the international community continues to widely ignore the cause, under such circumstances only, East Turkistan exile forces may be interested in recruiting and establishing military units under the East Turkistan flag. This would be fully under all applicable military laws if any state permitted them to form and train military units for East Turkistan as exiles through mutual cooperation. Currently, the exiled group of East Turkistani people who formed the East Turkistan Islamic Party have established their small armed forces in Syria's war zone to provide future national defense for the state of East Turkistan.[40]

External Dimensions

China's New Silk Road Project: Ambition of Controlling the World

Colonialism is not limited to Europeans, as the concept of colonialism is rooted in expansionist policies of extraction and settlement. This is precisely the character of China's "Open Up the West" policy that targets the vast land of East Turkistan for exploitation. "Open Up the West" is the basis for China's later China's Belt and Road Initiative (BRI), or New Silk Road, through which China seeks to expand economically from Central Asia to Europe and beyond. This has rendered East Turkistan even more geo-strategically significant, as the region is pivotal to accomplishing such a project.[41] It is more difficult for China to challenge US hegemony and expand through the sea, but it is far easier for them to do so through the land as long as the East Turkistan issue is resolved, as there are no significant adversaries to China's expansion across Central Asia to the rest of the world. As East Asia and military history specialist professor Miles M. Yu stated, "Xinjiang region [is China's] ultimate strategic rear from where to counter the U.S.-led 'containment.'"[42]

The New Silk Road project creates economic connections between more than sixty-five countries. The purpose of this initiative is to erode the global democratic order by projecting China's economic power, wield capital exports as leverage to shape its interest in geo-strategic targets, and expand the dominance of its authoritarian political model.[43] For example, in 2017, the Chinese government established an international leadership academy that trains foreign officials to export China's governance and development model. This encompasses the use of online propaganda, methods for controlling online public opinion, suppressing dissent, encouraging foreign investment, and retaining foreign technologies.[44] The New Silk Road project is not limited to business and investments, it also includes networks of think tanks, media agreements, ties between cultural institutions and academic exchanges, sister city agreements, and people-to-people exchanges to spread China's political influence and control.[45]

This ambitious agenda is reflected in academic works such as Chinese scholar Zhao Tingyang's *Redefining a Philosophy for World Governance*, which promotes China's "Tianxia" (All-Under-Heaven) concept as a "leading world ideology." This text provides a framework for imposing China's new neo-imperialism, with an emphasis on a hierarchy that places China at the top.[46] East Turkistan become an experimental model for the achievement of their goal and Chinese leaders apparently believe that they cannot fulfill these imperialistic goals without an ideological war, genocide in East Turkistan if necessary, and achieving total Han Chinese settlers' dominance. Xi Jinping also emphasized this point in his top-secret speech by stating that "New Silk Road" requires stabilizing security in Xinjiang.[47] Evidently, the fundamental characteristics of Chinese colonialism include not only military and demographic occupation, and systematic and planned extermination of the colonized, but also manifesting Xi Jinping's "China Dream" under the banner of the "New Silk Road." It is also apparent that they intend to secure their genocide policy in East Turkistan by demonstrating their so-called "five principles" as the basis of a new world order, one of which is "non-interference in each other's internal affairs and territorial integrity."[48] China has been successful in establishing this new global order by selling its totalitarian political model to puppet states and UN Human Rights Council officials. So much is clear from UN Senior High Commissioner for Human Rights Michelle Bachelet and her team's visit to East Turkistan in May 2022, which did not include the "unfettered access" she demanded before her visit. Her team finally published their report at very last minute before her stepped out from her position as she complied with China's pressure and strongly resist to publish report.[49] It is well known how China renders international law ineffectual in its own interests, notably when it comes to East Turkistan, Tibet, and Taiwan's sovereignty. By pushing this new world order,

China attempts not only to weaken the US-led Western world order and replace US hegemony but also deliberately to obstruct the moral imperative of states to intervene in human rights violations, allowing any power to engage in any aggression and transforming the world into a cesspool of violence. In this regard, attaining East Turkistan's independence is not only meant to protect the people in the region and ensure peace and security but also significant to prevent China's ambitious plan of distorting international law and colonizing the world.

Strategic Location and Geopolitics

East Turkistan's geopolitical situation has a significant impact on its independence movement. Historically, great powers have always been interested in the region due to its geographical location, which plays a pivotal role in the heart of Asia as a main corridor of the ancient Silk Road. Despite the fact that the people of the region defeated Chinese Nationalist warlords and colonizers in most of East Turkistan and established their independent statehood twice, victory did not last, and the region fell into the hands of the Chinese Communists. Fear of Japanese influence in the region during the 1930s and of British and American influence during the 1940s drove Stalin to cooperate with China and destroy East Turkistan's independence. Today, neighboring Central Asian countries are not entirely free of Russian influence, and these newly independent countries are weak and autocratic, squeezed between two aggressive countries—Russia and China. However, as Russia's position in the Ukraine war deteriorates, these countries are more inclined to favor the West or see the West as a counterbalance to China. China also has close ties with Pakistan and Afghanistan. Turkey has very little influence in Central Asia and does not want to get into conflict with China alone. However, China's genocide reveals how China aggressively secures its geopolitical ambitions. China's clashes with Japan and other countries in the East China Sea, tensions with India over Aksai Chin, and its ongoing entanglements in North Korea's aggression all reveal China's dangerous imperialistic character. Furthermore, China's ambitions for geographical expansion through access and control of major sea lanes in South Asian harbors, which threatens Taiwan and US hegemony, as well as the national interests of Japan, Vietnam, the Philippines, Indonesia, and other states, are not hidden from the rest of the world.

Many states may believe that China's ambitions are limited to the East Asian region. In fact, the New Silk Road project, which places Central Asia and Europe in a position of dependence on China, and China's genocide in East Turkistan, which intends to "cleanse" its colony as a gateway to Europe before marching to the west, both illustrate that the country has ambitions to extend through Central Asia. In other words, China's New Silk Road project and ambition of expanding to the west have become the main motivations for their genocidal intent. Governments that have signed on to this project should conduct extensive research on China's "Open Up the West" policy in East Turkistan and learn from East Turkistan's current tragedy in order to protect their own sovereignty. China's aggressive policy in Hong Kong, as well as genocide in East Turkistan and gross human rights violations in Tibet, should serve as a serious wake-up call to the international community about what might happen if China succeeds in its ambitious plan to colonize the world via the geographical, economic, digital, cultural, and political New Silk Road project. Furthermore, ignoring these regions' issue will allow China's autocratic expansion to accelerate. It is critical to obstruct China's expansion in order to preserve the world's free and democratic values. In this geopolitical strategy, the legitimate right to regain sovereignty of East Turkistan must play a significant part.

China's Veto Power and East Turkistan's Sovereignty

China's veto power as a permanent member of the UN Security Council provides it opportunities to obstruct justice. East Turkistan's goal of attaining independence to prevent genocide through international law could face objection if China's veto power is not invalidated in this case. Historical examples show that China's respect for the Genocide Convention is highly political: China established its own special military tribunal in Shenyang and Taiyuan to try Japanese Imperial officials in 1956, and Chinese delegations actively support the creation of criminal tribunals for the former Yugoslavia and for Rwanda, while actively participating in the United Nations and its special agencies.[50] However, China did not sign and ratify the Rome Statute of the International Criminal Court (ICC). As several commentators stated, China may have failed to do so in order to avoid the ICC's intervention in its implementation of genocide and other oppressive policies.[51] As a result, it is unproductive to file complaints with the ICC against Chinese leaders. China did not make a declaration under Article 36(2) on the compulsory jurisdiction of the Court.[52] China also does not consider itself bound by Article IX of the Genocide Convention. Nevertheless, this convention is a norm of international law that can be imposed as a binding obligation on any state party. An Advisory Opinion of the ICJ further clarified: "The principles underpinning the Convention are accepted by civilized nations as binding on States even without any conventional obligation."[53] Consequently, any contracting state party could take China's genocide to the ICJ as a dispute per Article IX related to "the responsibility of a State for genocide."[54]

In this respect, the UN Security Council can consider the case of China's genocide, since all UN members are obliged to cooperate with ICC investigations in order to maintain peace and security. However, China may use its veto power among the Big Five to block the Security Council's decision. Allowing China's veto power, despite China's self-declared non-party status to the Genocide Convention, would permit China to jeopardize peace and endanger the peace principles of the United Nations. Russia's use of veto power to block UN Security Council resolutions in its current invasion of Ukraine should serve as a wake-up call that the democratic world order must be protected and that more responsible institutions of the international rule of law should be reformed. Willful ignorance toward an autocratic, imperialistic country's illegal occupation and settler colonialism may lead to the destruction of international law and the principles of the democratic world order, opening the door to war, chaos, and genocide.

SUMMARY

Whatever the future holds, East Turkistan's people will most likely pursue independence in order to ensure their survival as a nation and to put an end to China's genocide, as they are deeply dissatisfied with Chinese colonialism. Only total liberation and independence can guarantee the East Turkistani people's right to sovereignty over their land. They must fight for these liberations for their survival:

- Liberation from the Xinjiang Production and Construction Corps and People's Liberation Army's military colonization.
- Independence from China's economic exploitation and sovereignty over the territory of East Turkistan.
- Liberation from China's political control and the settler colonialism that aims to destroy the people of East Turkistan by means of genocide and replace them with Chinese settlers.

At the moment, even if China provides self-governance and internal self-determination, it will not guarantee long-term peace. The East Turkistan issue is about the illegal occupation of one state by another, political and ethnic conflict, state genocide, and settler colonialism. These complex characteristics are related not simply to what both parties want but also to who is eliminating whom and their identity. Political, territorial, and economic exclusion, as well as genocide against the Uyghurs and other Turkic Muslims in the region, added to the colonized people's deep distrust of China's rule, could never be effectively resolved without total separation from China. However, states are very cautious when it comes to the topic of East Turkistan's sovereignty, fearing that it will be impossible to persuade China to comply with international norms and principles in their state relations if China believes it must give up advantages in occupied East Turkistan. Unfortunately, these governments did not realize that China has already seriously violated many international norms and principles by implementing genocide in East Turkistan despite the fact that it had complete assurance of reaping immense economic, political, and geo-strategic gains from that territory. So, the question is not whether upsetting China would result in negative consequences, but whether pleasing China would result in negative consequences.

It is important to note here why East Turkestan should be free and what would it mean if East Turkestan regains its independence. If East Turkistan regains its sovereign status and becomes an independent nation, the world and the people of East Turkistan will experience the following key outcomes:

1. Protection of Uyghur and other Turkic Muslims in East Turkistan from the Chinese genocide will be the most guaranteed outcome of establishing an independent East Turkestan.
2. East Turkistan has historically seen the establishment of sovereign democratic republics, and an independent East Turkistan will be democratic. East

Turkistan independence movement diaspora organizations are also training and working diligently to lay the foundation for the country's democratic future.

3. When East Turkistan achieves independence, its democratic and just government will attract the world's talented individuals by utilizing its immense natural resources and vast territory.

4. Independent East Turkistan will be the gateway for the West and East's healthy and peaceful relationship.

5. Independent East Turkistan will maintain regional balance and play a crucial role in fostering world peace by obstructing Chinese imperialism.

In short, the responsible international community should respect and support East Turkistan's legitimate right to choose sovereignty in order to limit China's autocratic rule from expanding further.

NOTES

1. International Convention on the Elimination of All Forms of Racial Discrimination art. 5(c), December 21, 1965, S. Exec. Doc. C, 95-2 (1978); S. Treaty Doc. 95-18; 660 U.N.T.S. 195, 212.

2. Reference re Secession of Quebec, Supreme Court Judgments [1998] 2 S.C.R. 217. Para134 (Can.). Accessed October 11, 2020, https://scc-csc.lexum.com/scc-csc/scc-csc/en/item/1643/index.do.

3. G.A. Res. 2625 (XXV), UN.Doc. A/8082 (October 24, 1970).

4. Lee C. Buchheit, Secession: *The Legitimacy of Self-Determination* (New Haven: Yale University Press, 1978), 222.

5. Cedric Ryngaert and Christine Griffioen, "The Relevance of the Right to Self-Determination in the Kosovo Matter: In Partial Response to the Agora Papers," *Chinese Journal of International Law* 8, no. 3 (2009): 575. SSRN: https://ssrn.com/abstract=1505168 or http://dx.doi.org/jmp021.

6. Chris Buckley. "Brushing Off Criticism, China's Xi Calls Policies in Xinjiang 'Totally Correct,'" *New York Times*, September 26, 2020, accessed October 17, 2020.
https://www.nytimes.com/2020/09/26/world/asia/xi-jinping-china-xinjiang.html.

7. U.N. Charter art. 1, ¶ 2. See also Convention on the Prevention and Punishment of the Crime of Genocide December 9 1948, 78 U.N.T.S. 277, S. Exec. Doc. O, 81-1 (1949).

8. U.N. Charter art. 55.

9. Aureliu Cristescu (Special Rapporteur on the Right to Self- determination), *The Right to Self Determination: Historical and Current Development on the Basis of United Nations,* 21, 122, U.N. Doc. E/CN.4/Sub.2/404/Rev.1(1981).

10. *Id.* at 11, ¶ 59.

11. G.A. Res. 2621(XXV), Programme of Action For the Full Implementation of the Declaration on the Granting of Independence to Colonial Countries and Peoples (October 12, 1970).

12. *Id.* action (7).

13. G.A. Res, 32/155, Declaration on the Deepening and Consolidation of International Détente (December 19, 1977).

14. Cristescu, supra note, at 20, ¶ 117.

15. International Covenant on Civil and Political Rights, December 16, 1966, 999 U.N.T.S. 171; S. Exec. Doc. E, 95-2 (1978); S. Treaty Doc. 95-20; 6 I.L.M. 368 (1967).

16. International Covenant on Economic, Social and Cultural Rights, December 16, 1966 993 U.N.T.S. 3; S. Exec. Doc. D, 95-2 (1978); S. Treaty Doc. No. 95-19; 6 I.L.M. 360 (1967).

17. African Charter on Human and People's Rights, June 27, 1981, 1520 U.N.T.S. 217; 21 I.L.M. 58 (1982).

18. World Conference on Human Rights, *Vienna Declaration and Programme of Action*, ¶ 2, U.N. Doc. A/CONF.157/23 (June 25, 1993).

19. G.A. Res, A/RES/738(VIII), The Right of Peoples and Nations to Self Determination (November 28, 1953).

20. Declaration on the Granting of Independence to Colonial Countries and Peoples, ¶ 4, December 14, 1960, 1960 UN Yearbook 40; GA res. 1514 (XV); UN Doc. A/4684 (1961).

21. Accordance with International Law of the Unilateral Declaration of Independence in Respect of Kosovo, Advisory Opinion, 2010, I.C.J. No. 141, at 31, ¶ 82 (July 22).

22. *Id.* at 31, ¶ 83.

23. S.C. Res.1244, Annex.1 principle VI; Annex. 2, ¶ 8 (June 10, 1999).

24. G.A. Res. A/RES/1541(XV), Principles which Should Guide Members in Determining Whether or Not an Obligation Exists to Transmit the Information Called for Under Article 73 e of the Charter (December 15, 1960).

25. G.A. Res. A/RES/742 (VIII), Annex. part 1 (November 27, 1953).

26. The Qur'an 58, *an-Nisa*, Translated by Dr. Mustafa Khattab, who is a Canadian-Egyptian authority on interpreting the Qur'an.

27. The Qur'an 90, *an-Nahl* Translated by Muhammad Taqi Usmani, who is a Pakistani Islamic scholar, former judge, and president of the Wifaq ul Madaris Al-Arabia and the vice president and Hadith professor of the Darul Uloom Karachi.

28. Alimjan Bughda, *East Turkistan Islamic State and Its Constitution in Historical Documents* (Istanbul: Sutuk Bugrahan Press, 2018), 76.

29. These interpretations of drafted principles of statehood agenda are not statutory. They have been elaborated and developed by the author, needs future discussion and amendment.

30. The Constitution of The East Turkistan Republic Government in Exile, November 22, 2004, art. 9 (United States), https://east-turkistan.net/constitution/.

31. Political Program of East Turkistan Youth Congress, February 15, 2022, art. 2. http://et-yc.org.

32. Constitution of World Uyghur Congress, art. 5(1) (The World Uyghur Congress's constitution is not available on their website. Original copy accessed by author).

33. Constitution of World Uyghur Congress, art. 5(3).

34. *Id.* art. 5(2).

35. Documents of International Union of the East Turkistan organizations Constitution obtained by author. Constitution is not publicly published yet.

36. Ibid.

37. Protocol Additional to the Geneva Conventions of 12 August 1949, and relating to the Protection of Victims of International Armed Conflicts (Protocol I), art.1, ¶ 4, June 8, 1977, 1125 U.N.T.S. 3.

38. Geneva Convention For the Amelioration of the Condition of the Wounded and Sick in Armed Forces in the Field, art. 3, ¶ 4, August 12, 1949, 75 U.N.TS.31.

39. Commentary of 1987 Legal Status of the Parties to the Conflict, art. 4, ¶ 165, Protocol Additional to the Geneva Conventions of August 12, 1949, and Relating to the Protection of Victims of International Armed Conflicts (Protocol I), June 8, 1977, 1125 U.N.T.S. 3 https://ihl-databases.icrc.org/applic/ihl/ihl.nsf/1a13044f3bbb5b8ec12563fb0066f226/12f dc8fb498225afc12563cd0042fca3.

40. G.A. Res 742 (VIII), supra note 23, ¶ 4. See also: Sultan Al- Kanj, "How Will US Removal of Turkestan Islamic Party From Terrorism List Affect Syrian File?," *Al Monitor,* November 13, 2020, accessed December 13, 2021, : https://www.al-monitor.com/originals /2020/11/syria-uyghur-fighters-idlib-us-remove-turkestan-terrorism.html#ixzz7SvKyI9RT.

41. Jeff Desjardins, "Mapped: China's Most Ambitious Megaproject — The New Silk Road," *Business Insider,* March 18, 2018, accessed May 14, 2020, https://www.businessinsider .com/chinas-most-ambitious-megaproject-the-new-silk-road-mapped-2018-3.

42. Miles Maochun Yu, *China's Final Solution in Xinjiang* (Washington, DC: *Hoover Institution,* October 9, 2018), accessed January 12, 2022, https://www.hoover.org/research/ chinas-final-solution-xinjiang.

43. Elizabeth C. Economy, "Yes, Virginia, China Is Exporting Its Model," *Council on Foreign Relations* (blog), December 11, 2019, accessed May 14, 2020, https://www.cfr.org/ blog/yes-virginia-china-exporting-its-model.

44. Hu Heifeng, "In a Remote Corner of China, Beijing Is Trying to Export Its Model by Training Foreign Officials the Chinese Way," *South China Morning Post,* June 14, 2018, accessed May 16, 2021, https://www.scmp.com/news/china/economy/article/2155203/ remote-corner-china-beijing-trying-export-its-model-training.

45. Clive Hamilton and Mareike Ohlberg, *Hidden Hand* (Winnipeg: Optimum Publishing International, 2020), 30, eBooks.

46. Zhao Tingyang, *Redefining A Philosophy for World Governance,* foreign language edition (Beijing: Foreign Language Teaching and Research Press, 2019), eBooks.

47. Adrien Zenz, "The Xinjiang Papers: An Introduction" *Uyghur Tribunal,* November 27, 2021, https://uyghurtribunal.com/wp-content/uploads/2021/11/The-Xinjiang-Papers-An -Introduction-01.pdf.

48. Embassy of the People's Republic of China in United States of America, "China Wants New World Order," https://www.mfa.gov.cn/ce/ceus//eng/zmgx/zgwjzc/t35080.htm.

49. Michelle Bachelet, Statement by UN High Commissioner for Human Rights Michelle Bachelet After Official Visit to China (May 28, 2022), https://www.ohchr.org/en/statements /2022/05/statement-un-high-commissioner-human-rights-michelle-bachelet-after-official; Edward White, "'Under Tremendous Pressure': The Battle Behind UN Report on China's Xinjiang Abuses," *Financial Times,* Sept 13, 2022, accessed Sept 14, 2022, https://archive .ph/XLrBG.

50. A. Elena Ursu, "No Place to Hide: Why China Will Ratify the Rome Statue," FICHL Policy Brief Series, No. 60, 2016, accessed December 11, 2021, https://www.toaep.org/pbs -pdf/60-ursu.

51. Harriet Moynihan, *China's Evolving Approach to International Dispute Settlement* (London: Chatham House, March 2017), accessed in December 11, 2021, https:// www.chathamhouse.org/sites/default/files/publications/research/2017-03-29-chinas-evolving -approach-international-dispute-settlement-moynihan-final.pdf.

52. Statute of the International Court of Justice, art. 36. ¶ 2.

53. Reservation to the Convention on the Prevention and Punishment of the Crime of Genocide, Advisory Opinion, 1951, I.C.J. at 19, second Phase, ¶ 4 (May 28), https://www.icj-cij.org/public/files/case-related/12/4285.pdf.

54. Convention on the Prevention and Punishment of the Crime of Genocide, December 9, 1948, 78 U.N.T.S. 277, S. Exec. Doc. O, 81-1 (1949). Article IX stated that "[d]isputes between the Contracting Parties relating to the interpretation, application or fulfilment of the present Convention, including those relating to the responsibility of a State for genocide or for any of the other acts enumerated in article III, shall be submitted to the International Court of Justice at the request of any of the parties to the dispute."

Appendix

The Constitution of the Islamic Republic of East Turkistan in 1933

Prepared by the academic group of the East Turkistan Independence Association

Following the people of East Turkistan's awakening, a tremendous national revolution emerged in East Turkistan. The people of East Turkistan received the mercy of Allah (God) and, led by heroic fighter Kohja Niyaz Haji and our faithful, patriotic mujahideen (freedom fighters), finally established the Islamic Republic of East Turkistan. The people of East Turkistan have no tolerance for Chinese colonization and harsh oppression. Thank you, Allah! Allah has heard and answered East Turkistani people's fifty-seven years of prayers for independence and national aspiration. The religious and civic national government of East Turkistan is established.

The academic group of the Independence Association prepared this Constitution. The Constitution provides the fundamental rules and principles that govern the country.

ARTICLE ONE

The Constitution of the Islamic Republic of East Turkistan is written based on Islamic Sharia [Law] and the unchanging words of God, the source of knowledge and glory, the Qur'an.

ARTICLE TWO

The country of East Turkistan established a republican government. This government provides religious, cultural, and economic prosperity to the people of East Turkistan. It ensures freedom and the sovereign status of East Turkistan by declaring its independence to the Nanjing government, international nations, and governments worldwide.

ARTICLE THREE

The Constitution establishes a central government and defines its power. The President seat is the center of the government, and the country is governed based on Islamic Sharia.

ARTICLE FOUR

The government was established based on populism, focusing on the needs of the people, consensus, and public discussion. The people elect parliamentarian representatives to represent and serve their interests.

The elected representatives are responsible for listening to the people's voice and helping all the people in the country.

ARTICLE 5: ESTABLISHMENT OF GOVERNMENTAL DEPARTMENTS

The central government minister's office was established under the leadership of the President.

The President appoints a Prime minister. The Prime ministers will have two cabinet ministers.

Departments of Government of the Islamic Republic of East Turkistan

1. Ministry of Religious and Judicial Affairs
2. Ministry of National Defense
3. Ministry of Finance
4. Ministry of Foreign Affairs
5. Ministry of Internal Affairs
6. Ministry of Trade and Agriculture
7. Ministry of Education
8. Ministry of Endowments
9. Ministry of Health

The above departments are separated into two cabinets.

Cabinet One: Civil and Political Affairs
Ministry of National Defense
Ministry of Foreign Affairs

Ministry of Internal Affairs
Ministry of Religious and Judicial Affairs
Ministry of Endowments
Cabinet Two: Social and Cultural Affairs:
Ministry of Finance
Ministry of Trade and Agriculture
Ministry of Education
Ministry of Health

ARTICLE 6: RESPONSIBILITIES OF THE PRESIDENT

1. The President of East Turkistan is the official upon whom the chief executive power of the state's security and peaceful development of the nation of the Islamic Republic of East Turkistan and their religion is reliant.
2. The President will be elected by Parliament every four years. However, the founder of the Islamic Republic of East Turkistan, Khoja Niyaz Haji, the Commander Chief of the Armed Forces, which fought for the freedom of East Turkistan, is accepted by the people of East Turkistan as President for life.
3. The President appoints the Prime minister and government ministers.
      Note: The President appoints a prime minister and submits a request for approval by the Parliament.
4. The President can sign legislation introduced by the ministers and members of Parliament into law. If the President refuses to sign the legislation, the President will return the legislation to Parliament for review.
5. When there is a conflict between the President, prime minister, and Head of the ministries of the government (members of the Prime Minister's cabinet), the prime minister will resign. The President then appoints a new prime minister, and the new prime minister appoints new cabinet members.
6. The President accepts and meets with the Ministry of Foreign Affairs and foreign diplomats to the Islamic Republic of East Turkistan in the Ministry of Foreign Affairs Office.
7. The President is the Commander in Chief of the Armed Forces and has the power to control the military through the powers vested in the Ministry of National Defense.
8. The Islamic Republic of East Turkistan was established based on consensus. The President approves most decisions and resolutions regarding governmental policies and programs agreed upon by the prime minister and the cabinet members.

ARTICLE 7: RESPONSIBILITIES OF
THE PRIME MINISTER

The Prime minister is the Head of ministers; he can directly administer and be involved in the administration of each governmental department through the ministers. The Prime Minister is also called the Head Minister of Ministers Office or the cabinet minister.

The Prime minister meets with the various ministers of government once a week or at any time when extraordinary situations arise or when it is necessary. The meeting where government affairs are discussed is called the meeting of the *'Hey'iti Nazir' [Committee of Ministers]*. Legislation, policies, programs, and regulations are introduced in this meeting and called "ministers' agreements."

If these agreements are introduced in the Parliament and passed with the majority vote, they will become law. Whereas if no parliamentary session is held, then the 'ministers' agreement' will be sent to President's desk for signature. If the President signs the 'minister' agreement, it will become public law, officially known as regulation.

ARTICLE 8. EXECUTIVE DEPARTMENTS

Responsibilities of the Ministry of Religious and Judicial Affairs:

The Islamic Republic of East Turkistan is established based on Islamic law principles and created the Ministry of Religious and Judicial Affairs. The Minister of Religious and Judicial Affairs is called the "Shaykh al-Islam."

The government's judicial branch has a religious affairs office called "*Bayutteqwa,*" administrated by a "*Mufti.*"

In developed countries, the government's judicial branch is responsible for coordinating between the government and the supreme court. Because in developed countries, judges have a permanent position. The judges presiding over the lower courts in the Islamic Republic of East Turkistan are appointed and approved by a collective decision of judges of the Supreme Court (*Qazikalan*) and the Ministry of the Judiciary (*Ediliye Naziri*).

The Ministry of the Judiciary appoints judges of Sharia court (*Qazilar*). The Ministry of Judiciary has the power to use appropriate measures to ensure justice.

The Ministry of Judiciary can also observe government regulations' applicability to Islamic Sharia law.

The Ministry of Judiciary also establishes prisons to provide prisoners with a clean and civilized conditions to correct their ethics or behaviors.

ARTICLE 9. RESPONSIBILITIES
OF NATIONAL DEFENSE

The first duty of the Department of National Defense of the Islamic Republic of East Turkistan is to establish advanced armed forces to deter war and protect the security of our country from foreign threats.

To do that Department of National Defense will establish military academies with the assistance of foreign military experts to train professionally skilled military leaders. The Department of National Defense has the power to develop factories and manufacture armaments. The Department of National Defense is responsible for designing and formulating military strategy and intelligence service. Now, the most essential and highest responsibility of national defense is establishing military institutions consisting of military experts to work side by side with East Turkistan armed forces. Experts and researchers of the military institute must have professional skills in the combat field of the air force, land force, utilization of armed equipment, and heavy machinery weapons. They should be the instructors of heavy machinery and advanced weapons. The National Defense Department military institution must also train chemical warfare experts to prepare the necessary equipment to protect the nation.

ARTICLE 10. MINISTRY OF FOREIGN AFFAIRS

The Ministry of Foreign Affairs is responsible for establishing East Turkistan Embassies and appointing diplomats in foreign countries. The Ministry of Foreign Affairs sends high-level ambassadors and mid-level ambassadors to the host countries separately based on the political power of the host country.

The Ambassadors establish consulates out of the capital city of the host country. Each consulate will be under the guidance of the embassy in their located country.

The Ambassadors shall receive instructions from the Ministry of Foreign Affairs.

The Consulates' primary responsibilities are to serve and protect East Turkistan citizens in foreign countries and to issue travel documents and visas for the citizens of East Turkistan that reside in a foreign host country for the person to return to the homeland.

The Ministry of Foreign affairs is responsible for resolving various business and trade tariffs with foreign countries.

The other primary responsibility of the Embassy of the Islamic Republic of East Turkistan is to maintain peace with foreign countries and establish friendly relations through diplomatic missions in a host country. The embassy also protects East Turkistan citizens who traveled or resided in the host state from prosecution.

The Ministry of Foreign Affairs has no power in the internal affairs of East Turkistan. However, they will issue passports and travel documents for citizens of East Turkistan if they want to travel to Afghanistan. East Turkistan citizens who would like to travel to other countries can apply for travel documents or passports at the nearest urban police stations near their homes. The mayor must approve their application and issue a travel document.

ARTICLE 11. MINISTRY OF INTERNAL AFFAIRS

For the new governments, the Department of Internal Affairs has utmost importance.

The most significant responsibility of the Ministry of Internal Affairs is to appoint governors (*vali*) in each Province of East Turkistan.

Governors are the heads of all government officials in the provinces and are responsible for keeping a peaceful and stable society. Governors have direct power to establish and control the urban armed police services and rural armed police services.

Urban armed police services and rural armed police services have the government's executive power. Their responsibilities include but are not limited to preventing crime, arresting criminals, carrying court orders, inspecting travel documents of foreigners, and detecting suspicious people or foreign spies. In the remote areas that have no police force, responsibility will be maintained by the armed forces.

The Ministry of internal affairs shall establish a post office. The post office is responsible for ensuring the delivery service of mail and parcels in time and in good shape. Provinces prepare blueprints related to borders and areas and submit them to the minister's office. The responsibility of the Ministry of Internal Affairs is also to build and develop the infrastructure of the country. The most important responsibility is to issue residents or citizens a residential paper or citizenship ID. Provide property ownership, manage and administer land title.

ARTICLE 12. MINISTRY OF ENDOWMENTS AND FOUNDATIONS (WAQFS)

Responsible for providing government funding and property to the schools under the guardianship of the Ministry of Education. Regulations of the Ministry of Endowments use examples of the endowment system of Turkey and Egypt.

CULTURAL AND SOCIAL CABINET

ARTICLE 13. MINISTRY OF FINANCE

The highest responsibility of the Ministry of Finance is to calculate government revenue and expenses; distribute government salaries.

The revenue of our government has direct and indirect revenue.

Direct revenue includes donations, tax, and other revenues. Indirect income includes tariffs collected from foreign goods. Tariffs are usually collected at the border as a so-called border or import tax.

Foreign trade tax will be increased or decreased based on the necessary needs of the government and agreements between foreign countries.

Ministry of Finance prepares blueprint resolution for appropriate taxation and introduces it into law. The Ministry of Finance has the power to forgive the tax burden of the citizens under the advice of ministers.

Ministry of Finance also prints banknotes and money. Yearbook of revenue called "*Botqe*" or "*Mizaniye.*"

ARTICLE 14. MINISTRY OF TRADE AND AGRICULTURE

The Ministry of Trade and Agriculture is responsible for developing agricultural products, cotton, and cotton product mining, animal husbandry, and various agricultural, industrial, and natural resources.

The Ministry is responsible for raising silkworms, increasing silk and cotton production, increasing agricultural harvests, and inviting foreign agriculture specialists to develop agriculture in East Turkistan.

ARTICLE 15. MINISTRY OF EDUCATION

The responsibility of the Ministry of Education is to ensure governance of the educational policies, regulations, and educational system across the country. The Ministry of Education is responsible for establishing primary and secondary schools and hiring qualified teachers knowledgeable in mathematics, geometry, and religion. Teachers must have good teaching ethics and be able to educate children with patriotism.

The Ministry of Education also builds and improves middle and high schools recruit students from high schools to the university. It is also responsible for introducing overseas exchange programs and sending students to study at universities abroad. The Ministry of Education shall also invite foreign scholars and academics to gain professional help for all educational affairs. The Ministry of Education also builds and improves various media, publishing houses, and publish textbooks. It is also authorized to import necessary textbooks until national publishing houses are established. The Ministry of Education should also develop libraries and bookstores.

ARTICLE 16. MINISTRY OF HEALTH

The Ministry of Health is responsible for building a government organization to cope with pandemics, administrating the health system, fighting diseases, building hospitals, and detecting the regions that lack clean water, food, and facilities of the medical supplies. The Ministry of Health is also responsible for preventing environmental pollution. The Ministry of Health shall hire at least twelve foreign doctors to get support for these responsibilities. The Ministry of Health shall also establish mental health hospitals, orphanages, veterinarian hospitals, and drug addiction treatment centers. The Ministry of Health is also responsible for importing advanced medical equipment and drug and pharmaceutical products and funding pharmacists and dentists.

ARTICLE 17. ESTABLISHING PROVINCES

The Ministry of Internal Affairs shall establish provinces and appoint governors in the provinces to manage civil affairs; it shall also observe and maintain the security of provinces if necessary.

ARTICLE 18. GOVERNORS OF PROVINCES

Governors are responsible for establishing and administering branch offices of each central government department in their Province.

ARTICLE 19. ESTABLISHING COURTS

Educational institutions, judicial offices, and endowments shall be established in the provinces under the direct control of the courts.

ARTICLE 20.

The central government shall establish branch offices of the Ministry of Finance and Trade office to manage the treasury, export-import business, governmental economic affairs, donations, income, and expenses in each Province.

ARTICLE 21

The Ministry of Foreign Affairs shall appoint diplomats to represent the government in the nations' embassies and consulates in the host cities of the foreign countries.

ARTICLE 22

Provincial Governors shall provide services and financial assistance to the military officials and soldiers.

ARTICLE 23: ESTABLISHING COUNTIES

The provinces shall appoint officials in every county and has to be approved by the Ministry of Internal Affairs.

ARTICLE 24

The Ministry of Internal Affairs is responsible for establishing guards and urban and county police stations to protect the security of the people. The Ministry of Religious and Judicial Affairs is responsible for establishing lower courts and judges in the counties. The provincial government appoints county judges with the Ministry of Religious and Judicial Affairs approval.

ARTICLE 25

The provincial government appoints government officials in each county to build and administer schools, government funding, and government properties. These government officials work with the support of county officials.

ARTICLE 26

The provincial governor appoints Water Management Officials known as *'Mirap'* in each county with the approval of the Ministry of Internal Affairs to administer water sources and agriculture. The Governor of the prefecture also appoints county government officials with the support of the Ministry of Agriculture to extract and develop mining and other natural resources.

ARTICLE 27

Cities belong to provinces and are administered by a city mayor or a special governor in the cases of unique cities.

ARTICLE 28: ESTABLISHING VILLAGES

County rulers appoint administrators known as *"Emin"* in each village with the approval of the provincial government to administer agricultural and animal husbandry affairs, cultural affairs, religious schools, and other public schools. The Emin implements government policies and county rulers' orders.

ARTICLE 29

The people will elect a village head in the town with the approval of the province's governor. The village head is responsible for protecting the peace and security of the population in the mountainous village and remote areas. The Head of the town administers religious schools and public schools. They also collect the opinions and demands of the villagers to implement government orders and policies. The head of the village keeps a record of government property and funds, and the village head is also responsible for enforcing government policies and court orders.

ARTICLE 30. INSPECTOR GENERAL

The Inspector General, known as the Buyuk Memur, is the eyes and ears of the government. The Inspector General checks all governmental affairs to <u>overview</u> and administrate them based on legal principles. The Inspector General is the government representative who has the power to access all offices of the departmental government offices.

In the provinces and counties, freelance government inspectors observe government affairs. All inspection reports shall be submitted to the Inspector General's office. If the reports reveal corruption or violations of government regulations, these reports will be forwarded to the Judicial Affairs Ministry by the Inspector General.

This document translated by author and reviewed by Salih Hudayar.

Bibliography

ARCHIVAL SOURCES

"Cable, No. 3582 from Filippov [Stalin] to Cde. Mao Zedong, 2 September 1949, RGASPI, f. 558, op. 11, d. 332, l. 8." Translated by Gary Goldberg. China-Soviet Relations Collection. History and Public Policy Program Digital Archive. Wilson Center, Washington, DC. https://digitalarchive.wilsoncenter.org/document/176340.

"Cable, Mao Zedong to Comrade Filippov [Stalin], 25 October 1949." Sino-Soviet Relations Collection. History and Public Policy Program Digital Archive. Wilson Center, Washington, DC. https://digitalarchive.wilsoncenter.org/document/176641.

"Cable with Message from Mao Zedong to Stalin, 26 September 1949, RGASPI, f. 558, op. 11, d. 332, ll. 54-56." Translated Gary Goldberg. China and Soviet Union 1934–1949 . Collection. History and Public Policy Program Digital Archive. Wilson Center, Washington DC. https://digitalarchive.wilsoncenter.org/document/176341.

"Ciphered Telegram No. 4159 from Filipov [Stalin] to Kovalev, 14 October 1949, RGASPI, f. 558, op. 11, d. 332, I,116." Translated by Gary Goldberg. Sino-Soviet Relations Collection. History and Public Policy Program Digital Archive. Wilson Center, Washington DC. https://digitalarchive.wilsoncenter.org/document/176342.

"Hon. John M. Murphy of New York, in the House of Representatives, 'Isa Yusuf Alptekin— Defender of Freedom'." Congressional Record (Bound Edition), Volume 116, Part 5 (March 3, 1970 to March 11, 1970), Extensions of Remarks, March 3, 1970, 5795-5796. History and Public Policy Program Digital Archive. Wilson Center, Washington DC. https://digitalarchive.wilsoncenter.org/document/208600.

"Isa Yusuf Alptekin, 'Memorandum Sent to Richard Nixon, President of the United States of America.' " July 12, 1969. History and Public Policy Program Digital Archive. Wilson Center, Washington, DC. https://digitalarchive.wilsoncenter.org/document/208601.

"Letter from L. Beria to Cde. I.V.Stalin, May 11, 1945, GARF, Fond R-9401ss, Opis' 2, Delo 95, II. 352-359." Obtained by Jamil Hasanli and translated by Gary Goldberg. China and Soviet Union in Xinjiang 1934–1949 Collection. History and Public Policy Program

Digital Archive. Wilson Center, Washington DC. https://digitalarchive.wilsoncenter.org/document/121725.

"Letter from Mohammad Emin Bugra, Former Deputy Chairman of Xinjiang Province, to Yolbars Khan, Chairman of the Office for the Xinjiang Provincial Government." May 10, 1954. History and Public Policy Program Digital Archive. 11-04-01-09-02-005. "Xinjiang nanmin yiju Tuerqi." West Asia Division, Ministry of Foreign Affairs. Archives of the Institute of Modern History. Academia Sinica. Obtained by Justin Jacobs and translated by Caixia Lu. https://digitalarchive.wilsoncenter.org/document/123643.

"Letter, Muhammad Amin Bughra, Isa Yusuf Alptekin, and Colonel Adam Sabri to Owen Lattimore. April 6, 1950. Folder 14 "Sinkiang Refugees 1950–1951," Box 5, Subseries 3 (Correspondence), Series 4 (Owen Lattimore), Subgroup 2 (Administrative Records, 1924-1955), Record Group 08.010. Records of Walter Hines Page School of International Relations 1923/1955. Ferdinand Hamburger Archives. Sheridan Libraries. Johns Hopkins University." Obtained by Charles Kraus. History and Public Policy Program Digital Archive. Wilson Center, Washington DC. https://digitalarchive.wilsoncenter.org/document/134644.

"Letter from Ahmetjan Qasimi and Rahim Jan Sabri to Mr. Savel'yev, Consul General of the USSR in Urumqi, 12 July 1947, RGASPI F. 17, Op. 128, D. 391, ll. 115-119." Obtained by Jamil Hasanli and translated by Gary Goldberg. China and Soviet Union in Xinjiang 1934–1949 Collection. History and Public Policy Program Digital Archive. Wilson Center, Washington, DC. https://digitalarchive.wilsoncenter.org/document/121803.

"Main Speech by Premier Chou En-lai [Zhou Enlai], Head of the Delegation of the People's Republic of China, Distributed at the Plenary Session of the Asian-African Conference." April 19, 1955. History and Public Policy Program Digital Archive. Wilson Center, Washington, DC. http://digitalarchive.wilsoncenter.org/document/121623.

"Memorandum of Conversation Between Stalin and CCP Delegation, 27 June 1949, APRF:F.45,Op.1, D.329, LI.1-7." Translated by Sergey Radchenko. Sino-Soviet Relations Collection. History and Public Policy Program Digital Archive. Wilson Center, Washington, DC. Online at https://digitalarchive.wilsoncenter.org/document/113380.

"Memorandum of a Discussion held by USSR Consul-General in Ürümchi, G. S. Dobashin, with First Secretary of the Party Committee of the Xinjiang Uyghur Autonomous Region, Comrade Wang Enmao, and Chair of the People's Committee, Comrade S. Äzizov. RGANI, fond 5, opis 49, delo 130, listy 54-56." January 17, 1958. Translated by David Brophy. "Local Nationalism" in Xinjiang 1957–1958. History and Public Policy Program Digital Archive. Wilson Center, Washington DC. https://digitalarchive.wilsoncenter.org/document/175894.

"Memorandum on a Discussion Held by the Consul-General of the USSR in Ürümchi, G.S. Dobashin, with Deputy Chairman of the People's Committee of the Xinjiang Uyghur Autonomous Region, Comrade Xin Lanting." January 12, 1958. "Local Nationalism" in Xinjiang 1957–1958. History and Public Policy Program Digital Archive. Wilson Center, Washington, DC. https://digitalarchive.wilsoncenter.org/document/175895.

"Telegram, Mao Zedong to [Liu] Shaoqi and [Zhou] Enlai, 7 January 1950." China at the United Nations Collection. History and Public Policy Program Digital Archive. Wilson Center, Washington, DC. https://digitalarchive.wilsoncenter.org/document/112681.

Yuan, Ming. "Missed Historic Opportunity Recalled." JPRS Report. *Foreign Broadcast Information Service*. US Department of Commerce National Technical Information Service, June 11, 1992. https://apps.dtic.mil/sti/pdfs/ADA335616.pdf.

GOVERNMENT RECORDS

"2012 Annual Report." US Congressional-Executive Commission on China, October 10, 2012. https://www.cecc.gov/publications/annual-reports/2012-annual-report#IV.%20Xinjiang.

U.S. Department of Defense. *Assistant Secretary of Defense for Indo-Pacific Security Affairs Schriver Press Briefing on the 2019 Report on Military and Security Developments in China.* Washington DC, 2019. https://www.defense.gov/News/Transcripts/Transcript/Article/1837011/assistant-secretary-of-defense-for-indo-pacific-security-affairs-schriver-press/.

Government Information Public Platform of Kashi. "Guanyu yinfa 'Kashi diqu 2018 nian jiancha gongzuo yaodian zeren fenjie fang'an' de tongzhi" 关于印发《喀什地区2018年督查工作要点责任分解方案》的通知. [Notice on the Publication and Distribution of the "Plan for Distributing Essential Inspection Work Tasks in the Kashgar Region, 2018"]. *Government Information Public Platform of Kashi*, March 6, 2018. https://web.archive.org/web/20180813115300/http:/www.kashi.gov.cn/Government/PublicInfoShow.aspx?ID=2851.

People's Republic of China. "2-8 Total Population and Birth Rate, Death Rate and Natural Growth Rate by Region." *China's Statistical Yearbooks, 2019.* http://www.stats.gov.cn/tjsj/ndsj/2019/indexeh.htm.

———. "4-3 Total Population and Birth Rate, Death Rate and Natural Growth Rate by Region." *China's Statistical Yearbooks, 1998.* http://www.stats.gov.cn/english/statisticaldata/yearlydata/YB1999e/d03e.htm.

The Constitution of The East Turkistan Republic Government in Exile. Adopted November 22, 2004. https://east-turkistan.net/constitution/.

US Central Intelligence Agency (CIA). *CIA-RDP79T01018A000100070001-3, Autonomous Governments in Minority Inhabited Areas of Communist China.* Washington, DC: CIA, August 17, 1998. https://www.cia.gov/library/readingroom/docs/CIA-RDP79T01018A000100070001-3.pdf.

———. *CIA-RDP80-00810A001400020009-5, Chinese Communist Regine in Sinkiang Province.* Washington, DC: CIA, May 29, 1958. https://www.cia.gov/readingroom/document/cia-rdp80-00810a001400020009-5.

———. *CIA-RDP82-00047R000200210003-2, The Chinese Population of Sinkiang.* Washington, DC: CIA, November 24, 1952. https://www.cia.gov/readingroom/document/cia-rdp82-00047r000200210003-2.

SECONDARY SOURCES

AFP. "UN Scraps Plans for Statement on Ethiopia's Tigray Region: Diplomats." *JusticeInfo. Net*, March 5, 2021. https://www.justiceinfo.net/en/74599-un-scraps-plans-for-statement-on-ethiopias-tigray-region-diplomats.html.

Al Jazeera. "Troops Deployed in Uighur City." *Al Jazeera*, July 7, 2009. https://www.aljazeera.com/news/2009/7/7/troops-deployed-in-uighur-city.

Al- Kanj, Sultan "How Will US Removal of Turkestan Islamic Party from Terrorism List Affect Syrian File?," *Al Monitor,* November 13, 2020, accessed December 13, 2021. https://www.al-monitor.com/originals/2020/11/syria-uyghur-fighters-idlib-us-remove-turkestan-terrorism.html#ixzz7SvKyI9RT.

Allievi, Stefano, and Jørgen Nielsen, eds. "Virtual Transnationalism: Uygur Communities in Europe and the Quest for Eastern Turkestan Independence." In *Muslim Networks and Transnational Communities in and across Europe*, 281–311. Leiden: Brill, 2003.

Almas, Turghun. *Uyghurs*. Munchen: World Uyghur Congress, 2010.

Alptekin, Isa Yusuf. *Doğu Türkistan İnsanlıktan Yardım İstiyor* (East Turkistan Expects Help from Humankind). Otağ Matbaası, 1974.

Australian Strategic Policy Institute. "The Xinjiang Data Project." *Australian Strategic Policy Institute*, 2020. https://xjdp.aspi.org.au/.

Bai, Jiayi 白嘉懿. "Shou ji Xinjiang nongcun fuyu laodongli zhuanyi jiuye chao 52.66 wanrenci" 首季 新疆农村富余劳动力转移就业52.66万人次 [In the First Quarter of Xinjiang, Rural Surplus Labor Transferred Employment exceeded 526,600 person Times]. *Chinanews.com*. https://www.chinanews.com.cn/cj/2019/04-04/8800898.shtml.

Bai Yunyi and Liu Xin. "White Paper Clarifies Historical Facts of Xinjiang." *Global Times*, July 19, 2019. http://www.globaltimes.cn/content/1158660.shtml.

Baidu. "Guowuyuan guanyu jichu jiaoyu gaige yu fazhan de jueding" 国务院关于基础教育改革与发展的决定 [Decision of the State Council on the Reform and Development of Basic Education]. *Baidu*, May 29, 2001. https://baike.baidu.com/item/国务院关于基础教育改革与发展的决定.

Bao, Yajun. "The Xinjiang Production and Construction Corps: An Insider's Perspective." *China: An International Journal* 18, no. 2 (May 2020): 161–74. https://muse.jhu.edu/article/756368.

BBC News. "What Does Xi Jinping's China Dream Mean." *BBC News*, June 6, 2013. https://www.bbc.com/news/world-asia-china-22726375.

Becquelin, Nicolas. "Staged Development in Xinjiang." *The China Quarterly*, no. 178 (June 2004): 358–78.

Bell, Abraham, and Eugene Kontorovich. "Palestine, *Uti Possidetis Juris*, and the Borders of Israel." *Arizona Law Review* 58, no. 3 (2016): 633–92.

Benson, Linda. *The Ili Rebellion: The Moslem Challenge to Chinese Authority in Xinjiang, 1944–1949*. Armonk, NY: M.E. Sharpe, 1990.

Blua, Antoine. "China Says Ethnic Violence In Check Amid Heavy Troop Presence." *Radio Free Europe and Radio Liberty*, July 8, 2009. https://www.rferl.org/a/Chinas_Ethnic_Violence_In_Check_Amid_Heavy_Troop_Presence/1772210.html.

Bovingdon, Gardner. *Autonomy in Xinjiang: Han Nationalist Imperatives and Uyghur Discontent*. Policy Studies 11. Washington, DC: East-West Center Washington, 2004.

———. *The Uyghurs: Strangers in Their Own Land*. New York: Columbia University Press, 2010.

Brophy, David John. *Uyghur Nation: Reform and Revolution on the Russia-China Frontier*. Cambridge, MA: Harvard University Press, 2016.

Buchheit, Lee C. *Secession: The Legitimacy of Self-Determination*. New Haven, CT: Yale University Press, 1978.

Buckley, Chris. "Brushing Off Criticism, China's Xi Calls Policies in Xinjiang 'Totally Correct.'" *New York Times*, September 26, 2020. https://www.nytimes.com/2020/09/26/world/asia/xi-jinping-china-xinjiang.html.

———. "China's Prisons Swell After Deluge of Arrests Engulfs Muslims." *New York Times*, August 31, 2019. https://www.nytimes.com/2019/08/31/world/asia/xinjiang-china-uighurs-prisons.html.

Bughda, Alimjan. *East Turkistan Islamic State and Its Constitution in Historical Documents*. Istanbul: Sutuk Baghran Press, 2018.

Bughra, Muhemmed Emin. *History of East Turkistan*. Ankara: Ankara Publishing, 1987.

Byler, Darren. "Why Xinjiang Is an Internal Settler Colony." *SupChina*, September 1, 2021. https://supchina.com/2021/09/01/why-xinjiang-is-an-internal-settler-colony/.

———. "Xinjiang Education Reform and Eradication of Uyghur Language Books." *SupChina*, October 2, 2019. https://supchina.com/2019/10/02/xinjiang-education-reform -and-the-eradication-of-uyghur-language-books/.

Cappelletti, Alessandra. "Socio-Economic Disparities and Economic Gap in Xinjiang: The Cases of Kashgar and Shihezi." In *Inside Xinjiang: Space, Place and Power in China's Muslim Far Northwest*, edited by Anna Hayes and Michael E. Clarke, 151–83. Routledge Contemporary China Series 137. London: Routledge, 2015.

Castellino, Joshua. "International Law and Self-Determination." In *Self-Determination and Secession in International Law*, edited by Christian Walter, Antje von Ungern-Sternberg, and Kavus Abushov, 27–44. Oxford: Oxford University Press, 2014.

Chen, Ping 陈平. "Xinjiang shengchan jianshe bingtuan de ruogan lishi wenti sikao" 新疆生产建设兵团的若干历史问题思考 [Analysis of Several Historical Issues of Xinjiang Production and Construction Corps]. http://www.shehui.pku.edu.cn/upload/editor/ file/20180829/20180829184531_5822.pdf.

Cheng, Li. "Ethnic Minority Elites in China's Party-State Leadership: An Empirical Assessment." *Brookings*, June 20, 2008. https://www.brookings.edu/articles/ethnic-minority -elites-in-chinas-party-state-leadership-an-empirical-assessment.

China Daily. "Full Text: The History and Development of the Xinjiang Production and Construction Corps." *China Daily*, October 5, 2014. https://www.chinadaily.com.cn/china /2014-10/05/content_18698088.html.

China Law Translate. "Decision to Revise the 'Xinjiang Uighur Autonomous Region Regulation on De-Extremification.' " *China Law Translate*, October 10, 2018. https:// www.chinalawtranslate.com/en/decision-to-revise-the-xinjiang-uighur-autonomous-region -regulation-on-de-extremification/.

China News. "Xinjiang sheng chan jianli she bingtuan guo jia an chuan ju chengli" 新疆生产建设兵团国家安全局成立 [Xinjiang Production and Construction Corps National Security Bureau Was Established]. *China News*, March 28, 2012. http://www .chinanews.com/gn/2012/03-28/3779628.shtml.

Chow, Kai-wing. "Imagining Boundaries of Blood: Zhang Binglin and the Invention of the Han 'Race' In Modern China." In *The Construction of Racial Identities in China and Japan: Historical and Contemporary Perspectives*, edited by Frank Dikötter, 34–52. Honolulu: University of Hawai'i Press, 1997.

Clarke, Michael E. *Xinjiang and China's Rise in Central Asia: A History*. Routledge Contemporary China Series 64. London: Routledge, 2011.

Cooper, John. *Raphael Lemkin and the Struggle for the Genocide Convention*. Basingstoke; New York: Palgrave Macmillan, 2008.

Dautcher, Jay. *Down a Narrow Road: Identity and Masculinity in a Uyghur Community in a Uyghur Community in Xinjiang China*. Harvard East Asian Monographs 312. Cambridge, MA: Harvard University Asia Center, 2009.

Davidson, Helen. "China Hands Death Sentences to Uyghur Former Officials." *The Guardian*. April 9, 2021. https://www.theguardian.com/world/2021/apr/09/china-uyghur-death -sentences-xinjiang-education-directors.

Desjardins, Jeff. "Mapped: China's Most Ambitious Megaproject—The New Silk Road." *Business Insider*, March 18, 2018. https://www.businessinsider.com/chinas-most-ambitious -megaproject-the-new-silk-road-mapped-2018-3.

Dillon, Michael. *Xinjiang: China's Muslim Far Northwest*. Durham East-Asia Series. London; New York: Routledge, 2004.

Doherty, Ben. "Chinese Government May Have Falsified Organ Donation Numbers, Study Says." *The Guardian*, November 14, 2019. https://www.theguardian.com/world/2019/nov/15/chinese-government-may-have-falsified-organ-donation-numbers-study-says.

Dong Yang 董洋. "Nongcun shengyu laodongli liudong dui Xinjiang jingji de yingxiang" 农村剩余劳动力流动对新疆经济的影响 [Flow of Rural Surplus Labor Force's Influence on Xinjiang's Economy]. *Jingji luntan* 经济论坛, no. 3 (2007). http://cdmd.cnki.com.cn/Article/CDMD-10755-2007165567.htm.

East Turkistan Youth Congress. *Political Program*. February 15, 2022. http://et-yc.org.

Ebrahimian, Bethany Allen. "Exposed: China's Operating Manuals for Mass Internment and Arrest by Algorithm." *International Consortium Investigative Journalist: China Cable*, November 24, 2019. https://www.icij.org/investigations/china-cables/exposed-chinas-operating-manuals-for-mass-internment-and-arrest-by-algorithm/.

Economy, Elizabeth C. "Yes, Virginia, China Is Exporting Its Model." *Council on Foreign Relations* (blog), December 11, 2019. Accessed May 14, 2020, https://www.cfr.org/blog/yes-virginia-china-exporting-its-model.

Embassy of the Peoples Republic of China in the Republic of Estonia. "Terrorist Activities Perpetrated by 'Eastern Turkistan' Organizations and Their Links with Osama Bin Laden and the Taliban." *Embassy of the Peoples Republic of China in the Republic of Estonia*, November 29, 2001. http://ee.china-embassy.org/eng/ztlm/fdkbzy/t112733.htm.

Ercilasun, Güljanat Kurmangaliyeva, and Konuralp Ercilasun, eds. *The Uyghur Community: Diaspora, Identity and Geopolitics. Politics and History in Central Asia*. New York: Palgrave Macmillan, 2018.

Everington, Keoni. "Saudis Allegedly Buy 'Halal Organs' From 'Slaughtered' Xinjiang Muslims." *Taiwan News*, January 22, 2020. https://www.taiwannews.com.tw/en/news/3862578.

Fang, Yingkai方英楷. *Xinjiang Bingtuan tunken shubian shi* 新疆兵团屯垦戍边史 [History of the Xinjiang Production and Construction Corps in Farming and Defending the Frontier]. edited by Li Fusheng 李福生. Wulumuqi: Xinjiang keji weisheng chubanshe 新疆科技卫生出版社, 1997.

Fei, Xiaotong. "Plurality and Unity in the Configuration of the Chinese." Lecture, University of Hong Kong, November 15–18, 1998.

———. *Zhonghua minzu duoyuan yiti geju* 中華民族多元一題格局 [The Pattern of Plurality and Unity in the Chinese Nation]. 2nd ed. Beijing: Zhongyang Minzu Daxue chubanshe, 2003.

Fiskesjö, Magnus. "China's 'Re-Education' / Concentration Camps in Xinjiang / East Turkestan and the Wider Campaign of Forced Assimilation Targeting Uyghurs, Kazakhs, etc.: Bibliography of Select News Reports & Academic Works." *Uyghur Human Rights Project*, April 18, 2022. https://uhrp.org/wp-content/uploads/2022/04/Chinas-genocide-in-Xinjiang-BIBLIOGRAPHY.pdf.

———. "Rescuing the Empire: Chinese Nation-Building in the Twentieth Century." *European Journal of East Asian Studies* 5, no. 1 (2006): 15–44. doi:10.1163/157006106777998106.

France 24. "Chinese Police Could Prevent Millions of Minority Births in Xinjiang: Report." *France 24*, August 6, 2021. https://www.france24.com/en/live-news/20210608-chinese-policies-could-prevent-millions-of-minority-births-in-xinjiang-report.

Front Line Defenders. "Ilham Tohti Sentenced to Life Imprisonment." *Front Line Defenders*, January 15, 2018. https://www.frontlinedefenders.org/en/case/ilham-tohti-sentenced-life-imprisonment.

"Fundamentals of National Reconstruction." *China Copy Right and Media Blog* (blog) ed. Rogier Creemers. November 24, 2014. https://chinacopyrightandmedia.wordpress.com/1924/04/12/fundamentals-of-national-reconstruction/.

Gan, Nectar. "Xi Jinping Thought: The Communist Party's Tighter Grip on China in 16th Characters." *South China Morning Post*, October 25, 2017. https://www.scmp.com/news/china/policies-politics/article/2116836/xi-jinping-thought-communist-partys-tighter-grip-china.

Global Times. "Populations of Han, Ethnic Minorities in Xinjiang Rise Markedly Over Past Decade: Communiqué." *Global Times*, June 14, 2021. https://www.globaltimes.cn/page/202106/1226080.shtml.

Grauer, Yael. "Revealed: Massive Chinese Police Database." *The Intercept*, January 29, 2021. https://theintercept.com/2021/01/29/china-uyghur-muslim-surveillance-police/.

Guo, Rongxing. *China's Spatial (Dis)Integration: Political Economy of the Interethnic Unrest in Xinjiang*. Elsevier Asian Studies Series. Waltham: Chandos Publishing, 2015.

Guo, Rui. "Chinese State Media Denounces 'Two-Faced' Xinjiang Officials Accused of Colluding with Extremists." *South China Morning Post*, April 3, 2021. https://www.scmp.com/news/china/politics/article/3128169/chinese-state-media-denoucestwo-faced-xinjiang-officials.

Haitiwaji, Gulbahar, and Rosenn Morgat. "'Our Souls Are Dead:' How I Survived a Chinese 'Re-Education Camp' for Uyghurs." *The Guardian*, January 12, 2021. https://www.theguardian.com/world/2021/jan/12/uighur-xinjiang-re-education-camp-china-gulbahar-haitiwaji?CMP=share_btn_tw.

Hall, Benjamin. "Uyghur Internment Camp Survivor Reveals China's Horrifying Re-Education Tactics." *Fox News*, February 6, 2021. https://www.foxnews.com/world/uighur-internment-camp-survivor-reveals-chinas-horrifying-re-education-tactics.

Hamilton, Clive, and Mareike Ohlberg. *Hidden Hand: Exposing How the Chinese Communist Party Is Reshaping the World*. London: Oneworld, 2020.

Harwel, Drew, and Eva Dou. "Huawei Tested AI Software That Could Recognize Uighur Minorities and Alert Police, Report Says." *Washington Post*, December 8, 2020. https://www.washingtonpost.com/technology/2020/12/08/huawei-tested-ai-software-that-could-recognize-uighur-minorities-alert-police-report-says/.

Hasanli, Jamil. *Soviet Policy in Xinjiang: Stalin and the National Movement in Eastern Turkistan*. The Harvard Cold War Studies Book Series. Lanham: Lexington Books, 2021.

Hawkins, Amy. "Beijing's Big Brother Tech Needs African Faces." *Foreign Policy*, July 24, 2018. https://foreignpolicy.com/2018/07/24/beijings-big-brother-tech-needs-african-faces/.

Hille, Kathrin, and Richard McGregor. "Trouble at the Margin." *Financial Times*, July 10, 2009. https://www.ft.com/content/fe6d1666-6d92-11de-8b19-00144feabdc0.

Hoja, Gulchehra, and Shohret Hoshur. "Children of Detained Uyghurs Face 'Terrible' Conditions in Overcrowded Xinjiang Orphanages." *Radio Free Asia*, October 18, 2017. https://www.rfa.org/english/news/uyghur/children-10182017144425.html.

Hoshur, Shohret. "At Least 150 Detainees Have Died in One Xinjiang Internment Camp: Police Officer." *Radio Free Asia*, October 29, 2019. https://www.rfa.org/english/news/uyghur/deaths-10292019181322.html.

———. "Chinese Authorities Continue to Destroy Mosques in Xinjiang." *Radio Free Asia*, September 7, 2018. https://www.rfa.org/english/news/uyghur/chinese-authorities-continue-to-destroy-mosques-in-xinjiang-09072018171910.html.

———. "Chinese Authorities Jail Four Wealthiest Uyghurs in Xinjiang's Kashgar in New Purge." Translated by Alim Seytoff, Mamatjan Juma, and Joshua Lipes. *Radio Free Asia*, January 5, 2018. https://www.rfa.org/english/news/uyghur/wealthiest-01052018144327.html.

———. "Prominent Uyghur Intellectual Given Two-Year Suspended Death Sentence for 'Separatism.'" *Radio Free Asia*, September 28, 2018. https://www.rfa.org/english/news/uyghur/sentence-09282018145150.html.

———. "Uyghur Muslim Scholar Dies in Chinese Police Custody." *Radio Free Asia*, January 29, 2018. https://www.rfa.org/english/news/uyghur/scholar-death-01292018180427.html.

―――. "Young Uyghur Tour Director Dies Under Questioning by Xinjiang Authorities: Mother." *Radio Free Asia*, June 24, 2019. https://www.rfa.org/english/news/uyghur/death-06242019143149.html.

Howell, Anthony. "Chinese Minority Income Disparity in Urumqi: An Analysis of Han-Ugyhur Labour Market Outcomes in the Formal and Informal Economies." *China: An International Journal* 11, no. 3 (May 2013): 1–23.

Howell, Anthony, and C. Cindy Fan. "Migration and Inequality in Xinjiang: A Survey of Han and Uyghur Migrants in Urumqi." *Eurasian Geography and Economics* 52, no. 1 (January 2011): 119–39. doi:10.2747/1539-7216.52.1.119.

Hu, A., and L. Hu. "第二代民族政策:促进民族交融一体和繁荣一体" [Second Generation Ethnic Policy: Promoting National Integration and Prosperity]. *Xinhua Digest* 新华文摘 24 (2011). https://www.sinoss.net/uploadfile/2011/1229/20111229100022433.pdf.

Hu, Heifeng. "In a Remote Corner of China, Beijing Is Trying to Export Its Model by Training Foreign Officials the Chinese Way." *South China Morning Post*, June 14, 2018. https://www.scmp.com/news/china/economy/article/2155203/remote-corner-china-beijing-trying-export-its-model-training.

Hua, Xia. "Xinjiang's GDP Grows 7.2 Pct Annually from 2014 to 2019." *Xinhua Net*, February 5, 2021. http://www.xinhuanet.com/english/2021-02/05/c_139724143.htm.

Human Rights Watch. "China: Minority Region Collects DNA from Millions." New York: Human Rights Watch, 2017. https://www.hrw.org/news/2017/12/13/china-minority-region-collects-dna-millions.

―――. "Devastating Blows: Religious Repression of Uyghurs in Xinjiang." New York,NY: Human Rights Watch, April 11, 2005. https://www.hrw.org/report/2005/04/11/devastating-blows/religious-repression-uighurs-xinjiang.

―――. "Eradicating Ideological Viruses: China's Campaign of Repression Against Xinjiang's Muslims." New York: Human Rights Watch, September 2018. https://www.hrw.org/report/2018/09/09/eradicating-ideological-viruses/chinas-campaign-repression-against-xinjiangs.

―――. "We Are Afraid to Even Look for Them." New York: Human Rights Watch, October 2019. https://www.hrw.org/sites/default/files/reports/xinjiang1009webwcover.pdf.

Illmer, Andreas. "Tashpolat Tiyip: Uyghur Leading Geographer Who Vanished in China." *BBC News*, October 11, 2019. https://www.bbc.com/news/world-asia-china-49956088.

Imin Bugra, Muhammed. *History of East Turkistan*. Ankara: Ankara Publishing, 1987.

Introvigne, Massimo. "Uyghur Traditional House Destroyed by the CCP: Another Tool of Cultural Genocide." *Bitter Winter*, November 7, 2020. https://bitterwinter.org/uyghur-traditional-houses-destroyed-by-the-ccp/.

Jacobs, Justin. *Xinjiang and the Modern Chinese State*. Studies on Ethnic Groups in China. Seattle; London: University of Washington Press, 2016.

Ji, Zen Tu. "Energy and Natural Resources of Xinjiang." In *Xinjiang: China's Northwest Frontier*, edited by K. Warikoo, 22–29. Central Asia Research Forum. London; New York: Routledge, 2016.

Jiang Xianhuan 蒋先欢. "'Minzu guojia' heyi jiangou Zhonghua minzu?: Sun Zhongshan de minzu tonghua sixiang jiqi shidai nanti zhong" "民族国家"何以建构中华民族?:孙中山的民族同化思想及其时代难题中 [Is the "Nation-State" Suitable for the Construction of the Chinese Nation?: Sun Yat-Sen 's Thought on Ethnic Assimilation and Its Dilemma]. *Lingdao kexue luntan* 领导科学论坛, no. 17 (2017): 42–54. doi:10.19299/j.cnki.42-1837/C.2017.17.006.

Jingji Ribao–Zhonguo Jingji wang 经济日报–中国经济网. "Jiaotong gaishan daidong tese chanye jiasu fazhan! Xinjiang zai tuijin xibu da kaifa zhong qianghua jichu sheshi guihua jianshe" 交通改善带动特色产业加速发展！新疆在推进西部大开发中强化基础设施规划建设 [Improved Transportation to Accelerate Special Characteristic Industries Development! In the Process of Development of Western Region, Strengthen Infrastructure Planning and Construction]. *Jingji Ribao–Zhonguo Jingji wang* 经济日报–中国经济网, January 4, 2021. http://www.ce.cn/xwzx/gnsz/gdxw/202101/04/t20210104_36184892.shtml.

Joske, Alex. "Reorganizing the United Front Work Department: New Structures for a New Era of Diaspora and Religious Affairs Work." *China Brief* 19, no. 9 (May 2019). https://jamestown.org/program/reorganizing-the-united-front-work-department-new-structures-for-a-new-era-of-diaspora-and-religious-affairs-work/.

Khalid, Adeeb. *Central Asia: A New History from the Imperial Conquests to the Present*. Princeton: Princeton University Press, 2021.

Kine, Phelim. "How China Hijacked the War on Terror." *Politico*, September 9, 2021. https://www.politico.com/news/2021/09/09/china-hijacked-war-on-terror-511032.

Kirby, William C. "When Did China Become China? Thoughts on the Twentieth Century." In *The Teleology of the Modern Nation-State*, edited by Joshua A. Fogel, 105–14. University of Pennsylvania Press, 2004.

Kurmangaliyeva, Ercilasun and Konuralp Ercilasun, eds. *The Uyghur Community: Diaspora, Identity, and Geopolitics*. New York: Palgrave Macmillan, 2018.

Landau, Jacob M. *Radical Politics in Modern Turkey*. New York: Routledge, 2016.

Lee, Joy R. "The Islamic Republic of Eastern Turkestan and the Formation of Modern Uyghur Identity in Xinjiang." MA, Kansas State University, 2006. https://apps.dtic.mil/sti/citations/ADA455923.

Leibold, James. *Reconfiguring Chinese Nationalism: How the Qing Frontier and Its Indigenes Became Chinese*. New York: Palgrave Macmillan, 2007.

Lemkin, Raphael. *Axis Rule in Occupied Europe: Laws of Occupation, Analysis of Government, Proposals for Redress*. Clark, NJ: Lawbook Exchange, 2005.

Levitz, Eric. "China Declared Islam a Contagious Disease – and Quarantined 1 Million Muslims." *Intelligencer*, August 2, 2018. https://nymag.com/intelligencer/2018/08/china-muslims-camps-uighur-communist-party-islam-mental-illness.html?gtm=bottom&gtm=top.

Li Jianxin 李建新 and Chang Qingling 常庆玲. "Xinjing ge zhuyao minzu renkou xianzhuang ji bianhua tezheng" 新疆各主要民族人口 现状及变化特征 [The Current Situation and Changing Characteristics of Major Ethnic Group Population in Xinjiang]. *Xibei minzu yanjiu* 西北民族研究 3, no. 16 (2015): 21–37. http://www.shehui.pku.edu.cn/upload/editor/file/20171212/20171212180106_2459.pdf.

Li Xiao Xia. "An Analysis Report on Population Change in Xinjiang." *Global Times*, January 7, 2021. https://www.globaltimes.cn/page/202101/1212073.shtml.

Li Zaili 李在立. "Fumu bei guan jizhongying, Weizu ertong cheng 'gu'er' " 母被關集中營, 維族兒童成 孤兒 [Parents Are Held in Concentration Camps, Uyghur Children Become 'Orphans']. *Bitter Winter*, June 28, 2018. https://zh.bitterwinter.org/china-muslim-parents-arrested-in-re-education-camps/.

———. "Uyghurs Secretly Moved to Hide Mass Detentions." *Bitter Winter*, December 17, 2018. https://bitterwinter.org/uyghurs-moved-to-hide-mass-detentions/.

Liang, Zai. "The Age of Migration in China." *Population and Development Review* 27, no. 3 (September 2001): 499–524. doi:10.1111/j.1728-4457.2001.00499.x.

Lipes, Joshua. "Expert Says 1.8 Million Uyghurs, Muslim Minorities Held in Xinjiang's Internment Camps." *Radio Free Asia*, November 24, 2019. https://www.rfa.org/english/news/uyghur/detainees-11232019223242.html.

Liu, Mingfu, *China Dream: Great Power Thinking and Strategic Posture in the Post American Era.* New York: CN Times books Inc, 2015.

Liu Xin and Fan Lingzhi. "Xinjiang Regional Government Introduces Democracy Practices, Lashes Out at US Democratic Hegemony." *Global Times*, December 6, 2021. https://www.globaltimes.cn/page/202112/1240812.shtml.

Lone, Fozia. "*Uti Possidetis Iuris.*" In *International Law.* Oxford Bibliographies. Oxford: Oxford University Press, 2012.

Ma, Alexandra. "China Is Reportedly Sending Men to Sleep in The Same Beds as Uyghur Women While Their Husbands Are in Prison Camps." *Business Insider*, November 4, 2019. https://www.businessinsider.com/china-uighur-monitor-home-shared-bed-report -2019-11.

———. "Chinese Ambassador to the US Says Mass Surveillance and Oppression of Muslim Minority Is to Make Them 'Normal Persons.'" *Business Insider*, November 28, 2018. https://www.businessinsider.com/china-ambassador-muslim-uighur-crackdown-make -normal-persons-2018-11.

Mair, Victor H. "The North (West) Ern Peoples and the Recurrent Origins of the 'Chinese' State." In *The Teleology of the Modern Nation-State*, edited by Joshua A. Fogel, 46–84. Philadelphia: University of Pennsylvania Press, 2004.

Mao Weihua, and Zheng Caixiong. "Xinjiang Still China's Largest Cotton Producer in 2019." *China Daily*, January 8, 2020. https://www.chinadaily.com.cn/a/202001/08/WS5 e156c70a310cf3e3558336b.html.

Mao, Zedong. *Quotations from Chairman Mao Tse-Tung.* Peking: Foreign Languages Press, 1966. https://www.marxists.org/reference/archive/mao/works/red-book/index.htm.

———. *Selected Works of Mao Tse-Tung.* Peking: Foreign Languages Press, 1961. https://www.marxists.org/reference/archive/mao/selected-works/index.htm.

McMillen, Donald H. "Chinese Communist Power and Policy in Sinkiang, 1949–73: Revolutionary Integration vs. Regionalism." PhD dissertation, University of Colorado at Boulder, 1976.

———. "Xinjiang and the Production and Construction Corps: A Han Organisation in a Non-Han Region." *The Australian Journal of Chinese Affairs* 6 (July 1981): 65–96. https://doi.org/10.2307/2159052.

Millward, James A. *Eurasian Crossroads: A History of Xinjiang.* New York: Columbia University Press, 2007.

Miles, Maochun Yu. "China's Final Solution in Xinjiang." *Hoover Institution,* October 9, 2018. Accessed January 12, 2022. https://www.hoover.org/research/chinas-final-solution -xinjiang.

Minster, Christopher. "Spain's American Colonies and the Encomienda System." *Thought. Co,* May 30, 2019. https://www.thoughtco.com/spains-american-colonies-encomienda -system-2136545.

Moynihan, Harriet. "China's Evolving Approach to International Dispute Settlement." London: Chatham House, 2017. https://www.chathamhouse.org/sites/files/chathamhouse /publications/research/2017-03-29-chinas-evolving-approach-international-dispute-settle -ment-moynihan-final.pdf.

NTDTV. "Tuiwu junren jie Zhonggong zhenya Jiang Zang Gang ren de kongbu jingli" 退伍军人揭中共镇压疆藏港人的恐怖经历 [Veterans Expose the Chinese Communist Party's Horrific Oppression in Xinjiang and Tibet]. *NTDTV*, April 11, 2020. https://www .ntdtv.com/gb/2020/04/10/a102820365.html.

Oeter, Stefan. "The Role of Recognition and Non-Recognition with Regard to Secession." In *Self-Determination and Secession in International Law*, edited by Christian Walter, Antje von Ungern-Sternberg, and Kavus Abushov, 45–67. Oxford: Oxford University Press, 2014.

Office of United States Chief of Council For Prosecution of Axis Criminality. *Nazi Conspiracy and Aggression, Office of the United States Chief of Counsel for Prosecution of Axis Criminality 'Red Series': Volume 8*. Periodical, 1945. https://www.loc.gov/item/2011525363_NT_Nazi _Vol-VIII/.

Peters, Anne. "The Principle of Uti Possidetis Juris." In *Self-Determination and Secession in International Law*, edited by Christian Walter, Antje von Ungern-Sternberg, and Kavus Abushov, 95–137. Oxford: Oxford University Press, 2014.

Qazanchi, Abdullah. "Briefing the Disappearance of Uyghur Intellectual and Cultural Elites." Washington, DC: Uyghur Human Rights Project. Accessed December 9, 2021. https:// uhrp.org.

Qiao Long and Yang Fen. "China Bans Use of Uyghur, Kazakh Textbooks, Materials in Xinjiang Schools." *Radio Free Asia*, October 13, 2017. https://www.rfa.org/english/news/ uyghur/ethnic-textbooks-10132017135316.html/.

Qin, Amy. "In China's Crackdown on Muslims, Children Have Not Been Spared." *New York Times*, December 28, 2019. https://www.nytimes.com/2019/12/28/world/asia/china -xinjiang-children-boarding-schools.html.

Qin, Hancai. *Zuo zongtang quan zhuan* 左宗棠全传 [The Complete Biography of Zuo Zong-tang]. Beijing shi: Zhonghua shuju, 2016.

Radio Free Asia. "Han Migrant Influx Threatens Uyghur Farms." *Radio Free Asia*, March 11, 2013. https://www.rfa.org/english/news/uyghur/farmers-03112013164151.html/.

———. "Xinjiang Political 'Re-Education Camps' Treat Uyghurs 'Infected by Religious Extremism': CCP Youth League." *Radio Free Asia*, August 8, 2018. https://www.rfa.org/ english/news/uyghur/infected-08082018173807.html.

Rahim, Zamira. "Muslim Prisoners in China's Xinjiang Concentration Camps Subjected To Gang Rape and Medical Experiments, Former Detainee Says." *The Independent*, October 22, 2019. https://www.independent.co.uk/news/world/asia/china-xinjiang-uighur-muslim -detention-camps-xi-jinping-persecution-a9165896.html.

Raič, David. *Statehood and the Law of Self-Determination*. Vol. 43. Developments in International Law. The Hague; New York: Kluwer Law International, 2002.

Rajagopalan, Meghan, Alison Killing, and Christo Buscheck. "China Secretly Built A Vast New Infrastructure To Imprison Muslims." *BuzzfeedNews*, January 29, 2020. https:// www.buzzfeednews.com/article/meghara/china-new-internment-camps-xinjiang-uighurs -muslims.

Ramdani, Nabila. "Uyghur Camps Risk Being Turned Into 'Organ Banks.'" *The Independent*, September 26, 2019. https://www.gulftoday.ae/opinion/2019/09/26/uighur-camps-risk -being-turned-into-organ-banks.

Ramzy, Austin, and Chris Buckley. "'Absolutely No Mercy': Leaked Files Expose How China Organized Mass Detentions of Muslims." *New York Times*, November 16, 2019. https://www.nytimes.com/interactive/2019/11/16/world/asia/china-xinjiang-documents .html.

Roberts, Sean R. *The War on the Uyghurs: China's Internal Campaign against a Muslim Minority.* Princeton Studies in Muslim Politics. Princeton: Princeton University Press, 2020.

Robertson, Matthew P., Raymond L. Hinde, and Jacob Lavee. "Analysis of Official Deceased Organ Donation Data Casts Doubt on the Credibility of China's Organ Transplant Reform." *BMC Medical Ethics* 20, no. 1 (December 2019): 79. doi:10.1186/s12910-019-0406-6.

Ruser, Nathan, James Leibold, Kelsey Munro, and Tilla Hoja. "Cultural Erasure: Tracing the Destruction of Uyghur and Islamic Spaces in Xinjiang." Australian Strategic Policy Institute, 2020. https://www.aspi.org.au/report/cultural-erasure.

Ryngaert, C., and C. Griffioen. "The Relevance of the Right to Self-Determination in the Kosovo Matter: In Partial Response to the Agora Papers." *Chinese Journal of International Law* 8, no. 3 (2009): 573–87. doi:10.1093/chinesejil/jmp021.

Sautman, Barry. "Preferential Policies for Ethnic Minorities in China: The Case of Xinjiang." *Nationalism and Ethnic Politics* 4, no. 1–2 (March 1998): 86–118. doi:10.1080/13537119808428530.

Schabas, William A. *Genocide in International Law: The Crimes of Crimes.* Cambridge, UK: Cambridge University Press, 2000.

———. "State Policy as an Element of International Crimes." *The Journal of Criminal Law & Criminology* 98, no. 3 (2008): 953–82.

———. *Unimaginable Atrocities: Justice, Politics, and Rights at the War Crimes Tribunals.* Oxford: Oxford University Press, 2012.

Schuster, Brenda L. "Gaps in the Silk Road: An Analysis of Population Health Disparities in the Xinjiang Uyghur Autonomous Region of China." *The China Quarterly* 198 (June 2009): 433–41. doi:10.1017/S0305741009000393.

Shahit Biz. "Xinjiang Victim Database." *Shahit Biz.* Accessed May 16, 2022. https://shahit.biz/eng/#home.

Shan Wei and Weng Cuifen. "China's New Policy in Xinjiang and Its Challenges." *East Asia Policy* 2, no. 3 (2010): 60.

Shaw, Malcolm N. *International Law.* 7th ed. Cambridge, UK: Cambridge Univ. Press, 2014.

Shawt, M. N. "The Heritage of States: The Principle of *Uti Possidetis Juris* Today." *British Yearbook of International Law* 67, no. 1 (January 1, 1997): 75–154. doi:10.1093/bybil/67.1.75.

Shichor, Yitzhak. "Dialogue of the Deaf: The Role of Uyghur Diaspora Organizations Versus Beijing." In *The Uyghur Community: Diaspora, Identity and Geopolitics,* edited by Güljanat Kurmangaliyeva Ercilasun and Konuralp Ercilasun, 121–36. New York: Palgrave Macmillan US, 2018.

———. "Virtual Transnationalism: Uyghur Communities in Europe and the Quest for Eastern Turkistan Independence." *In Muslim Networks and Transnational Communities in and Across Europe,* edited by S. Allievi and J. S. Nielsen, 288–311. Leiden: Brill, 2003.

Smith, Anthony D. *National Identity. Ethnonationalism in Comparative Perspective.* Reno: University of Nevada Press, 1991.

Smith, Nicola. "China Destroys Dozens of Cemeteries in Drive to 'Eradicate' Cultural History of Muslims." *The Telegraph,* October 9, 2019. https://www.telegraph.co.uk/news/2019/10/09/china-destroys-dozens-uighur-cemeteries-drive-eradicate-cultural/.

South China Morning Post. "China Plans to Send Uygur Muslims From Xinjiang Re-Education Camps to Work in Other Parts of Country." *South China Morning Post.* May 2, 2020. https://www.scmp.com/news/china/politics/article/3082602/china-plans-send-ugyur-muslims-xinjiang-re-education-camps-work.

Stanton, Gregory H. "The Ten Stages of Genocide." *Genocide Watch*, 1996. https://www .genocidewatch.com/tenstages.

Starke, J. G. "The Acquisition of Territorial Sovereignty by Newly Emerged States." *The Australian Year Book of International Law Online* 2, no. 1 (1968): 9–15. doi:10.1163/26660229-002-01-900000003.

Sudworth, John. "China Muslims: Xinjiang Schools Used to Separate Children From Families." *BBC News*, July 4, 2019. https://www.bbc.com/news/world-asia-china-48825090.

Sun, Yat-sen. "Fundamentals of National Reconstruction." *China Copyright and Media*, April 24, 2013. https://chinacopyrightandmedia.wordpress.com/1924/04/12/fundamentals-of -national-reconstruction/.

———. *Fundamentals of National Reconstruction*. Taipei: China Cultural Service, 1953.

———. *The Complete Works of Sun Yat-Sen*. Volume 5. Beijing: Zhonghua Shu Ju, 1985.

The Economist. "How Xinjiang's Gulag Tears Families Apart." *The Economist*, October 17, 2020. https://www.economist.com/china/2020/10/17/how-xinjiangs-gulag-tears-families -apart.

The State Council Information Office of the People's Republic of China. *Employment and Labor Rights in Xinjiang*. Beijing: Foreign Languages Press, 2020. http://english.www.gov .cn/archive/whitepaper/202009/17/content_WS5f62cef6c6d0f7257693c192.html.

———. *Guiding Opinions of the Central Committee of the Communist Party of China and the State Council on Promoting the Development of the Western Region in the New Era to Form a New Pattern*. Beijing: ChinaLawInfo, 2020.

———. *Historical Matters Concerning Xinjiang*. China: Foreign Languages Press, 2019. http://english.www.gov.cn/archive/whitepaper/201907/21/content_WS5d33fed5c6d00 d362f668a0a.html.

———. *White Paper on History and Development of Xinjiang*. Beijing: Foreign Languages Press, 2003. http://en.people.cn/200305/26/eng20030526_117240.shtml.

Thum, Rian. "The Spatial Cleansing of Xinjiang: Mazar Desecration in Context." *Made in China Journal*, August 24, 2020. https://madeinchinajournal.com/2020/08/24/the-spatial -cleansing-of-xinjiang-mazar-desecration-in-context/.

———. "The Uyghurs in Modern China." In *Oxford Research Encyclopedia of Asian History*. Oxford: Oxford University Press, 2018.

Tohti, Ilham. "Diaocha: 12.3% de Weiwuer ren yao duli jianguo, er 81.3% yao gaodu zizhi" 调查: 12.3%维吾尔人希望建立独立国家, 81.3%希望高度自治 [Survey: 12.3% of Uighurs Want to Establish an Independent Country, While 81.3% Want a High Degree of Autonomy]. November 12, 2010. Original: www.uighurbiz.net, deleted by the Chinese government. Now online at https://uyghurbiz.org/%E8%B0%83%E6%9F%A5%EF%BC %9A12-3%E7%9A%84%E7%BB%B4%E5%90%BE%E5%B0%94%E4%BA%BA%E8 %A6%81%E7%8B%AC%E7%AB%8B%E5%BB%BA%E5%9B%BD%EF%BC%8C %E8%80%8C81-3%E8%A6%81%E9%AB%98%E5%BA%A6%E8%87%AA%E6%B2 %BB/.

———. "My Ideals and the Career Path I Have Chosen." *Ilham Tohti Institute*, March 2020. http://www.ilhamtohtiinstitute.org/?p=108.

———. "Yilihamu: heping, gongkai, pingdeng, zunzhong, shanyi, cai shi jiejue wenti de genben" 伊力哈木:和平、公开、平等、尊重、善意、才是解决问题的根本 [Ilham: Peace, Openness, Equality, Respect, Goodwill, Is the Root of the Problem]. *Still Darkness*, July 7, 2009.

———. "Yilihamu Toheti: Beijing de zhengce rang xinjiang hui jiao tu geng bu man" 伊力哈木·土赫提:北京的政策让新疆回教徒更不满 [Ilham Tohti: Policy of Beijing

Dissatisfied Muslims in Xinjiang More Than Ever]. *Da Jiyuan*. June 14, 2010. https://
www.epochtimes.com/b5/10/6/14/n2937204.htm.

————. "Yilihamu: women shi yi ge ziji zuo bu liao zhu de minzu" 伊力哈木:
我们是一个对自己作不了主的民族 [Ilham: We Are a People Who Cannot Rule Them-
selves]. *Weiwuer zai xian*, December 13, 2012. uighurbiz.net.

Toops, Stanley. *Demographics and Development of Xinjiang After 1949*. Working Papers 1.
Washington, DC: East-West Center Washington, 2004. https://www.eastwestcenter.org/
system/tdf/private/EWCWwp001.pdf?file=1&type=node&id=32004.

————. "Spatial Results of the 2010 Census in Xinjiang." *Asia Dialog*, March 7, 2016.
https://theasiadialogue.com/2016/03/07/spatial-results-of-the-2010-census-in-xinjiang/.

Turdush, Rukiye. "Genocide as Nation Building: China's Historically Evolving Policy in
East Turkistan." *Journal of Political Risk* 7, no. 8 (August 2019). https://www.jpolrisk.com
/genocide-as-nation-building-chinas-historically-evolving-policy-in-east-turkistan/.

————. "Right to Self-Determination of East Turkistan." *Grin*, October 26, 2020.

Turdush, Rukiye, and Magnus Fiskesjö. "Dossier: Uyghur Women in China's Genocide." *Genocide Studies and Prevention* 15, no. 1 (May 2021): 22–43.
doi:10.5038/1911-9933.15.1.1834.

Tursun, Nebijan. *General History of Uyghurs*. Uyghur. Volume 7. Ankara: Uyghur Research
Institute, 2020.

Ursu, A. Elena. *No Place to Hide: Why China Will Ratify Rome Statute*. Brussels: Torkel
Opsahl Academic E-Publisher, 2016.

Uyghur Human Rights Project. "Detained and Disappeared: Intellectuals Under Assault in
the Uyghur Homeland." Press Release. Washington, DC: Uyghur Human Rights Project, May 21, 2019. https://uhrp.org/report/update-detained-and-disappeared-intellectuals
-under-assault-in-the-uyghur-homeland/.

————. "Simulated Autonomy: Uyghur Underrepresentation in Political Office." Washington, DC: Uyghur Human Rights Project, October 30, 2017. https://uhrp.org/report/
simulated-autonomy-uyghur-underrepresentation-political-office-html/.

————. "The Bingtuan: China's Paramilitary Colonizing Force in East Turkestan." Washington, DC: Uyghur Human Rights Project, April 26, 2018. https://uhrp.org/report/uhrp
-releases-new-report-bingtuan-chinas-paramilitary-colonizing-force-east/.

————. "Under the Gavel: Evidence of Uyghur-Owned Property Seized and Sold Online."
Washington, DC: Uyghur Human Rights Project, 2021. https://uhrp.org/report/under
-the-gavel-evidence-of-uyghur-owned-property-seized-and-sold-online/.

Uyghur Research Institute. *Genocide in East Turkistan*. Ankara: Uyghur Research Institute,
February 2019. https://www.uysi.org/en/?p=774.

Uyghur Tribunal. "The Xinjiang Papers." *Uyghur Tribunal*, November 27, 2021. https://
uyghurtribunal.com/statements/.

Vermander, Benoît. "Sinicizing Religions, Sinicizing Religious Studies." *Religions* 10, no. 2
(2019): 137. doi:10.3390/rel10020137.

Victims of Communism Memorial Foundation. "China's Minister of Public Security
Zhao Keji's June 2018 Speech on the Progress of Xinjiang Security Regime." In *Xinjiang Police File*. Washington, DC: Victims of Communism Memorial Foundation,
May 23, 2022. https://victimsofcommunism.org/xinjiang-police-files-summary-policy
-recommendations/.

————. *Xinjiang Police File*. Washington DC: Victims of Communism Memorial Foundation, May 23, 2022, https://victimsofcommunism.org/xinjiang-police-files-summary
-policy-recommendations/.

Wakeman, Frederic E. *The Fall of Imperial China. The Transformation of Modern China*. New York: Free Press, 1975.

Walter, Christian. "The Kosovo Advisory Opinion." In *Self-Determination and Secession in International Law*, edited by Christian Walter, Antje von Ungern-Sternberg, and Kavus Abushov, 13–26. Oxford: Oxford University Press, 2014.

Wan, William. "What Separation From Parents Does To Children: 'The Effect Is Catastrophic'." *Washington Post*, June 18, 2018. https://www.washingtonpost.com/national /health-science/what-separation-from-parents-does-to-children-the-effect-is-catastrophic /2018/06/18/c00c30ec-732c-11e8-805c-4b67019fcfe4_story.html.

Wang Ke. *The East Turkestan Independence Movement, 1930s–1940s*. Translated by Carissa Fletcher. Hong Kong: The Chinese University Press, 2018.

Wang Luobu. "Guoji fa da jiangtang di sishiyi qi: ruhe zuo hao Xinjiang shehui wending yu changzhi jiu'an di qiyan" 国际法大讲堂第四十一期—如何做活新疆社会稳定与长治久安的棋眼 [41st Session of International Law Lecture: How to Thread the Needle of Social Stability in Xinjiang]. Lecture presented at the 41st Session of International Law, China University of Political Science and Law, April 2, 2015. http://web.archive.org/web/20210305011946/http://sil.cupl.edu.cn/info/1040/1013.htm.

Wang, Maya. *"Eradicating Ideological Viruses": China's Campaign of Repression against Xinjiang's Muslims*. New York: Human Rights Watch, 2018. https://www.ecoi.net/en/file/local /1443021/4792_1536632022_china0918-web.pdf.

Warikoo, K. *Xinjiang: China's Northwest Frontier*. Milton Park, Abingdon, Oxon: Routledge, 2016. https://search.ebscohost.com/login.aspx?direct=true&scope=site&db=nlebk &db=nlabk&AN=1194330.

Watts, Arthur. *The International Law Commission, 1949–1998*. Oxford; New York: Oxford University Press, 1999.

White, Edward "'Under Tremendous Pressure': The Battle Behind UN Report on China's Xinjiang Abuses." *Financial Times*. Sept 13, 2022. Accessed Sept 14, 2022, https://archive .ph/XLrBG.

Wines, Michael. "A Strongman Is China's Rock in Ethnic Strife." *New York Times*, July 20, 2009. https://www.nytimes.com/2009/07/11/world/asia/11xinjiang.html.

Wong, Edward. "China Invests in Region Rich in Oil, Coal and Also Strife." *New York Times*, December 20, 2014. https://www.nytimes.com/2014/12/21/world/asia/china-invests-in -xinjiang-region-rich-in-oil-coal-and-also-strife.html.

World Uyghur Congress. "Mission Statement." https://www.uyghurcongress.org/en/introducing-the-world-uyghur-congress/.

World Watch Monitor. "China's Communist Party Increases Control Over Religious Affairs." *World Watch Monitor*, March 27, 2018. https://www.worldwatchmonitor.org/coe /chinas-communist-party-increases-control-over-religious-affairs/.

Wright, Rebecca, Ivan Watson, Zahid Mahmood, and Tom Booth. "'Some Are Just Psychopaths': Chinese Detective in Exile Reveals Extent of Torture Against Uyghurs." *CNN*, October 5, 2021. https://www.cnn.com/2021/10/04/china/xinjiang-detective-torture-intl -hnk-dst/index.html.

Wu, Zhe. "Caught between Opposing Han Chauvinism and Opposing Local Nationalism: The Drift toward Ethnic Antagonism in Xinjiang Society, 1952–1963." In *Maoism at the Grassroots: Everyday Life in China's Era of High Socialism*, edited by Jeremy Brown. Cambridge, MA: Harvard University Press, 2015.

Xelq Imza Herikiti. "World Uyghur Congress Does Not Represent the Collective Interest of Uyghurs." *Xelq imza herikiti*, January 2022. https://xelqimzaherikiti.net/.

Xi Jinping. "Secure a Decisive Victory in Building a Moderately Prosperous Society in All Respects and Strive for the Great Success of Socialism with Chinese Characteristics for a New Era." Speech presented at the 19th National Congress of the Communist Party of China, Beijing, October 18, 2017. http://www.xinhuanet.com/english/download/Xi_Jin-ping's_report_at_19th_CPC_National_Congress.pdf.

Xinhua Net. "Innocent Civilians Make Up 156 in Urumqi Riot Death Toll." *Xinhua Net*, August 5, 200AD. http://www.xinhuanet.com/english/urumqiriot/latestnews.htm.

———. "Xi Stresses Developing Religions in Chinese Context." *Xinhua Net*, December 4, 2021. http://www.news.cn/english/2021-12/04/c_1310352026.htm.

Xinjiang Ribao 新疆日报. "Zizhiqu dangwei hui zhuchi huiyi chenchuanguo jiang hua" 自治区党委常委会主持会议 陈全国讲话 [The Standing Committee of the Autonomous Region Party Committee Holds a Meeting: Chen Quanguo's Speech]. *Xinjiang Ribao* 新疆日报, October 11, 2020. http://news.ts.cn/system/2020/10/11/036459586.shtml.

———. "Zizhiqu dangwei jiu jie shi ci quanhui zhaokai" 自治区党委九届十次全会召开 [The Tenth Plenary Session of the Ninth Party Committee Meeting of the Autonomous Region Was Held]. *Xinjiang ribao* 新疆日报, October 11, 2020. http://wap.xjdaily.com/xjrb/20201011/app_163015.html.

Xu, Vicky Xiuzhong, Danielle Cave, James Leibold, Kelsey Munro, and Nathan Ruser. "Uyghurs for Sale: 'Re-Education', Forced Labour and Surveillance beyond Xinjiang." Australian Strategic Policy Institute, March 1, 2020. https://www.aspi.org.au/report/uyghurs-sale.

Xu, Vicky Xiuzhong, James Leibold, and Daria Impiombato. "Exposing the Chinese Government's Oppression of Xinjiang's Uyghurs." Australian Strategic Policy Institute, October 2021. https://www.aspistrategist.org.au/exposing-the-chinese-governments-oppression-of-xinjiangs-uyghurs/.

Yidu. "Xuan jiang gao: dao jiaoyu zhuanhuaban xuexi shi dui sixiang shang huan-bing qunzhong de yici mianfei zhuyuan zhiliao" 宣讲稿: 到教育转换班学习是对思想上患病群众的一次免费住院治疗 [Presentation: Studying in the Educational Transformation Facilities Is Free Hospitalization for Ideologically Ill Individuals]. *Yidu*, March 31, 2017. http://web.archive.org/web/20211117160618/https:/read01.com/zh-sg/n3L6Do.html.

Yojana, Sharma. "Alarm Over Choice of New Leader for Xinjiang University." *University World News*, October 2020. https://www.universityworldnews.com/post.php?story=20201015084137568.

Zenz, Adrian. "'End the Dominance of the Uyghur Ethnic Group': An Analysis of Beijing's Population Optimization Strategy in Southern Xinjiang." *Central Asian Survey* 40, no. 3 (July 3, 2021): 291–312. doi:10.1080/02634937.2021.1946483.

———. *Sterilizations, IUDs, and Mandatory Birth Control: The CCP's Campaign to Suppress Uyghur Birthrates in Xinjiang.* Washington, DC: The Jamestown Foundation, 2020. https://jamestown.org/wp-content/uploads/2020/06/Zenz-Sterilizations-IUDs-and-Mandatory-Birth-Control-FINAL-27June.pdf?x71937.

———. "The Karakax List: Dissecting the Anatomy of Beijing's Internment Drive in Xinjiang." *Journal of Political Risk* 8, no. 2 (2020). https://xinjiang.sppga.ubc.ca/the-karakax-list/.

———. "The Xinjiang Papers: An Analysis of Key Findings and Implications for the Uyghur Tribunal in London." *Uyghur Tribunal*, December 9, 2021. https://uyghurtribunal.com/wp-content/uploads/2021/12/The-Xinjiang-Papers-An-Analysis-for-the-Uyghur-Tribunal.pdf.

———. "The Xinjiang Papers: An Introduction." *Uyghur Tribunal*, November 27, 2021. https://uyghurtribunal.com/wp-content/uploads/2021/11/The-Xinjiang-Papers-An-Introduction-01.pdf.

———. "'Wash Brains, Cleanse Hearts': Evidence From Chinese Government Documents About the Nature and Extent of Xinjiang's Extrajudicial Internment Campaign." *Journal of Political Risk* 7, no. 11 (2019). http://www.jpolrisk.com/wash-brains-cleanse-hearts.

Zhang Fan and Li Jingquan 张凡, 李景全 "Xinjiang bingtuan tunken shubian hefa xing ji qian-zai hefa xing weiji tanxi" 新疆兵团屯垦戌边合法性及潜在合法性危机探析 [Analysis on the Legality and Potential Legality Crisis of Xinjiang Corps]. *South China University Gazette* 18, no. 2 (2012). http://www.zndxsk.com.cn/upfile/soft/20120329/17-p101-skbs4.pdf.

Zhao, Gang. "Reinventing China: Imperial Qing Ideology and the Rise of Modern Chinese National Identity in the Early Twentieth Century." *Modern China* 32, no. 1 (January 2006): 3–30. doi:10.1177/0097700405282349.

Zhao, Tingyang. *Redefining a Philosophy for World Governance.* Translated by Liqing Tao. Palgrave Pivot. Singapore: Palgrave Macmillan, 2019.

Zhongguo Xinwen wang. "Xinjiang sheng chan jianli she bingtuan guo jia an chuan ju chengli" 新疆生产建设兵团国家安全局成立 [Xinjiang Production and Construction Corps National Security Bureau was Established], *Zhonguo Xinwen wang* 中国新闻网, March 28, 2012. Accessed December 12, 2021. http://www.chinanews.com/gn/2012/03-28/3779628.shtml.

AUDIO-VISUAL AND SOCIAL MEDIA SOURCES

Istiqlal TV. "Exposed Silence (11) Unimaginable Oppression." *YouTube* video, 23:32. September 5, 2018. https://youtu.be/AGfPqG7f2F4.

Lude Press 路德. "Lude fangwen Mina nüshi: jiang shu zai Xinjiang zao shou Zhonggong guo-bao pohai, shiqu yi ge ji ge yue da de haizi, bei qiangpo tuoyi jiancha de jingli" 路德访谈米娜女士：讲述在新疆遭受中共国宝迫害，失去一个几个月大的孩子，被强迫脱衣检查的经历 [Lude Press Interview with Mihrigul Tursun: Recounting the Experience of Being Persecuted by the CCP, Losing a Few-Months-Old Child, and Being Forced to Strip Naked for Inspections]. *YouTube* video, 1:46. January 18, 2019. https://www.youtube.com/watch?v=P_By_N8U_YY&feature=youtu.be.

Mahsut, Guly. Neq meydan: Beshinchi Iyul Ürümchi qirghinchiliqi eslimilirim: Dunya körüp baqmighan resim widiolirim [Eyewitness: My recollections of the July 5 Massacre in Ürümchi: My photos and videos that the world has never seen before]. YouTube video, 2:00:50. July 4, 2020. https://www.youtube.com/watch?v=axzAasB6wzI.

Photographer and Traveller. "Speaking Turkish with Turkish Uyghurs—Xinjiang Uyghur Autonomous Region in China-2." *YouTube* video, 10:12. Posted December 22, 2018.

Turdush, Rukiye. "Chinese settlers destroying beautifully decorated Uyghur houses." Twitter, April 17, 2020, 12:37 pm. https://twitter.com/parlabest/status/1251188000832327682.

———. "He Was a 32 years Old Healthy Man." Twitter, September 23, 2029, 11:44 am. https://twitter.com/parlabest/status/1308794408406593537.

———. "Uyghur Kids Struggling to Understand Why Their Healthy Parents Mentally and Physically Harmed." Twitter, April 29, 2029, 2:09pm. https://twitter.com/parlabest/status/1167137218240159750.

———. "Uyghur Language Totally Banned." Twitter, March 6, 2021, 10:28 pm. https://twitter.com/parlabest/status/1368403090840432641?s=12.

Uyghur, Rita. "China's Live Organ Harvesting in Uyghur Region, This Signs Is in Urumchi Airport, It says : Special Passengers, Human Organs Transport Corridor." Twitter, February 28, 2019, 6:41 am. https://twitter.com/0715Rita/status/1101085027809574912.

War on Fear. "Xinjiang: A New Explanation." *YouTube* video, 1:45. September 17, 2019. https://www.youtube.com/watch?v=gGYoeJ5U7cQ.
Youku. "【四月大讲堂】艾跃进: 中国国防政策的历史沿革(二)" [April Lecture: Ai Yuejin: The History of China's National Defence Policy]. *Youku* video, 38:02. April 26, 2013. https://v.youku.com/v_show/id_XNTQ4Mjg5NTcy.html.

REFERENCE WORKS

The Editors of Encyclopaedia Britannica, and Amy McKenna. "Minority." In *Encyclopaedia Britannica*, September 18, 2019. https://www.britannica.com/topic/minority.

INTERVIEWS

All interviews conducted by the author were confidential. To protect the interviewees' identities, the author and select interviewees have mutually agreed to use pseudonym * and/or redact their last names. Where no special symbols appear, interviewees' original names were retained. (Names are ordered by first and then last name.)
Abdulehet Mehmet, Phone interview. September 6, 2021.
Araphat Ablimit, in- person interview. April, 12 2022. Toronto, Canada.
*Asiye Yasin (friends of Elfira Nury, currently asked political asylum in Europe), pseudonym is used to protect the identity for the victim and interviewee. phone interview with author. March 12, 2022.
*Adile Kamran, in discussion with author, July 12, 2021. Pseudonyms are used to protect interviewee's identity.
*Erkin Muhemmmed. In discussion with author, July 14, 2021.
Ehmet Igembedi. Former president of East Turkistan Government in Exile. phone interview. March 2, 2021.
Gulemhan Dawut, Osman Haji, Abdukadir Yasinbay. In discussion with author. Ghulja, Xinjiang. March 1998. (All of these interviewees are deceased.)
Gulbahar Jelilova, phone interview with author, March 24, 2021.
Hannekezi. Aisa, phone interview, April 20, 2022.
Halmurat Eziz. Uyghur farmer in Ghulja. Social media chat conversation, July 23, 2018.
Muhemmet Ehmet. Eyewitness. Phone interview, April 15, 2022.
*Miyesser. In-person interview with author, May 21, 2021, Toronto, Canada.
Qemer, Sajide, Tursun, Mehmet, Nurgul. Group interview, conducted by author in Ghulja, April 1998. Surnames redacted for the protection of interviewees' identity.
*Rishat Ibrahim, *Aliye Qurban, and Ismail. Uyghur Refugees in Canada and Europe. Interview. October 2021.
Rishat Elkun, Phone interview, September 13, 2021.
Sureyya Abdurahman. Currently seeking political asylum in Turkey. Phone interview, July 26, 2018.
Turdush Kasim. Eyewitness. Phone interview, April 16, 2022.
Tursunay Ziyawudun. Chinese concentration camp survivor. Phone interview with author. March 25, 2021.
*Xiaoli. In-person interview with author, November 2001, Beijing, China.
Zumret Dawut. Chinese concentration camp survivor. Phone interview. September 3, 2021.
*Zunun and Amine. Interview with parents of child camp survivor. October 9, 2021.

Index

Note: Italic page numbers refer to figures and tables; Page numbers followed by "n" denote endnotes.

51; against people of East Turkistan, 43; precondition of, 47–49; ten stages of, 47; in Xi era, nation-building as, 53–56
Genocide Convention: Article IV of, 56; Article IX of, 157; Article 2 of, 54; cultural genocide, 86–88; violation of Article II(a), 62–67; violation of Article II(b), 67–80; violation of Article II(d), 80–86; violations of Article II(c) and (d), 83–85
Genocide Convention law, xiv
Ghulja Uprising (1997), 117
Global War on Terrorism, 120
governmental departments, establishment of, 164–65
Governors, 170
Griffioen, Christine, 145

Hague Regulations (1907), Article 42 of, 31
Hakimbeg Hoja, 19
Halmurat Ghopur, 66, 67
Han Chinese, 13, 53; cadres in East Turkistan, 116; ethnic group, 53; ethnicity, 49; ethnic tensions between Uyghurs and, 121; identity, 26, 50; mass movement of, 102; migrants, 80; migration of, 6; settlement, history of, 98; settlement of, 86; voluntarily inter-marriages, 82–83
Han Chinese nation, xiii, 48, 50, 51, 53, 121
Han Chinese population, 24, 78, 97; proportion of, 100–101
Han Chinese settlers, 48, 100–103, 106, 117, 145, 152
Helsinki Final Act, 3
Holy Qur'an, 149, 150
Howell, Anthony, 104
Hui Muslims, 13
Hu Yaobang, 116

Idiqut Kingdom of Qocho (843–1370s), 11–13
Ilham Tohti, 125; ideology of, 120–22; nonviolent strategy, 121
illegal children, 82
"illegally occupied nation," 5
independence movements, 114–18

India, Uyghur refugees in, 123
independence, 158
indigenous peoples, 5
internal self-determination, 8, 11, 124, 143–45, 158
"international capitalism," 53
international community, xii, xiv, 7–9, 23, 34–35, 37, 47, 106, 128, 133, 145, 154, 157, 159
International Convention on the Elimination of All Forms of Racial Discrimination: Article 5 of, 143
International Court of Justice (ICJ), 147
International Covenant on Civil and Political Rights, 146
International Covenant on Economic, Social, and Cultural Rights, 146
International Criminal Court (ICC), 157
International Criminal Court (ICC) Statute, Article 30 of, 77
internationalism, 51, 134
international peace, 34–35, 147
International Trusteeship System, 146
International Union of the East Turkistan Organizations (IUETO), 153
Islam, 137–38, 149–51
Islamic law, 149
IUETO. *See* International Union of the East Turkistan Organizations (IUETO)

Jin Shuren (1883–1941), 13
justice, 119, 150–52

Kashgar, 23, 55, 62, 70, 80, 104, 120
Kashgaria, 17
Kazaks, 6, 7, 13, 32; independence movements, 114–18
killings: in concentration camps, 62–63; through organ harvesting, 64–66; during Uyghur protests, 62
Kingdom of Moghulistan (1347–1514), 11
knowledge and science, 152
Kohja Niyaz Haji, 163
Kosovo, 8, 143, 147, 148

Labor Law, 135
Land Reform program, 114

Tianxia, 155
Turghun Almas, 66
Turkic Muslims, xiii, 43–44; arrests and
    murders of, 99; destruction of, 35; directly
    demanded end of Chinese colonization,
    117; elimination of, 56; incarcerated in
    concentration camps, 49; internal enemies,
    53; leadership positions, 134; legal value
    of land, 101; mass detention camps,
    44; murder of, 64; oppression of, 120;
    religious activities of, 86–87; territorial
    rights of, 45; torture and killing of, 54;
    trust and tolerance between Chinese
    settlers and, 47; violations of rights, 113

UN Charter: Article 1 of, 3, 145; Article
    2(4), 8; Article 2(4) of, 144; Article
    55 of, 3; Article 73 of, 148
unemployment rate, of Uyghurs, 48
UN General Assembly Resolution 1514, 8
UN General Assembly Resolution 2625
    (XXV), 32
UN General Assembly Resolution 3314
    (XXIX): Article 5(3) of, 33
UN General Assembly's Friendly Relations
    Declaration (1970), 144
Union of Burma, 24
United Front Work Department, 138
United Nations Convention on the
    Prevention and Punishment of the Crime
    of Genocide (1948): Article II of, 62
United Nations (UN) law, principle of, 3
UN Security Council resolution, 7, 157
UN Security Council Resolution 1244, 8
UN Security Council Resolution 1514, 6, 117
UN's International Covenant on Civil and
    Political Rights, 103–4
Ürümchi Abdurehim Saidov, 115
Urumchi protests (2009), 118
Uyghur children, 72–73; experience mental
    and physical abuse in camps, *74*, 74–76,
    75; intentional removal of younger
    generation, 77–78; not allowed to speak
    language/practice culture and religion,
    73; not allowed to travel out of China,
    76, *77*; potential consequences of child
    separation, 78–80; removed from
    communities and culture, 73–74

Uyghur ethnic group, xii
Uyghur Human Rights Project, 67, 101,
    135
Uyghur Online, 121
Uyghur protests, killings during, 62
Uyghurs, 5–7, 11, 13, 26, 32; arrests and
    murders of, 99; criminalization of,
    47–49; destruction of, 35; directly
    demanded end of Chinese colonization,
    117; eliminating bloodline of, 82;
    elimination of, 56; ethnic tensions
    between Han Chinese and, 121; for
    forced labor manufacturing jobs, 136;
    genocide, 26; independence movements,
    114–18; internal enemies, 53; land
    ownership rights, 136; legal value of
    land, 101; mass detention camps, 44;
    oppression of, 120; peaceful resistance
    of, 149; as "pickpockets" and "wild
    outsiders," 48; political activities of
    exiled, 122–26, *127*, 128; population
    in rural areas, 104; religious activities
    of, 86–87; territorial rights of, 45;
    unemployment rate of, 48; unfair
    regulations and ill-treatment of, 119
Uyghur scholars, detention and death
    sentences for, 66–67
Uyghurs protest, in Ghulja, 119

Vienna Declaration of 1993, 3, 146;
    Section 2 of, 43
violation of Article II(a): detention and
    death sentences for Uyghur scholars,
    66–67; killings during Uyghur protests,
    62; killings in concentration camps, 62–
    63; killings through organ harvesting,
    64–66; mass killings, 64
violation of Article II(b): sexual violence,
    67–72, *68*; transferring children, 72–83
violation of Article II(d), 80; deportation
    to secret locations, 85–86; forced labor
    and deportation, 83–85; forced marriage
    policy, 82–83; prevention of birth,
    80–82

Wang Lequan, 120
Wang Zhen, 98, 114, 116, 134
Water Management Officials, 171

welfare state, 151
West-East Gas Pipeline, 105
Western Han dynasty, 11
World Conference on Human Rights, 146
World Uyghur Congress (WUC), 120,
    124–26, 128; Constitution of, 153
World Uyghur Youth Congress, 124

Xi Jinping, 44, 52, 53, 81, 85, 87, 118,
    137–39, 145, 155; articulation of
    "China Dream," 122; nation-building as
    genocide, 53–56; order of "no mercy," 68
Xinjiang, xii, 11–12, 33, 116, 121, 134,
    135, 137
Xinjiang Production and Construction
    Corps (XPCC), xiii, 85–86, 98–100,
    102, 106, 116
Xinjiang Religious Affairs Regulation, 49, 87
Xinjiang Uyghur Autonomous Region
    (XUAR), xii, 26, 97, 98, 114, 134, 135,
    139, 144

Xinjiang Work Bureau, 138
Xin Lanting, 114

Yalkun Rozi, 66
Yang Zengxin (1864–1928), 13, 14
Ya'qūb Beg, 17
Yarkand Khanate (1514–1705), 11
Youth League, 55
Yuan Shikai, 13
Yu, Miles M., 155

Zenz, Adrian, 72, 81, 85
Zhang Binglin, 50
Zhaokeji, 62
Zhao Tingyang, 155
Zhou Enlai, 26, 37
Zirip Kari Haji, 19
Ziya Sämädi, 114
Zuo Zongtang, xii

About the Author

Rukiye Turdush is a former Uyghur Research Institute researcher who is now affiliated with the Centre for East Turkistan National Interest, recently elected as an president of East Turkistanian Federation of Canada. She had written several articles and books in both English and Uyghur languages. Her work is dedicated to the people of East Turkistan who are suffering under Chinese colonialism.

www.ingramcontent.com/pod-product-compliance
Lightning Source LLC
Chambersburg PA
CBHW022313280326
41932CB00010B/1087